Resurrecting Slavery

This book is dedicated to my mother, Barbara Jean;

my grandmother Betty-Ann;

and my godmother, Hannah

CRYSTAL MARIE FLEMING

Resurrecting Slavery

RACIAL LEGACIES AND
WHITE SUPREMACY IN FRANCE

TEMPLE UNIVERSITY PRESS
Philadelphia | *Rome* | *Tokyo*

TEMPLE UNIVERSITY PRESS
Philadelphia, Pennsylvania 19122
www.temple.edu/tempress

Photographs and graphics by Crystal Marie Fleming

Portions of Chapter 3 were originally published as Crystal M. Fleming, "White Cruelty or Republican Sins? Competing Frames of Stigma Reversal in French Commemorations of Slavery," Ethnic and Racial Studies *35, no. 3 (2012): 488–505, available at www.tandfonline.com.*

Portions of Chapters 6 and 7 and the Conclusion were originally published as Crystal M. Fleming and Aldon Morris, "Theorizing Ethnic and Racial Movements in the Global Age: Lessons from the Civil Rights Movement," Sociology of Race and Ethnicity *1, no. 1 (2015): 105–126.*

Library of Congress Cataloging-in-Publication Data

Names: Fleming, Crystal Marie, 1981– author.
Title: Resurrecting slavery : racial legacies and white supremacy in France /
  Crystal Marie Fleming.
Other titles: Racial legacies and white supremacy in France
Description: Philadelphia : Temple University Press, [2017] | Includes
  bibliographical references and index.
Identifiers: LCCN 2016022899 (print) | LCCN 2016048533 (ebook) |
ISBN 9781439914083 (cloth : alk. paper) | ISBN 9781439914090 (paper : alk.
  paper) | ISBN 9781439914106 (E-book)
Subjects: LCSH: Blacks—France—History. | Blacks—Race identity—France. |
  Whites—Race identity—France. | France—Race relations—History. |
  Slavery—France—History. | Slavery—French colonies—History.
Classification: LCC DC34.5.B55 F54 2017 (print) | LCC DC34.5.B55 (ebook) |
  DDC 305.896/044—dc23
LC record available at https://lccn.loc.gov/2016022899

Printed in the United States of America

9 8 7 6 5 4 3 2

Contents

Acknowledgments

I would first like to acknowledge the French people who took the time to talk with me over the course of this project. I am especially grateful to the French black people and people of color who shared their deeply personal experiences of trauma and triumph. These conversations—held in private homes, cafés, restaurants, classrooms, and cultural venues throughout the Paris region—indelibly shaped my understanding of racial inequality in France.

The Institut d'Études Politiques in Paris provided administrative and intellectual support during my fieldwork. I am grateful to the Centre des Amériques and the Centre de Recherches Internationales for providing an intellectual community, office space, and access to Science Po's immense intellectual resources. I also acknowledge the many French scholars who consulted with me over the course of this project, including Christine Chivallon, Olivier Pétré-Grenouilleau, Marcel Dorigny, Daniel Sabbagh, Abdellali Hajjat, Clarisse Fordant, Emannuelle Sibeud, Sylvain Pattieu, Michel Giraud, Bruno Cousin, Patrick Simon, Myriam Cottias, Eric Fassin, Pap Ndiaye, Patrick Weil, and Audrey Célestine. I am especially grateful to Audrey for being an extraordinarily generous colleague over the years. Our ongoing dialogues and spirited debates continue to sharpen my understanding of race and Antillean identities in France. Meetings with the staff of Les Anneaux de la Mémoire in Paris and Nantes, including Mathilde Bossard, Jacky Charmant, and Babacar Lam, provided important contextual background on the metropolitan commemorative movement in the 1990s. Jean-Marc Masseaut in particular helped connect me to many other activists and commemorators in the Paris region, including Odile Lantier of *L'Ombre du Silence*. Daniel Goldberg, a member of the French National Assembly and the deputy of Seine-Saint-Denis, allowed me to work with Christophe Piercy, his parliamentary assistant, to recruit study participants through announcements in municipal newspapers whose readerships included significant populations of French Caribbean migrants.

I learned much from my doctoral committee at Harvard University: Michèle Lamont, Orlando Patterson, Chris Winship, and Mary Lewis. During my graduate studies, this work was greatly improved by the pointed questions and comments of participants in the Sociology Department's Cultural and Social Analysis workshop; the Justice, Welfare, and Economics workshop; the Graduate Student Associate workshop at the Weatherhead Center for International Affairs; and the Qualitative Data Analysis working group. Clare Putnam, coordinator of student programs and fellowships at Weatherhead, was a wonderful source of support. When I found myself struggling with debilitating pain from repetitive strain injuries, Harvard's Student Disability Services provided not only accommodations but also a generous grant to support the transcription of my interviews. I am grateful to my excellent team of Francophone transcribers at Harvard and Stony Brook, including Bettina Fatal, Ouloide Yannick Goue, Aurélie Tichoux, Jean Biem, and Renee Ragin. Other research assistants, including Vanessa Lynn, Hewan Girma, Ramsha Begum, Genarro Aliperti, and Jalana Harris, helped with literature reviews and data analysis at various stages of the project.

My colleagues in the Department of Sociology and the Department of Africana Studies at Stony Brook helped me establish an intellectual community in New York. I am especially appreciative of Tracey Walters, Daniel Levy, Oyeronke Oyeumi, Norman Goodman, John Shandra, Katy Fallon, Ian Roxborough, Michael Schwartz, Abena Asare, Zebulon Miletsky, Anthony Hurley, Tiffany Joseph, Georges Fouron, Kathleen Wilson, and Gene Lebovics. A chance meeting with Charles Mills at Stony Brook in 2012 (re)introduced me to critical race theory and completely changed the course of this project. Participants in our Race, Ethnicity, and Inequality workshop and the Critical Race and Intersectionality reading group have all been extremely valuable interlocutors. Many people were generous enough to read and comment on drafts and portions of the manuscript, including Barbara Moore, Michael Flaherty, Vilna Bashi-Treitler, Kei Petersen, Jessica Welburn, Audrey Célestine, Chinyere Osuji, Onoso Imoagene, and Michel Giraud. I also acknowledge my editor at Temple University Press, Aaron Javsicas, for supporting this project.

Invitations from universities and cultural centers to talk about the project helped me develop my analysis and respond to much needed criticism. I thank the French American Foundation for inviting me to discuss my work in 2014; Christèle Fraïssé for asking me to speak at the Université de Bretagne Occidentale; Rokhaya Diallo and Yasmina Edwards for an invitation to WNYC's "Greene Space"; Ellen McClure for inviting me to the University of Illinois, Chicago; Audrey Célestine, Sylvain Pattieu, Emanuelle Sibeud, and Tyler Stovall for bringing me to Berkeley, as well as Paris-8's Populations Noires en France research seminar; Carla Shedd and the Institute for Research in African-American Studies at Columbia University; and discussants at numerous conference presentations at meetings of the American Sociological Association, the Eastern Sociological Society, and the Social Science History Association. A visiting professorship at the Université Lille-3 sponsored by the European Union's Erasmus Mundus Intercultural Mediation: Identities, Mobilities, Conflicts (MITRA) program allowed me to spend the glorious spring months of 2015 writing, sharing drafts of chapters with French scholars, and delivering a series of talks. In the fall of 2015, I had the opportunity to visit Paris again to refine my ideas (especially my conceptualization of French white supremacy) by participating in a conference on the memory of slavery at the École des Hautes Études en Sciences Sociales, organized by Abdoulaye Gueye and Johann Michel. Finally, the Creative Connections writing retreat in 2014 in Yosemite, organized by the sociologists Tanya Golash-Boza, France Winddance Twine, and Zulema Valdez, helped me move the manuscript forward in a rich intellectual environment that also included holistic practices of well-being.

This work was funded by a number of grants and fellowships from the Center for Work and Service at Wellesley College; the Weatherhead Center for International Affairs and the Center for European Studies at Harvard University; the Ford Foundation; the Woodrow Wilson Foundation; the Mellon Foundation; the Social Science Research Council; the Dean of the College of Arts and Sciences at Stony Brook; and the State University of New York Office of Diversity, Equity and Inclusion. I completed the most significant revisions during a research leave funded by the Woodrow Wilson Career Enhancement Fellowship, which provided the precious time and breathing space I needed to read new literatures and develop a fresh analytical perspective on the data.

This book would not have come to fruition without the many sources of emotional and spiritual support I am fortunate to enjoy. Over the years, the Ford Foundation Fellows have been a continuing source of inspiration and generosity. My gratitude goes, as well, to the thousands of people who have connected with me and commented on my work through my blog and social media. I owe a special shout-out to black (and especially black French) Twitter—for responding to my writing as I worked out ideas for this book (very often in real time). Their instant commentary, positive feedback, critique, and thoughtful suggestions nurtured my enthusiasm for the project and helped push me to the finish line. My "kitchen table" of mentors, friends, and family sprinkled across the globe have carried me through all kinds of crises (existential and otherwise). My beloved and brilliant mother, Barbara—who read and commented on much of the dissertation and the final book—continues to be a shining light of inspiration, kindness, wisdom, and spiritual support. I thank her for teaching me to prioritize God, personal growth, and self-care and well-being beyond all else. I am grateful for my Chicago family: Dianna, Tracey, Isaac, and Stanley. Lori and Jonathan Roses, Joy Renjilian-Burgy, Chinyere Osuji, Jessica Louison, and the incomparable Velma Bury lift me up with laughter, inspiration, wisdom, and emotional support. Vilna Bashi-Treitler provided encouragement, sage advice—and a much-needed intervention at a critical juncture. On the home front, Kei has been the most patient, thoughtful, and supportive partner I could ask for during the stressful completion phase of this book. She steadfastly held the vision of this completed work and believed in my abilities as a writer when the proverbial shit hit the fan.

Finally, I owe my interest in French to Mother Hannah, my Haitian godmother, who began teaching me the language when I was nine years old. Growing up, I would periodically spend a night or two at her immaculate home in South Philly, around the corner from the church we attended on Bainbridge Street. We would sit together at her enormous, plastic-covered wooden dining room table with a Berlitz French book and a tape recorder. There, Mother Hannah would record her warm, craggy voice, carefully pronouncing basic phrases such as *Je m'appelle* and *Comment allez-vous*. Although I made nothing of it at the time, the cartoons shown in the Berlitz book depicted a French nation filled exclusively with white people. Weekends with Mother Hannah were inflected with her transnational journey: the melody of her accent, the aroma of rice and beans with fried plantains, her devout Christian faith, and her memories of growing up in Haiti. Mother Hannah came from a generation of Haitians who turned away from *kreyòl* in favor of French. In our lessons, she never expressed any negativity toward France. It would take me years to finally direct the language she taught me toward learning about the horrors of French slavery and colonialism—but without her influence and encouragement, I never would have begun that journey.

The last time I saw Mother Hannah, just a few months before her passing, I told her once again, in French and English, just how much I appreciated and loved her. Our relationship exemplifies the theme of global connections woven throughout this text. Mother Hannah permanently shaped my sociological imagination, expanding its limits and sparking the transatlantic curiosity that animates this project. In nurturing that curiosity, learning French, and eventually moving to France, I came to understand that our histories are not our own—our oppressions are interconnected. I am not, really, an outsider anywhere in the Black Atlantic. But I am not completely at home anywhere, either. This liminal status of blackness in modernity is, of course, what undergirds the continuities of white supremacy in France, the United States, and the many haunted spaces in between.

Resurrecting Slavery

Introduction

RACIAL RESURRECTIONS

For most of the French, 1998 is vividly remembered as the year that *les bleus* won their stunning 3–0 victory over Brazil in the FIFA World Cup championships. The diverse team, which included Zinedine Zidane and Lilian Thuram—popular players with ties to former French colonies—was widely represented in the media as the triumph of French multiculturalism. The phrase "*La France: black, blanc, beur*" (France: black, white, Arab) became a ubiquitous refrain in coverage of the event. The uplifting framing of the World Cup victory and its symbolism of multicultural solidarity eclipsed a far more troublesome development that year, as 1998 happened to be the 150th anniversary of the abolition of slavery in the French overseas territories.[1]

To mark the occasion, the French government planned a series of official events over the course of the year in both mainland France and the overseas departments of Guiana, Réunion Island, Guadeloupe, and Martinique.[2] This decision stood in marked contrast to the 100th anniversary of the abolition, which passed without much fanfare in 1948.[3] For the 150th anniversary, an inter-ministerial office was established under the leadership of the Guadeloupean writer Daniel Maximin to organize a series of commemorations (see Lutte Ouvrière 1998). In mainland France the commemorations included, among other events, the Déchaîne ta Citoyenneté (Unchain your Citizenship) exposition, which attracted more than fifty-five thousand primary school students. The National Assembly opened its doors on April 25 for a musical festival and display of "documents [and] objects illustrating the steps and evoking the great actors of the abolitionist fight."[4] The next day, the public television station France 3 aired a biography of Aimé Césaire, the Martinican intellectual and politician. Designed to attract a young audience, the show brought together popular Francophone rap artists such as MC Solaar, Stomy Bugsy, and "Positive Black Soul" to interpret the words of the *négritude* writer.

The national day of commemoration itself was reserved for April 27, the anniversary of the abolitionary proclamation. The flurry of commemorative activities included a ceremony at the Pantheon honoring two white abolitionists and one black colonial administrator: Victor Schoelcher, author of the abolitionary decree; Abbé Grégoire, a famous antislavery agitator; and Adolphe-Sylvestre-Félix Eboué, the governor-general of French Equatorial Africa. Two large plaques were erected in the lower level of the Pantheon, near Schoelcher's tomb. Visitors can now find the name of Louis Delgrès, the French Caribbean freedom fighter, stretched in massive, glistening gold script across a beige stone wall. He is described as a "hero of the struggle against the re-establishment of slavery in Guadeloupe." On the opposite wall, the Haitian revolutionary Toussaint L'Ouverture is lionized as a "combatant of freedom [and] artisan of the abolition." Five years later, on the anniversary of L'Ouverture's death, Jean-Bertrand Aristide, the erstwhile president of Haiti, would demand billions of dollars in reparations from France—a request that was swiftly rejected. Not long thereafter, Aristide was forcibly removed from power. French politicians, meanwhile, continue to refuse material reparations.

In 1998, the slogan that accompanied the French government's commemorative outreach was "Tous Nés en 1848" (We Were All Born in 1848), accompanied by an image that was meant to convey a hip, fun portrait of French multiculturalism. The photograph portrays a lower row of brown-skinned youth who are, not without some irony, flanked by several individuals who appear to be white or North African. The slogan became a source of consternation and offense, an emblem of all that was wrong with the Republic's awkward attempts to commemorate a difficult past by focusing on the glory of abolition.

It was also one of the factors that contributed to Afro-Caribbeans deciding to take their historical and contemporary grievances to the streets.[5] During an interview with me years later, one activist observed:

> The Socialist Party and [Lionel] Jospin in particular, at the time he was prime minister, recognized that they had actually made a small linguistic mistake, because in 1998, . . . at the time of the 150th anniversary of the abolition of slavery, they [said]: "We Were All Born in 1848"—therefore, [born] at the moment of abolition. That is to say that before abolition, nothing happened. [There was a] very big reaction and march. The march

. . . affirmed dignity, respect and the will to have slavery recognized as a crime against humanity.[6]

The march the activist refers to is not a well-known event in recent French history. Yet it was the first time that thousands of French people of Caribbean and sub-Saharan African origin formed a visible, collective community of protest in mainland France. Unlike the famous Marche des Beurs, which stretched from Marseille to Paris in 1983 and drew widespread attention to the plight of the Maghrebis and their French-born children, the march in memory of the victims of slavery that took place in Paris on May 23, 1998, was largely ignored by the media, to the chagrin of the activists involved. A note published in *Le Monde* some three days later mentioned the march only at the end of an article about the annual commemoration of abolition in Martinique. The brief dispatch reported:

> In Paris, several thousand people (twenty thousand, according to the organizers; eight thousand, according to the police), in great majority natives of the overseas departments, marched, Saturday May 23, from Republic to Nation, in homage to millions of victims of slavery, at the call of the Committee for a Unitary Commemoration of the 150th Anniversary of the Abolition of the Slavery of Negroes in the French Colonies, which gathers some three hundred associations of Guadeloupeans, Martinicans, Guianese, and Réunionese. The protestors marched in silence with banners carrying inscriptions such as, "Slavery: Crime against Humanity" [and] "We Are All the Daughters and Sons of Slaves."[7]

It is interesting to note that *Le Monde* does not refer to the event as a "black" march. Although it may seem odd to an American, this march by people of African descent—related to slavery—was not universally framed as a black mobilization, even by the activists themselves. The march brought together people and groups with divergent racial politics. One the one hand, certain activists—particularly those from the French Caribbean—eschewed race in favor of ethnicity, waving the banner of descendants of slaves. On the other hand, other activists with a variety of ancestral ties (Caribbean and African) embraced race and affirmed their blackness. French people of color on both sides of this divide have been involved in efforts to resurrect the slavery past.

Despite the atmosphere of general indifference that seemed to greet the protest, March 23, 1998, would prove to be a tipping point in efforts to break the silence surrounding the history of French slavery. This commemorative mobilization highlights the growing presence and political weight of postcolonial migrants and immigrants from both the French overseas departments and sub-Saharan Africa and laid the groundwork for the Taubira Law, passed three years later, which defines slavery as a "crime against humanity." The march also predates new black movements in France such as the moderate Conseil Representatif des Associations Noires (Representative Council of Black Associations [CRAN]) and the radical group Tribu Ka. The events of 1998 raise important questions about race in France. What present-day societal conditions motivated thousands of people to take to the streets in 1998 and subsequent years to resurrect the memory of those enslaved? How do commemorators grapple with the racial content of the slavery past (and present) in the context of French norms of color-blindness? Finally, what kinds of group identities are at stake today for activists and French people with ties to overseas territories where slavery took place?

These questions sent me to Paris nearly a decade after the 1998 march to study commemorations of slavery in France. On May 9, 2008, I joined more than one hundred people in an auditorium at the Hôtel de Ville (Paris City Hall) for a screening of *Africaphonie*, a new, fifty-two-minute documentary chronicling the rise of slavery commemorations in France. After the film, several panelists gathered on-stage for a roundtable discussion and question-and-answer session with the audience. The speakers included the director of a publishing house; a producer of the television series *Bitter Tropics*, about slavery; a journalist; and a few academics. After their opening remarks, a young black man in the audience stood up with a piece of paper in his hand and began speaking into the microphone. "I'm honored to be in the presence of the people who are involved," he said. "But I think that the real problem in France isn't simply a question of slavery but really a question of *race*." He paused, then continued: "We only have to look at the portrait you represent up there." The young man gestured dramatically toward the speakers, drawing some laughter from the audience as the panelists nervously looked at one another and smiled. His remarks drew my attention to the fact that none of the speakers appeared to be phenotypically black. He began reading from his paper:

> I'm going to read the definition of "Negro" from the 1905 Larousse dictionary: "Nègre, Négresse: Latin, Niger. Black: Man, woman with Black skin. It's the name especially given to inhabitants of certain regions in Africa that form a Black race inferior in intelligence to the white race, also known as the Caucasian race." . . . This is the real problem. Today's society doesn't want *blaaaaaaack* men [*saying the word "black" slowly, for emphasis, and raising his pitch*] to have access to positions of responsibility.

Today, at the National [Gendarmerie] Officers School, at the entrance to the cafeteria, we find a statue of a Negro servant [*le nègre serviteur*], the American kind [*he mimics the form of a figurine, bending his knees and opening his hands*], with his hands held out like this, at the entrance . . . , and it seems normal to everyone. The truth is that the Black man, for most people, is considered inferior in intelligence and considered a child. That's . . . why everything will be done to block him, to contain him.

The atmosphere in the room was electric. While a number of panelists discussed historical constructions of race, much of the earlier dialogue had centered on debates (such as whether Africans shared responsibility for the transatlantic slave trade) and sweeping overviews of the cultural legacies of slavery and the politics of commemoration. The young man managed to do what previous speakers had not: to make explicit links between past and present racism. With this audience member's intervention, white racism, anti-blackness, and black identity moved into the foreground.

This moment raises a central concern at the heart of this book: *To what extent do the French make connections between the history of slavery and race relations today?* Students of collective memory are concerned with how history comes to be framed, debated, and infused with meaning. These contested representations are linked to relations of power, as people with unequal resources and divergent interests produce competing perspectives on the past. Struggles over the meaning of racial history are, of course, informed by contemporary politics of race. One of the goals of this study is to show how people make sense of slavery in a nation where talking about race, colonialism, and slavery (not to mention their interconnections) remains taboo. In his masterly *Silencing the Past: Power and the Production of History* (1995: 98), Michel-Rolph Trouillot frames the suppression of the Haitian Revolution in French historiography as intimately connected to "the relegation to an historical backburner of the three themes to which it was linked: racism, slavery, and colonialism." The relegating of racism, slavery, and colonialism to the dustbin of an unspoken history explains not only inattention to the revolution in Saint-Domingue but also the difficulty the French have with acknowledging the social realities of racial inequality and oppression today.[8] Throughout this book, I inquire into the connections and disconnections that are made among these three themes—racism, slavery, and colonialism—in how French politicians, activists, and ordinary people interpret and frame transatlantic enslavement.

Such an inquiry requires unpacking the extent to which commemorators and members of the public *acknowledge* the racial and colonial content of the slavery past—and the social present. In the French case especially, the degree to which the racial content of slavery is acknowledged—and the meanings that are attached to it—cannot be taken for granted. This is arguably the case throughout the commemorative landscape in societies shaped by transatlantic slavery, but it is particularly true in nations like France and Brazil where politicians represent the nation as color-blind. Although we are no strangers to post-racial ideology in the United States, the denial of race is far more hegemonic in France.[9] As Bruce Crumley observes in *Time* magazine, the "accepted wisdom in France . . . is that acknowledging difference, and naming it, is bigotry itself."[10] This ideological and moral objection to using racial categories is what the sociologist Melissa Weiner refers to as "anti-racialism"—the view that making racial distinctions is "racist" (Weiner 2014; Goldberg 2009). In such a context, one might expect to find representations of slavery that downplay or obscure the concept of race.

The notion that one could talk about slavery without directly addressing race might strike most Americans as absurd. In France, however, public racial discourse has been largely suppressed since World War II, when more than seventy thousand French Jews were targeted by racist ideology and sent to death camps in Nazi Germany. With the aftershocks of the Vichy regime and the ongoing trauma of anti-Semitism, many French antiracist groups continue to argue that acknowledging race or using racial categories is incompatible with fighting racism. Erik Bleich (2003: 14) describes French color-blind ideology this way: "Prevailing French frames have downplayed or denied the categories of race and ethnicity, they have focused more on expressive racism and on anti-Semitism, and they have rejected the North American analogy, because of its perceived irrelevance to understanding France's domestic context of racism." Thus, the dominant mode of "dealing with race" in France consists of racial avoidance.

It is clear, however, that the political posture of color-blindness has not erased the legacies of race and racism. Sonia Dayan-Herzbrun (2015: xii) notes, "In France where the use of the word 'race' is prohibited if it applies to human beings, where a 1991 law prohibits all sorts of discriminations, African artists and craftsmen, from ten to fifty years old, coming from Ivory Coast were, not so long ago, exhibited in a large zoological park, as a part of an *African safari*. This exhibition took place in 1994." Twenty years later, when the white South African artist Brett Bailey brought his controversial *Exhibit B* human zoo to Saint-Denis, a suburb outside Paris, minorities protested the display of black bodies in dehumanizing portraits that revived colonial imagery (Breeden 2014). Yet antiracist groups such as SOS-Racisme supported the exhibition in the interest of promoting "reflection" (see Sopo 2014). At the same time, the group's leadership, including its (black) president, Dominique Sopo, have been vocal critics of using racial categories in research to measure and combat discrimination. This conflict—over race, memory, and representation—illustrates the extent to which French groups that seem to share the goal of fighting racism nonetheless embrace opposing racial politics and attitudes toward the colonial past.

As Trica Keaton (2010: 110) insightfully argues, France's official race-blindness "is actually a testament to the power of its 'race-blind' ideology that succeeds in diminishing the significance of the sociohistorical formation of 'race,' its on-going social potency, and its inherence in the objectivity and subjectivity of Blackness (and Whiteness) in the French context." Despite cultural and political pressure from French policy makers and intellectuals to remain race-mute (Bleich 2000), the reality on the ground demonstrates that racial exclusion remains a lived reality for minorities. Many view 2005 as a watershed year for raising consciousness about the weight of French racism. After highly publicized riots sparked by the death of minority youth fleeing the police, new antiracist organizations, including CRAN and the anticolonial group Indigènes de la République, highlighted the difficulties French racial and ethnic minorities face.[11] Thanks to a law proposed in 2001 by Christiane Taubira, France's first black (and female) minister of justice, there is now a national day of memory for slavery and the slave trade: May 10. New, powerful minority voices have emerged in the public sphere, including those of the filmmaker, TV personality, and activist Rokhaya Diallo and the scholar-activist Maboula Soumahoro, who spearheaded France's first "Black History Month" in 2012. That same year, a group of thirteen black and Arab men filed a suit accusing the French state of complicity in allowing police officers to practice racial discrimination. One of the victims included a black Frenchman stopped by police for "walking fast" while "wearing a hoodie" (Géraud 2015). In 2015, a court of appeals ruled in their favor, condemning *the French government itself* for racial profiling. French minorities are also beginning to challenge the overwhelming whiteness of the political establishment. A study published by CRAN showed that all of France's fifty largest cities have white mayors (Cassely 2014). The study also highlights ten French cities, including Bordeaux, Versailles, and Toulon, characterized by "apartheid," where the totality of elected officials is white. Another study commissioned by CRAN claims that the percentage of minority representatives in eighty departments in Hexagonal France is *zero*. With discrimination against non-whites gaining unprecedented attention, the question is whether—and how—French people are making connections between contemporary racism and the history of colonialism and slavery.

Race and Racialization

Before delving further into the racial politics of slavery and commemoration in France, it would be helpful to define several orienting concepts. *Race* refers to the categorization of human groups according to subjective perceptions of phenotypic features (such as skin tone, facial structure, and hair grade) and socially constructed ideas about biological difference.[12] *Ethnicity*, by contrast, refers to the categorization of human groups on the basis of perceived similarities in culture, religion, or nationality.[13] Sociologists often emphasize the fact that race has no biological basis (Roberts 2011; Smedley and Smedley 2005). As the sociologist Eduardo Bonilla-Silva points out, "The selection of certain human traits to designate a racial group is always socially rather than biologically based" (Bonilla-Silva 1997: 469). The *social constructivist perspective*, widely accepted by most sociologists, maintains that race is not essential, biological, or timeless. Instead, ideas about race are produced by human beings and vary across social contexts and historical periods. Racial conceptualizations (Morning 2011) are socially constructed and disseminated through institutions, discourse, and representations. Transformations in the meanings we attach to race and ethnicity are influenced by demographic changes, as well as by shifting relations of power. The concept of race was largely developed by Europeans seeking to justify colonization and enslavement of people they viewed as physically different—and inferior (Golash-Boza 2015). The sociologist Dorothy Roberts describes race as a "political" concept because it is primarily tied to the exercise of power and domination.

Racism is also a political concept as it relates to power relations within racialized social *systems*—societies in which "economic, political, social, and ideological levels are partially structured by the placement of actors in racial categories" (Bonilla-Silva 1997: 469). Racism involves the belief that "racial groups" are characterized by essential and permanent differences that, in turn, are used to justify "the practice of subordinating races believed to be inferior" (Golash-Boza 2015: 6). Racist ideology is inherently hierarchical: dominant racial groups are depicted as superior to minorities. While anyone can be *prejudiced*—biased against particular groups—racism, in strict terms, is accessible only to people who occupy dominant positions within a racialized society. This definition of racism, as a systematic feature of social life, is very different from the "interpersonal" understanding of racial prejudice often heard in public discourse.

I describe France not only as a racialized social system but also as a racist society for at least three reasons. First, racial bias is embedded within the nation's institutions. Discrimination against racial minorities in employment, housing, and public space has been well documented in recent years. As there cannot be systematic, institutionalized racism within a nonracist society, a society that produces systematic racial bias is obviously racist. Second, racial categories and stereotypes are prevalent in everyday life. The lack of formal racial categories in French law does not preclude the social construction of racial categories, labels, and stereotypes on the ground. Finally, present-day inequalities are related to historical racial categories and openly racist practices rooted in colonialism and slavery. Chattel enslavement and colonial domination provide clear precedents of white-supremacist racialization in France and its overseas empire. Given that the French engaged in racialized slavery and colonialism for several centuries, it would be unreasonable to imagine that the traces and legacies of race could have been magically erased in the postcolonial period.

I use the metaphor of resurrection to refer to various attempts to revive the history of slavery through commemorative ceremonies, pedagogy, consciousness-raising, artistic representations, and discourse. "To resurrect" generally means to bring something from the past back to life. Thus, the imagery of resurrection is useful for conveying the sense in which present-day constructions of memory and history seek to *revive the dead* by invoking the historical existence of people involved in relations of colonial enslavement and bring *renewed attention* to an obscured and often forgotten past. For many of those involved in commemorating slavery, the aim is not merely to unearth historical details but also to (re)construct a living history.

Racial Diversity in France

Understanding race politics in France requires some familiarity with the country's basic demographics. However, describing France's racial demographics in precise terms is difficult because of the government's refusal to recognize race officially in its census. A law passed in 1990 banned the use of racial categories in electronic data collected by the government, and as recently as 2013 French politicians were so averse to acknowledging "race" that they voted to remove the word from French legal texts. Nevertheless, various attempts have been made—particularly since the riots in 2005—to approximate the ethnoracial diversity of the population. Like all western European nations, France continues to be a majority-white society. The French black activist group CRAN estimates that 12 percent of France's population falls under the category of "visible minority," while whites constitute 88 percent. However, the population has diversified rapidly over the past thirty years, with increased immigration flows from former colonies in Africa, Asia, and the Caribbean. Of the 66 million people who live in France, approximately 20 percent are immigrants or children of immigrants. In the past most immigrants to France came from

Europe, but by the 2000s, nearly two-thirds of the immigrant population came from countries outside Europe (Bleich 2003; Breuil-Genier et al. 2011).[14] The growing population of immigrants and migrants from France's former colonies means that the physical appearance of the citizenry is changing. French politicians, journalists, and academics typically address this physical transformation euphemistically, referring obliquely to "visible minorities," by which they mean "non-whites."[15]

French people of Muslim confession or Maghrebi (North African) origin are widely considered the largest and most important minority population in France. A study commissioned by Pew in 2010 found that France's 4.7 million Muslims make up the second-largest Muslim population in Europe—second only to that in Germany.[16] The number of French people from the Maghreb is smaller, however, than the number of Muslims, and distinctions between the two groups should be kept in mind. Writing in 2008, the demographer Michèle Tribalat (2008) estimated the population of first-, second-, and third-generation French of North African descent at 3.5 million. Overall, the demographic and symbolic weight of Maghrebis—as well as growing attention to Islamophobia in the wake of the *Charlie Hebdo* terror attacks—tend to obscure the presence of other minority groups, including French of sub-Saharan African or Caribbean origin.

Determining the number of French black people is an unwieldy task. Estimates by CRAN put the number of blacks living in France (both in the mainland and in overseas departments and territories) at 1.88 million, or 3.86 percent of the general population. Most French blacks are of sub-Saharan African origin (Conseil Représentatif des Associations Noires 2007). Some suggest that about 80 percent of the "overseas" French population is "black," setting aside those who would identify as white or multiracial (see Mataillet 2007). French Caribbeans are a very important, though understudied, population. They include "descendants of slaves"—French people of color whose ancestors were enslaved in the overseas departments and territories. In contrast to the establishment of Haiti—which involved the first and only successful slave revolt in history—Martinique and Guadeloupe followed a path of political assimilation into the French nation. Following the second abolition of French slavery (in 1848), Martinique and Guadeloupe remained colonies until 1946 when they were administratively and legally absorbed into France as *départements*. French Caribbeans' uninterrupted status as citizens since the abolition of slavery in 1848 provides them with cultural and social resources, as well as avenues for political inclusion, that are denied to many black French people of sub-Saharan African origin. A complex apparatus of administrative offices and political representatives is specifically concerned with Guadeloupe and Martinique (which are both overseas departments and regions). Similarly, an entire ministry is dedicated to overseas affairs, a carryover from the colonial era. By contrast, no political office or ministry is specifically charged with the welfare of French people with immigrant ties to Africa. As a result of their special status—and their failure to follow in the footsteps of Haiti and attain independence—French Caribbeans are sometimes stereotyped by other Afro-descended minorities as "assimilated."

Migration from the French Caribbean to mainland France has grown steadily over the past fifty years, producing a large population of Afro-Caribbeans in Ile-de-France, the region where Paris is located.[17] Beginning in the 1960s, the Office for the Development of Migration in the Overseas Departments developed a state-sponsored program of mass migration from the Antilles to mainland France.[18] French Caribbean migrants were sought especially for jobs in the public sector (e.g., hospitals and post offices), where their status as citizens gave them pathways to upward mobility and assimilation that were not accessible to noncitizen residents and immigrants. More than three-quarters of French Caribbean migrants in mainland France are concentrated in the Paris region (Condon 2005). Census figures from 2008 (the first year I attended a commemoration of slavery in France) indicated a population of 455,000 first- and second-generation migrants from the *départements d'outre-mer* (overseas departments [DOM]) living in mainland France—more than the entire population of Guadeloupe (403,000) or Martinique (388,000).[19]

Toward a Critical Perspective on Race in France

Although *Resurrecting Slavery* is based on systematic empirical research, it is also unapologetically polemical. By bringing a critical race perspective to the study of French racism, I aim to critique and move beyond analyses that obscure (or outright deny) the existence of white domination in France. Unlike most scholars who work on race in Europe, I frame French racism in terms of oppression rather than "inequality." Further, I am explicit about the need to produce scholarly work that will help French people understand and resist systematic racism. In the contemporary period, many French academics and politicians have deployed color-blind ideology or revisionist denial (or both) to erase, justify, or grossly minimize France's history of racism. As late as 1950, Henri Blet, a prominent historian of French colonialism, affirmed that "Frenchmen . . . never adopted . . . racial doctrines affirming superiority of Whites over men of color" (quoted in Cohen 1980: xvi). Such denials of French racism are not only ahistorical and factually untrue. They are also *atemporal*. That is, portraying France as blind to race requires erasing French racism across time. It is against this backdrop of French racial denial that some activists and intellectuals are attempting not only to resurrect slavery and the history of French racism but also, crucially, to connect these inter-related subjects to the present.[20]

Despite being relegated to the margins of scholarship on race in France, French enslaving colonies in the Caribbean were central sites of white domina-tion and racial formation. William Cohen (1980: xxii) notes that for the French, the "most significant contact between Whites and Blacks occurred in the plantation colonies in the West Indies" in the early seventeenth century. French settler colonialism in the Americas and slave trading in West Africa combined to form a crucible of increasingly racialized thought that crystal-lized into a modern ideology of white (and Western) superiority over primi-tive non-white "others" in the mid-nineteenth century (Cohen 1980: 210). Throughout the 1800s, French academics played a central role in constructing and disseminating a white-supremacist racial hierarchy by crafting scientific racism, eugenics, and social Darwinism. Even Abbé Grégoire, the famous white French abolitionist and member of the antislavery group Société des Amis des Noirs (Society of the Friends of the Blacks), viewed black Africans as inferior beings and referred to them as "barbarians" (Cohen 1980: 210).

To be clear, my objective is not to reconstruct the history of French At-lantic slavery. While I draw on historical elements to understand the racial politics of slavery in contemporary France, this is not the work of a historian. Nor is my aim to identify "memorial regimes," as conceived by the French political scientist Johann Michel (2015), whose recent work provides a rich institutional history of slavery commemorations in France. Rather, my aim is to interrogate the racial ideas, narratives, categories, and images involved in the way French people resurrect the slavery past (Cottias, Fleming, and Boulbina 2009; Hourcade 2012, 2014; Schmidt 2012). In so doing, I ask this: *To what extent do commemorators and ordinary people make temporal connec-tions between past and present racism? How do representations of chattel slavery provide insight into race relations in France today?*

In addressing these questions, I draw attention to features of the French racial order that emerged in the aftermath of transatlantic slavery and con-tinue to shape group relations today: anti-blackness and white supremacy. It is unusual for scholars interested in race in France to center anti-black racism and white domination. This is ostensibly the case for at least three reasons. First, most students of inter-group relations in France have framed social problems in terms of "immigration" or social class. Second, those (relatively few) academics with interests in French racial discrimination tend to focus on the difficulties of the Maghrebis—French Arabs of North African descent. Finally, and perhaps most perplexingly, scholars working in a fledgling field one might call black European studies have produced important studies of contemporary and historical anti-black racism that, nonetheless, fail to dia-logue with critical race and whiteness studies. As a result, analyses that con-nect anti-blackness to white supremacy in France are exceedingly rare. This is a problem, I argue, because scholarship on race that ignores white suprem-acy—in France and elsewhere—unwittingly reinforces the domination of people who have come to be socially defined as "white."

My work is influenced by scholarship that takes a "critical approach" (Go-lash-Boza 2015) to the study of race and racism. This perspective foregrounds the systemic and structural nature of racial oppression (Bonilla-Silva 1997; Feagin 2006) as well as the impact of ideology in perpetuating racial privilege and disadvantage (Jung 2015). In a similar vein, critical race scholarship (Bell 1992; Delgado and Stefancic 2001; Harris 1993) has also informed my analysis of race in France.[21] Critical race theory (CRT) is an activist intellectual move-ment that emerged among legal theorists in the 1970s who were attempting to analyze and challenge the persistence of racism in the post–Civil Rights era (Delgado and Stefancic 2001: 3). While CRT is largely ignored in Europe, it has migrated into other disciplines in the United States, including philosophy (Mills 1997; Sullivan 2014) and the social sciences. I follow the sociologist Melissa Weiner (2012: 332), who calls for a global approach to CRT, examin-ing "the power of a dominant racial group to shape racial identities, knowl-edges, ideologies, and, thus, life chances and experiences of an oppressed racial group through coercion, violence and ideology." CRT represents a compel-ling—and underutilized—analytical framework for understanding French racism on the basis of its (1) critique of color-blind ideology and "race neutral" jurisprudence, (2) emphasis on systematic racism, and (3) insistence on mak-ing connections between the history of European imperialism and present-day inequalities.

A critical perspective is also helpful because of its conceptual specificity: instead of merely studying "race" or "racism," critical race scholars have been concerned with understanding white supremacy and interrelated forms of op-pression. Although it may seem surprising to write about white supremacy in relation to France, a society that is sometimes imagined as color-blind or post-racial, the persistence of white racial domination is key to understanding how matters of race, colonialism, and slavery are represented today. The phrase "white supremacy" generally brings to mind images of racial violence in the United States, exemplified by lynch mobs, the Ku Klux Klan, or the more recent terror attack in Charleston, South Carolina, where Dylann Roof, a twenty-one-year-old white man, murdered nine parishioners at Emanuel Af-rican Methodist Episcopal church. This caricature of white supremacy—as applicable only to extremist groups in the U.S. context—obscures the exis-tence of white supremacy as a global system of political and social domination.

Contrary to this narrow portrait, I follow the critical race philosopher Charles Mills (1997, 1998) in defining white supremacy as a "sociopolitical system" of racial dominance. This system, which he describes as the *racial contract*, is rooted in the history of European colonial domination of non-white others:

> The Racial Contract . . . is clearly historically locatable in the series of events marking the creation of the modern world by European colonialism and the voyages of "discovery" now increasingly and more appropriately called expeditions of conquest. . . . [W]e live in a world which has been foundationally shaped for the past five hundred years by the realities of European domination and the gradual consolidation of global White supremacy. (Mills 1997: 20)

After Europeans began colonizing non-European populations and territories in the fifteenth century, they eventually elaborated an ideology of *white supremacy* that justified their conquest and domination.[22] Mills, along with sociologists of race such as Eduardo Bonilla-Silva (1997, 2000), Joe Feagin (2006), Vilna Bashi-Treitler (2013), Melissa Weiner (2012, 2014b), and France Winddance Twine (1998) all examine how formations of white supremacy persist even after the fall of de jure racism.

By foregrounding the concept of global white supremacy and its particular manifestations in France, I attempt to move beyond the limitations of prior work on French racism. To that end, I advance two main arguments. First, I suggest that commemorations of slavery in mainland France are creating opportunities for the French to resurrect and (re)construct the intertwined taboos of race and colonialism. Yet I also argue that the hegemony of color-blindness and white racial dominance both limit the capacity of commemorations to foster antiracism. The racial context of French slavery commemorations—characterized by dominant rules of "political correctness," widespread resistance to talking frankly about race, and a lack of antiracist public policies—makes it difficult for activists and politicians to clearly link slavery to racism. For this reason, it is a mistake—in France and elsewhere—to believe that merely "breaking the silence" about slavery is itself antiracist.

The racial domination that reigned in the French Caribbean is inextricably linked to the racial biases that continue to shape France today. Few people realize that terms related to chattel enslavement are in some ways more racialized in French than in English. For example, the transatlantic slave trade is generally referred to as *la traite des noirs* (the trade in blacks) or *la traite negriere* (the Negro trade). This explicit racialization of slavery was built into the cultural and legal apparatus of French Atlantic slavery. Thus, in resurrecting slavery through commemoration, the French would have a hard time completely avoiding race simply because of the racial language that was used to describe the trade. Nonetheless, the lexicon used to describe French slavery is, in fact, embedded with forms of racial avoidance hiding in plain sight. One of the things you might notice about a term such as the "black trade" is that it racializes the victims of slavery without mentioning—or racializing—the perpetrators. This pattern is also on display in the Code Noir (Black Code), the 1685 document promulgated by Louis XIV that provided legal infrastructure and regulation of slavery in the French colonies. Throughout, the document—long forgotten by most of the French—systematically describes "slave masters" in nonracial terms yet designates slaves by the word *nègres* (which denotes "black," "Negro," and "nigger" in French).

In addition to asymmetrically racializing blacks and people of color (*gens du couleur*), some French texts and practices related to slavery included explicit references to whiteness. As Keaton (2010) notes, the decree of 1802 reestablishing slavery in the colonies (after its initial abolition in 1794) formally restricted citizenship to whites. Moreover, the name of the general—Antoine Richepanse—who wrote the white-supremacist text reenslaving blacks and stripping them of citizenship rights is engraved on the Arc de Triomphe in Paris.[23] Whiteness was also inscribed and institutionalized into French social, political, and cultural life through the writings of explorers, colonists, enslavers, politicians, and scientists (Cohen 1980). French intellectuals played a leading role in crafting scientific racism in the mid-1800s, which explicitly defined whiteness and Europeanness as superior to non-white and non-European groups. With his *Essays on the Inequality of the Human Races*, written in the 1850s, influential French thinker Arthur de Gobineau (1967) helped popularize racist thought and justified the ideology of white supremacy using the language of science (Biddiss 1970; Painter 2010). French advocates of social Darwinism and eugenics proliferated racist beliefs that defined whiteness as synonymous with intellectual, moral, and social achievement. Further, France's colonial encounter with and domination of Africans and their descendants both on the continent and in the West Indies solidified the ideology of white supremacy. On this subject, Alice Conklin (1997: 213) writes:

> The overwhelming superiority of French technology to any in Africa convinced the French that they held a monopoly on civilization. The belief in African laziness also derived from the absence of industrial achievements in Africa comparable to those in the West. . . . Both the apparent failure of freed slaves in the West Indies to prosper after emancipation . . . and the "scientific" findings of French physical anthropology after 1850, encouraged the image of the lazy African.

While Conklin's narrative is helpful for understanding the historical roots of French anti-blackness and anti-African sentiment, an important dimension of social construction is missing from this analysis. It is important to point out that rather than reproducing French colonial propaganda about their own technological superiority, French ideas about what the words "civilization" and "technology" mean shaped their perception of their own advancement. Thus, what emerges, to the critical eye, is not the "fact" of French technological superiority but, rather, that *the French framed their industrial practices as "advanced" and defined African technologies as non-existent or backward.* Thus, French ideas about their technical achievements (and their undervaluing or negating of African knowledge and achievement) facilitated the ideology of white (and European) superiority.

Racial Temporality

Much of this book concerns the extent to which the French imagine slavery and racism as *temporal* phenomena. Although the word "temporality" does not usually come up in everyday conversation, it is nonetheless a central component of our everyday lives. When we think or talk about time—or make connections among the past, present, and future—we are invoking temporality. Theories of time are of great interest to physicists, but temporality is also relevant to those who study the social world. Somewhat surprisingly, students of collective memory often neglect social perceptions of time and temporality. A significant exception to this trend is found in the work of Michael Flaherty (1999, 2011), whose contributions to the field of symbolic interactionism explore the ways people subjectively experience and attach meaning to the passage of time. In particular, Flaherty's notion of "time work" orients our attention to "how individuals control or manipulate their own experience of time" (Flaherty 2011: 10).[24] Flaherty's emphasis on agency is especially useful to this study, given my interest in the work of activists and officials involved in constructing and shifting the present-day representation of the colonial past. My study draws attention to an understudied form of time work at the heart of antiracist mobilizations: resistance to the collective forgetting, denial, or marginalizing of the racial past and its connections to the present. This resistance takes the form of social movements concerned with memorializing racial history that the state and other segments of the citizenry find embarrassing or inconvenient.

The concept of *racial temporality*, which I introduce and develop throughout the book, refers to social actors' representations of race. Representing race as temporal involves making claims about the *content* of the racial past, present, and future, as well as the *relationship* among racial categories, relations, and processes in these different time periods. Racial temporality involves

Figure I-1. *A monument dedicated to General Thomas-Alexandre Dumas, the son of a slave, installed in the Place du General Catroux (Seventeenth Arrondissement) in 2009 at the initiative of Claude Ribbe and the Association des Amis du Général Dumas.*

both time work and cognitive labor as social actors attempt to describe race in the past, present, and/or future. Claims about continuities and discontinuities are key to representations of race across time. Depictions of racial continuity emphasize what has not changed (e.g., similarities in patterns of racial discrimination over time). For example, in her work on the commemoration of Bristol's history of slavery in Britain, Olivette Otele (2012: 156) suggests that claims about continuity take the form of "discourses regarding the history of that trade and, by extension, the history of populations of African-Caribbean descent." Racial claims about temporal continuity might frame Africans and Caribbeans in the past and present as targets of racial domination. Other narratives and representations highlight *differences* between the racial past and present. For example, some people argue that racism existed in the past but no longer exists in the present. This kind of narrative is often referred to as *post-racial*—the claim that race and racism have disappeared in the contemporary moment. Still other depictions of racial temporality involve denial of race and racism in the past *and* present. This kind of temporal claim is at the heart of color-blind racial ideology, which denies or minimizes the existence of the racial past as well as of the racial present.

In my view, temporality is an understudied dimension of what Ann Morning (2011) refers to as *racial conceptualization*—the way people understand and define what race means. The way we invoke (or avoid) racial categories, narratives, and representations conveys certain understandings about race and time. Temporal representations of race not only are embedded in how we think about history; they also undergird our everyday conceptualizations of race. When we describe the legacies of racism, or speculate about racial progress in the present or the future, we are constructing racial temporality. By focusing on the racial temporalities constructed by activists, politicians, and ordinary people in

Figure I-2. *Flyers on racism at a commemoration of enslaved people on May 23, 2015, organized by the French Caribbean activist 1998 March Committee (CM98). The International League against Racism and Anti-Semitism hosted the table.*

France, this study aims to shed light on the role of social movements and political discourse in shaping the representation of racial processes across time.

My interest in this project reflects my impression that blacks broadly—and French Caribbeans specifically—are too often excluded from academic and political debates over racism, migration and immigration, diversity, and multiculturalism. As noted above, U.S. scholars studying France have framed anti-black racism as a side issue or as less important than anti-Arab sentiment—rather than developing an analysis of how racialized minorities are subject to white-supremacist oppression. Even scholarly treatments of race in France (already a rather narrow field) often fail to center the perspectives of black people—including the Martinican psychiatrist and theorist Frantz Fanon. Bizarrely, Fanon's trenchant analysis of French colonialism and anti-black racism, linking his experience with racial oppression as a Martinican to the Algerian struggle for independence, is curiously absent from much contemporary scholarship on French racism. While Fanon has garnered much more attention outside France than within it, the lack of engagement with his work among well-known scholars of French racism is striking. More than fifty years after his death, Fanon remains studiously ignored by most scholars in his native country.[25] As Sonia Dayan-Herzbrun (2015: xi) notes, Fanon still is "not yet completely accepted as an author legitimately to be read and discussed" by the French intelligentsia. This sidelining of Fanon and the minimization of French anti-blackness have produced an inaccurate portrait of racism in France, a distortion that I hope to correct with this book.

In addition to centering the voices of French Afro-descendants, my work contributes to scholarship on race by unpacking the representation of whiteness in France. Specifically, I ask how the French construct (or obscure) white people as a social group in relation to the history and legacies of slavery. One of the most persistent findings in my fieldwork is what I term *asymmetric racialization*, a pattern of unequal recognition for racialized groups that very often renders whiteness an invisible, unmarked category. When racial categories are used asymmetrically in depictions of the past, certain groups are named and explicitly marked, whereas others are either implicitly alluded to or ignored altogether. Take, for example, the Taubira Law of 2001, mentioned earlier, which made France the first (and to this day, the only) country in the world to recognize slavery as a "crime against humanity." On its face, this legislative development might seem like a significant step in the fight against racism. After all, no other Western nation has explicitly enshrined in law any recognition for the criminality of transatlantic slavery, a practice that European practitioners routinely legitimated and justified with explicitly racist ideology throughout its history. Yet a closer look at the text of the law reveals certain peculiarities. The three main articles of the legislation read this way:

ARTICLE 1
The French Republic recognizes that the transatlantic Negro slave trade as well as the trade in the Indian ocean on the one hand, and slavery on the other, perpetrated from the 15th century in the Americas and in the Caribbean, in the Indian Ocean and Europe against African, American-Indian, Malagasy and Indian populations constitutes a crime against humanity.

ARTICLE 2
The academic curriculum and programs of research in history and the human sciences will accord to the Negro trade and slavery the consequential place they deserve. Cooperation which permits and places in articulation written archives available in Europe with oral sources and archeological knowledge accumulated in Africa, the Americas, the Caribbean and in all other territories having known slavery will be encouraged and promoted.

ARTICLE 3

A request for recognition of the transatlantic Negro trade as well as the trade in the Indian ocean and slavery as a crime against humanity will be introduced before the European Council, international organizations and the United Nations. This request will equally target the selection of a common date on an international scale for commemorating abolition of the Negro trade and slavery, without preference for the commemorative dates of each overseas department.

The text of the law makes it clear that the French state now acknowledges that transatlantic slavery was criminal and calls for educational and commemorative efforts to resurrect this aspect of the past. This retroactive declaration is important, given that slavery was completely legal in France while it was practiced. The wording also singles out specific groups that were targeted and exploited: African, American Indian, Malagasy, and Indian populations. Further, the law implicitly reifies a racial category—in this case, blackness—with four references to the Negro trade (*traite negrière*). But how are those who carried out enslavement characterized? The first article declares that slavery was "perpetrated," yet no perpetrator (individual or collective) is mentioned. More to the point, the perpetrators of slavery not only are not named; they are not racialized. The slavery past is represented in terms that resurrect certain aspects of race, but only the race of the victims.

Black French Activism

While the commemorative activism at stake in this book involves people of diverse backgrounds, it is nonetheless deeply connected to prior activism and intellectual labor by Afro-descended populations in France. Black French mobilizations began to germinate in the social and cultural networks of intellectuals migrating to the metropole from Africa and the Caribbean after World War I (Boittin 2010; Jules-Rosette 2007). Literary scholars in particular have played a central role in unpacking the black identity work of *négritude* intellectuals (Ako 1984; Le Baron 1966; Edwards 2003; Sharpley-Whiting 2002). As Edward Ako (1984) points out, Césaire first invoked the term *négritude,* in his well-known *Cahier d'un retour au pays natal* (1947). For Bentley Le Baron (1966), writers such as Césaire, Léopold Sédar Senghor, and Léon-Gontran Damas affirmed cultural pride while embracing African roots and centering the collective memory of historical subjugation:

The persistent themes of négritude poetry include a remembrance of past indignities; but more significant is an emphasis on present and future greatness. Even in passages recalling slavery and humiliation, references to inherent Negro values are contrasted with the shallowness of the seemingly superior Whites. (Le Baron 1966: 268)

Tracy Sharpley-Whiting (2002) situates Jane and Paulette Nardal as precursors to *négritude*. The Martinican sisters held a weekly salon in the Parisian suburb of Clamart and spearheaded the groundbreaking though short-lived publication *La Revue du Monde Noir* (Review of the Black World [1931]), a "monthly bilingual, multiracial collaborative review" (Sharpley-Whiting 2002: 55). Taken together, the intellectual work of the Nardal sisters served to "raise consciousness," construct an international black identity, and promote interracial exchange (Sharpley-Whiting 2002: 55). In these settings, individuals from Africa, Europe, and the Americas circulated ideas and strategies for confronting colonial racism. Over the course of its six issues, *La Revue du Monde Noir* was a forum for commentary and literary work, in English and French, that explicitly called for the formulation of an international black identity. French Caribbean writers in the 1980s who rejected cultural and racial essentialism of *négritude* in favor of theories of *antilleanité* (Antilleanness) and *créolité* (Creole-ness) that emphasize the cultural syncretism and multiracialism of populations in Guadeloupe and Martinique would later criticize such efforts to promote a shared racial consciousness and solidarity among all people of African descent.

Overview of the Study

I examine the significance of recent commemorative movements using three main sources of data: in-depth interviews with commemorators and French Caribbean migrants outside the commemorative movement, ethnographic observation of commemorative events in the Paris region between 2007 and 2010, and a database of speeches delivered by French politicians over the past thirty years. I define commemorators as people involved in the production, management, and institutionalization of collective memory. This includes event organizers as well as journalists, politicians, civil servants, politicians, and activists. This case study of commemoration included a broad range of events in the Paris region, from official ceremonies to small meetings of grassroots organizations, marches, cultural shows, and educational exhibitions.

Finally, to assess the views of people outside the commemorative movement, I probe the perspectives of French Caribbeans through interviews with first- and second-generation migrants from Guadeloupe and Martinique. Despite being born French, Afro-descended French Caribbeans (often referred to in France as "Antillean") face racism due to their skin color and phenotype (Célestine 2009b; Giraud 2005). The specification of "Afro-descended" here is important, given the existence of a small white minority in the French Caribbean—descendants of white French slave owners and colonizers often referred to as the *békés*. Unlike French Arabs, most French Caribbeans do not face discrimination or stigmatization tied to their religion. Catholicism continues to be widely influential in Guadeloupe and Martinique. Yet Antillean migrants do experience some of the same difficulties that immigrants face, including discrimination in housing (Condon and Ogden 1993) and employment (Condon 2000), as well as exclusion due to their Caribbean accent. The sociologist Michel Giraud (2005: 101) captures the special dilemma faced by non-white French Caribbeans who feel entitled to fair treatment because of their citizenship, yet experience discrimination:

> Neither their citizenship nor their close relationship to French history and culture have been, for them, guarantees against discriminations and practices of exclusion, while they are continually told that they are rightfully and entirely French. . . . [D]escendants from the DOM living in metropolitan France discover that they are, according to the formulation of Aimé Césaire[,] "entirely apart." . . . [D]espite their not being, strictly speaking, foreigners, they are in fact considered as such by the nation.[26]

The forms of exclusion faced by blacks and people of color in the French Caribbean have always involved processes of colonial domination and racialization. Thus, in spite of their relatively small number vis-à-vis blacks in mainland France, Antilleans have much to teach us about past and present French racism.

Organization of the Book

The chapters in *Resurrecting Slavery* are organized as follows: The first suite of chapters provides historical context and examines the role of politicians and commemorative activists in shaping representations of race and slavery in France. Chapter 1 provides historical and theoretical background on the relationship between slavery and constructions of race in France. I make the case for using a critical race lens to understand the construction of race in France. Chapter 2 examines the political context in which slavery is commemorated. I discuss certain public controversies over the representation of slavery to illustrate some of the norms and taboos that characterize the commemorative field. The chapter also considers how French politicians and party leaders (most of whom are white) talk about the history and memory of slavery. Overall, I show that the state's efforts to commemorate slavery tend to avoid issues of race. In this way, the state generally commemorates slavery without historicizing race. When race is alluded to, whiteness is mostly avoided, leaving politicians to make statements about ethnic and racial minorities as historical actors without acknowledging whites—except as abolitionists. Chapter 3 introduces the perspectives of commemorative activists and officials (most of whom are non-white) to show the cleavages that exist between race-avoidant groups seeking symbolic recognition for French Caribbeans as ethnic "descendants of slaves" and race-conscious activists who assert black or African-diasporic identities and seek redress for contemporary and past racism. Chapter 4 draws on ethnographic observations at events in the Paris region to show how commemorative events allow experts, activists, and members of the public to construct racial temporality on the ground, particularly in settings where people of color are able to engage in discussion and make connections between past and present racism.

The second set of chapters turns our attention to the everyday racial politics of remembrance by including the views of people outside of the commemorative movements. Chapter 5 surveys the perspectives of non-activist French Caribbeans by exploring the place of slavery in relation to their identities. I explore what it means to be a descendant of slaves in France from the perspective of people outside of the commemorative movements. Finally, I compare ordinary and activist perspectives according to specific themes: the legacies of slavery (Chapter 6) and reparations (Chapter 7). The Conclusion situates the book's major findings in a discussion of broader issues related to racial domination in societies shaped by chattel slavery. In an age in which activists and ordinary people alike on both sides of the Atlantic are urgently insisting that black lives matter, the question is whether and how citizens will be able to make coherent and compelling connections between white supremacy in the past and the present. It is my modest hope that engaging French perspectives on slavery will not only contribute to a more nuanced understanding of racism among specialists of France but also provide new ways to think about the global dimensions of slavery, stigma, and anti-blackness.

1

Slavery and the Construction of Race in France

Most people think of France as a hexagon-shaped nation located on the European continent. The reality, however, is that France is composed of its mainland as well as its overseas departments and territories. A great many French officials, journalists, and everyday people still refer to the mainland as "metropolitan France," an appellation that harks back to the distance (both geographic and symbolic) between the colonizing *metropole*, on the one hand, and conquered territories, on the other. France's overseas expansion involved both settler colonialism and racial slavery. Unlike the United States, where slavery took place within the geographic boundaries of the nation, France established chattel enslavement in the Caribbean and Indian oceans, thousands of miles away from the mainland. In this respect, France is similar to other major European powers—Portugal, Great Britain, the Netherlands, and Spain—that engaged in chattel slavery within the context of colonial ambitions abroad. Indeed, the historian Sue Peabody (1996) illustrates that this physical and imaginative distance helps explain the persistence of a popular myth: that there are no (and never have been) slaves in France.[1] The relegation of slavery to the overseas territories means that many French people view slavery as a marginal issue—one that is relevant mostly to islands thousands of miles away. The work of many commemorators attempts to contest the ghettoization of enslavement by embedding the history and memory of slavery in the national narrative.

This chapter provides the historical and theoretical context needed to understand the significance of commemorative movements related to slavery. First, I show how the history of transatlantic slavery is linked to racism in

France today. Throughout the chapter, I argue that racial temporality is an essential cognitive tool that enables French minority groups involved in the commemoration of slavery to name and contest racism. At the same time, certain features of white supremacy in France, including norms of political correctness, color-blind ideology, and the stigmatization of group-based mobilizations, limit the ability of non-whites to resist domination with temporal representations of race. After explaining (and critiquing) how social scientists have examined race in France, I turn to research on collective memory and explain the importance of uncovering the temporal claims people make about how the racial past is connected to the present.

Understanding Transtlantic Slavery

Transatlantic slavery refers to the nearly four centuries of kidnapping and transportation of enslaved people from sub-Saharan Africa to the Americas by European colonial powers.[2] The majority of transatlantic slaves were taken from regions of West-Central Africa and the Bight of Benin (Burnard 2011; Lovejoy 1983). Portugal was the very first European colonial power to engage in the trade, while the Portuguese-descended Brazilians were the very last to abolish slavery, in 1888. Other European (or Euro-descended) enslavers include Britain, the United States, France, Spain, and the Netherlands. The first shipment of enslaved Africans arrived in the Americas in 1525, and trade continued until 1876, although slaves remained captive decades after the legal abolition of the trade.[3] For example, Britain and the United States ended their involvement in the slave trade in 1807 but did not abolish slavery itself until 1833 and 1865, respectively. France passed three different laws over the course of fourteen years (from 1817 to 1831) to withdraw from the trade but continued enslaving Africans and their descendants in French colonies until 1848.[4]

In his well-known global survey of the institution, the sociologist Orlando Patterson (1982: 13) defined slavery as "the permanent, violent, and personal domination of natally alienated and generally dishonored persons." For Patterson, the slave is "socially dead," meaning that he or she is unable to be positioned or recognized within "the legitimate social order" (Patterson 1982: 5). Enslavement is an ancient institution found in virtually every society across the globe. Even today, there are nearly 30 million slaves throughout the world, despite international conventions and laws banning human bondage and trafficking.[5] Yet while slavery is a global phenomenon that predates our modern notions of race, many people continue to associate slavery with black people *in particular*. Today, anti-black epithets such as *nègre* (in French) and "nigger" (in English) are imbued with the double meaning of "black" and "slave."[6] It is important to note, however, that the word "slave" is derived from the Latin *sclavus*, indicating a person of Slavic (Eastern European) origin.[7] As the historian Nell Painter (2010: xi) reminds us, the existence of "unfree White people slumbers in popular forgetfulness, though White slavery (like black slavery) moved people around and mixed up human genes on a massive scale." The perceived link between blackness, slave status, and negative stereotypes forms the backbone of contemporary anti-black racism. But where does this association between blackness and enslavement come from, and what does it have to do with race and racism today?

While scholarly consensus indicates that at least 10 million people were enslaved and deported from Africa to the Americas during the transatlantic trade, estimates vary greatly. The Transatlantic Slave Trade Database identifies 12,521,336 individuals who were enslaved and deported from Africa while only 10,702,656 people arrived in the Americas—meaning that nearly 2 million died during the horrific voyage across the Atlantic euphemistically known as the Middle Passage.[8] Paul Lovejoy (2012), a recognized authority on slavery, also pegs the number at about 12 million.[9] On the higher end of the scale, the Slave Route Project, an initiative of the United Nations Educational, Scientific and Cultural Organization (UNESCO), suggests that as many as 17 million Africans became transatlantic slaves.[10] Regardless of the exact number cited, the fact remains that the transatlantic trade was by far "the largest forced mass migration in history" (Burnard 2011: 94). Almost 50 percent of enslaved Africans captured during the transatlantic slave trade were sent to Brazil—a population of some 5,848,265 souls. This mass displacement of forced labor is the reason Brazil is now home to the largest population of African descent outside the African continent. Britain, the second-largest enslaver, deported 3,259,440 people to its colonies in the Americas. Of the six major Euro-descended enslavers, France ranks third, having enslaved at least 1,381,404 Africans—a figure that is 4.5 times greater than the number forced into bondage by the United States (305,326).[11]

Slavery and Anti-blackness

The scholarly literature on the subject of race and transatlantic slavery is vast and complex, with historians and sociologists disagreeing across and within disciplinary lines. Acknowledging these complexities and debates is important for students of commemoration because they point to the special difficulties involved in trying to understand—and represent—the history and legacies of slavery generally and of transatlantic slavery in particular. For example, some scholars, such as the sociologist Tanya Golash-Boza, portray transatlantic slavery as distinctive for its unique dehumanization of slaves.

"Until the eighteenth century," she writes, "no society categorically denied the humanity of slaves. It was not seen as necessary to rationalize slavery by denying that slaves were fully human" (Golash-Boza 2015: 9). This view is starkly different from the account of David Brion Davis, who argues that slaves have been portrayed throughout history as "human animals" insofar as they are made to embody "the so-called animal traits that all humans share and fear" while being deprived of "the redeeming rational and spiritual qualities that give humans a sense of pride" (Davis 2006: 32). On this point, Davis speculates that techniques for enslaving people emerged at some point after the so-called Neolithic Revolution in 7000 B.C., when Mesopotamians devised methods to domesticate animals: "To control such beasts, humans not only branded them but devised collars, chains, prods, and whips and also castrated and subjected certain animals to specific breeding patterns" (Davis 2006: 32). While the treatment and status of slaves varied across social and historical contexts, enslavement has always been a brutal affair involving forms of denigration, torture, and trauma (both physical and psychological). More specifically, it is important to understand that the institution of chattel slavery, which reduces human beings to a status somewhere between property and beast, existed before the transatlantic trade.

We return now to the business of examining the precise role of transatlantic slavery in producing anti-black racism. Davis (2003: 68) tells us that "human bondage carried no racial implications" during "biblical and early antiquity." However, at some point along the line, the perceived link between race and slavery came into being. To understand the process, several issues require untangling. The first regards the widespread stigmatization of enslaved people found wherever and whenever slavery took place. Many features of anti-black racism today—including negative stereotypes of mental inferiority, laziness, and sexual immorality—have been applied throughout history to enslaved and low-status populations throughout the world, including in Europe. Second, one of the main reasons that slaves were socially dishonored throughout history has to do with their status as *conquered foreigners* and *outsiders*. Patterson (1982: 178) argues convincingly that ethnic differences between masters and slaves were far more prevalent than racial differences, noting a "universal reluctance to enslave members of one's own community." As ethnic outsiders, slaves often did not speak the language of their conquerors and lacked familiarity with enslavers' social and political systems, factors that undoubtedly contributed to their vulnerability and domination (Patterson 1982).

There is also the more general relationship among slavery, stigmatization, and skin tone. In exploring this complicated terrain, it is necessary to consider the variety of meanings associated with dark skin and "blackness" *before* the modern concept of race. In other words, we must examine *pre-racial perceptions* of skin tone and status. There are different views on this question, even among specialists. One group of race scholars, *primordialists*, tend to argue that race relations and racial domination are the result of essential differences among groups, including variations in skin tone. This school of thought, exemplified by the work of Pierre van den Berghe, Thomas Gossett, Edward Shills, and Bernard Lewis, tends to project racial categories and conflict into the distant past (Smedley and Smedley 2012: 21). On the other end of the theoretical spectrum are *constructivists*, who view race as a social construction and tend to represent racism as historically contingent and, especially, linked to colonialism and transatlantic slavery. Constructivists are much more careful in their use of the term "race" and generally restrict it to the modern period.[12] Although he does not fit into the primordialist mold, Patterson also imagines race as a constituent element of social relations before the modern advent of racial ideology. Consider this passage in his analysis of color, "race," and slavery:

> Where the slave was of a different race or color, this fact tended to become associated with slave status—and not only in the Americas. A black skin in almost all the Islamic societies, including parts of the Sudan, was and still is associated with slavery. True, there were white slaves; true, it was possible to be black and free, even of high status—but this did not mean that blackness was not associated with slavery. Perceived racial differences between masters and slaves could be found in a significant number of other societies ranging from the Ethiopians, the Bemba, and even the Lozis of Africa, to the Gilyaks and Lolos of eastern Asia. (Patterson 1982: 58)

Patterson's approach—indeed, the writing of many scholars of slavery—begs the question: *does it make sense to consider so-called blacks and whites racial groups before the emergence of a racial worldview?* I am inclined to suggest that doing so is theoretically questionable, at best, and historically inaccurate, at worst.

Although black skin was not universally stigmatized in the ancient world, the historical record points to surprising instances of anti-blackness applied to populations *outside* Africa. Davis's work in this regard is enlightening. On the origins of anti-black racism, he writes, "In both the ancient and medieval worlds, there was a strong inclination to equate slaves with ugliness and dark skin, wholly apart from the reality of their appearance" (Davis 2006: 50). Moreover, "even when slaves and slavelike serfs belonged to the same ethnic group as their masters, as in eighteenth- and nineteenth-century Russia, they were said to be intrinsically lazy, childlike, licentious, and incapable of life without authoritative direction. Some Russian noblemen reinvented a sup-posedly separate historical origin of Russian serfs and even claimed that they had black bones" (Davis 2006: 50).[13]

While Europeans certainly viewed sub-Saharan Africans as having "black" skin at the onset of transatlantic slavery, they did not depict them as a distinctly inferior, biologically differentiated *racial group* until the second half of the eighteenth century. Against those who suggest that Africans were selected for transatlantic slavery for their skin tone or "ideological" reasons, the prolific historian Gwendolyn Midlo Hall (2005: 9–10) insists that eco-nomic motives, as well as the desire to maintain social order within Europe were primary factors. Further, in the earlier phases of transatlantic slavery, European enslavers sometimes described white and black servants in similarly degrading terms (Patterson 1982: 6–7). Golash-Boza (2015) stresses that peo-ple labeled "black" were not viewed negatively in antiquity. In her view, the global stigmatization of blackness as connoting both innate inferiority and racial belonging is a relatively recent development. Further, there is the ad-ditional factor of dark skin being associated with low status for reasons com-pletely unrelated to "race"—namely, the fact that throughout history, people with greater resources have been able to spend more time within physical dwellings, whereas lower-status workers tend to labor outside in the sun, thus acquiring darker skin (Davis 2006: 51).

With regard to whiteness before European colonization of the Americas, similar caveats apply. Painter's (2010: 33) observation that "in the land we now call Europe, most slaves were white, and that fact was unremarkable" requires a slight qualification. The fact of the matter is that the European populations we now typically think of as "white" were not routinely labeled as such until the past several centuries. Whiteness in its modern connotations is the unacknowledged bastard child of colonialism and transatlantic slavery. Painter herself admits as much, arguing that slavery was essential to the con-struction of whiteness in two ways. First, she posits that human bondage—particularly transatlantic enslavement—resulted in a "tradition [that] equates whiteness with freedom while consigning blackness to slavery." But she goes further, suggesting that the category "Caucasian" became infused with "con-cepts of beauty related to the white slave trade from eastern Europe," result-ing in the association between whiteness and "visions of beauty found in art history and popular culture" (Painter 2010: xi). The trouble here is that the "white slave trade," by which Painter means the extensive enslavement of Europeans by other Europeans, predated the emergence of whiteness as a *racial category*. Thus, while racial conceptualizations of whiteness are cer-tainly related to premodern social transformations, including the perception of dominant and non-dominant European ethnic groups, these representations cannot be properly considered analogues for what most people mean by "white" today.

Despite these complications, what we know for sure about race and transatlantic slavery is this: at the onset of the transatlantic slave trade, whiteness had not yet been consolidated into a widely shared racial identity for the diverse array of ethnic groups living in Europe. Nor, for that matter, were the thousands of ethnic groups living in Africa universally viewed as either "black" or "African," by themselves or by others. The scholarly consensus holds that the diverse peoples of sub-Saharan Africa came to be viewed as a single "black" group, rather than as members of various ethnicities, as the transatlantic slave trade progressed (Hall 2005). But as the transatlantic trade increased in volume during the eighteenth century, Europeans—the French prominent among them—began to develop modern concepts of race, along with scientific racism, to justify the colonization and enslavement of populations they defined as non-white. The new race concept was unique due to its representation of the human population as belonging to discrete, mutually exclusive biological categories arranged in a hierarchy with whites at the top and blacks at the bottom (Bashi-Treitler 2013; Roberts 2012).[14] These pseudo-scientific justifications came to replace—and complement—the Judeo-Christian ideology that was previously used to legitimate the enslavement, torture, and rape of transatlantic slaves.[15]

Prior to the modern notion of race as "biological" difference, people across the globe noticed variations in skin tone and developed ideas about what these distinctions might mean. But they did not establish categories of differentially ranked humans denoting innate superiority and inferiority that we are familiar with today. Dorothy Roberts (2011: 6) drives this point home in her analysis of the social construction of race. "Believing in the uniqueness and superiority of one's own group may be universal," she argues, "but it is not equivalent to race. These ancient attempts to describe and explain differences among peoples did not . . . treat these differences as markers of immutable distinctions that determine each group's permanent social value." This historical detail is important, as it highlights the racial legacies of transatlantic slavery, both in France and throughout the societies affected by the trade—namely, the emergence of racial categories and white-supremacist racism.

Problems in the Literature on Race in France

Having reviewed the links between transatlantic slavery, white supremacy, and anti-black racism, I now turn to some of the problems in the contemporary literature on race in France. These include the minimization of racism, the trivialization of anti-blackness, and the obfuscation of white supremacy.

Minimization of Racism

Traditionally, French scholars interested in inequality have avoided integrating race (and gender) into their analyses, preferring to focus on social class and immigration. As a result, French scholarship on race and racism is notoriously anemic. Despite progress over the past decade, social science research on race remains underdeveloped and even controversial in France. In this respect, the country lags far behind the United States and Great Britain, nations with long-established academic disciplines dedicated to the study of race. French research on inequality typically focuses on social class and immigration, with relatively few scholars directly examining race or gender. While intersectionality has become a buzzword of late in the French academic scene, black feminists and critical race theorists from across the Atlantic remain on the margins of intellectual discourse. "Black studies" as such does not exist as an institutionalized field of inquiry in France or Europe, although an increasing number of scholars are investigating the experiences and worldviews of Afro-descended Europeans.

Even scholars who work on race in France have portrayed French society as comparatively less ravaged by racism than countries such as South Africa and the United States. For example, the historian George Fredrickson (2005: 110) insisted, "There has been no equivalent in metropolitan France for the American colour line." Fredrickson (2005: 110) thus situates racism as a peripheral issue for the French—one "mainly in distant colonies and not in the metropole." Further, while noting "a rising tide of xenophobic hostility to North African Muslims," Fredrickson (2005: 110) was nonetheless reassured that "North Africans intermarry with French people of European antecedents at a substantially higher rate than Blacks do with Whites in the United States." Of course, comparatively high rates of intermarriage and the social integration of minorities can coexist with pervasive and systematic racism, as seen in Brazil and Great Britain.

Trivialization of Anti-blackness

An emerging body of work has challenged the hegemony of race-avoidant research by refocusing attention on French racism (Balibar and Wallerstein 1991; Bleich 2003; Chapman and Frader 2004; Hargreaves 1995, 2007; Peabody and Stovall 2003; Silverman 1992). However, one of the unfortunate characteristics of this literature is its penchant for trivializing the existence (or severity) of anti-black racism. In part, this minimization of French anti-blackness reflects the influence of scholars who argue that ethnic and racial minorities in France face exclusion mainly on the basis of *cultural racism*.

From this perspective, members of minority groups are stigmatized as "unassimilable" due to their perceived cultural differences vis-à-vis the majority population. Social scientists who embrace the cultural racism perspective argue that biological racism or phenotypic racism is passé and no longer broadly affirmed as a legitimate basis of exclusion. Thus, newer, cultural forms of racism have arisen to take the place of old-school racism.

One of the best-known theorists of cultural racism in France is the sociologist Michèle Lamont (2000, 2004), whose influential work examined the experiences of whites and Arabs in France. In *The Dignity of Working Men*, Lamont sought to complement the work of scholars interested in "symbolic racism"—forms of racial exclusion that are less explicit than overt violence or de jure segregation. This perspective downplays the importance of racial phenotype (e.g., skin tone, hair texture, or facial features) and emphasizes the role of cultural or "moral" values in determining how group membership and worthiness are defined. One of the downsides of the cultural racism perspective is that it minimizes the existence of anti-black racism in France. Indeed, Lamont describes the context of French racism as "one where Blacks are not salient and North African immigrants are" (Lamont 2000: 170). In so doing, she aims to contrast French racism with the U.S. case, where the legacies of whites' violent domination and stigmatization of African Americans loom large. Lamont's cultural racism thesis asserts that racial bias and discrimination—particularly subtle forms—are not closely related to skin color in France. Instead, racism is perpetuated through the "symbolic boundaries" and the cultural definitions of citizenship and belonging of the dominant group.[16]

Despite the important role of Lamont's work in unveiling the existence of French racism, the cultural racism perspective perpetuates the fallacious notion that phenotypic discrimination is not especially salient in France. Her portrayal of French racism as mainly "cultural"—and the focus on French Arabs—has been broadly influential in U.S. scholarship on immigration and migration in France. However, we need only look to Frantz Fanon and the Nardal sisters, as well as the many writers involved in the Negritude movement, to know that French black minorities themselves have long challenged the notion that skin color is a minor factor in French racism. Phenotypic racism is not a new phenomenon in France. According to Cris Beauchemin and colleagues (2010), 73 percent of people born to parents from the overseas departments (DOM) and 88 percent of those born to immigrants from sub-Saharan African cite skin color as the reason why they believe they experience discrimination. An increasing number of academic reports and public incidents of racism attest that while politicians portray *French law* as color-blind, *French society* is decidedly color-conscious. Despite the denial of race in politics and academic culture, French people themselves do not describe their nation as color-blind. A poll conducted by OpinonWay in 2013 shows that 78 percent of general population and 82 percent of citizens from DOM say discrimination is "common."

More recently, Lamont and Nicolas Duvoux (2014) have argued that anti-black racism has *become* salient over the past two decades as a result of neo-liberalism and changing demographics. This analysis, however, contradicts empirical evidence of systematic anti-blackness before Lamont completed her original study of racism in France. The very *first* (and rarely cited) audit study of French racism leveraged the experiences of French Caribbeans to demonstrate the link between skin color and discrimination.[17] In measuring discriminatory hiring practices, Frank Bovenkerk and his colleagues (1979) compared the results of male and female job candidates—white individuals born in mainland France and black migrants from the Caribbean who grew up in the Hexagon, matching candidates according to age, family background, education, and professional experience. Among the 682 job ads involved in the study, researchers found an overall discrimination rate of 66.7 percent, indicating significant bias against the black Antillean candidates. Demographic reports issued by Institut National d'Études Démographiques (National Institute of Demographic Studies [INED]) on Antillean migration to mainland France also documented cases of phenotypic discrimination through the 1980s and 1990s. More recent *testing* studies have confirmed the continuing significance of skin color in French racial exclusion. In 2014, SOS-Racisme initiated an undercover test of racial bias in twenty-five night-clubs in Paris, Reims, Bordeaux, Metz, and Besançon. The group identified racist practices at five clubs (three of which were located in Paris) that "refused people of color, then, a few minutes later, accepted White people without any other motive that could justify this difference in treatment."[18]

Recent studies also indicate that black French people report the same or higher levels of discrimination faced by Maghrebis. The landmark *Trajectoire et origines* study commissioned by INED shows that 31 percent of first-generation migrants from overseas France report being discriminated against "often" or "sometimes"—essentially the same level (30 percent) reported by first-generation immigrants from Algeria. Indeed, the very existence of racism against French Caribbeans, citizens for nearly two centuries, shows that the immigrant thesis is wrong. French from the DOM (many of whom are black) report higher levels of discrimination than French of Algerian origin. By contrast, French of sub-Saharan African origin report higher levels than that for both of these groups: 47 percent of the first generation feel targeted.[19] As the sociologist Eduardo Bonilla-Silva (2000: 207) argues, while "Arabs seem to have captured the popular imagination of the French . . . Caribbean French and Blacks from Africa suffer, too, from high levels of discrimination." These data underscore the continuing significance of anti-African sentiment *and* anti-black racism in France. The empirical facts have proved wrong those who portray French racism as mainly "cultural" in nature; patterns of bias and mistreatment cannot be reduced to symbolic racism, xenophobia, or anti-immigrant sentiment.

Beyond the minimization of anti-blackness among analysts of cultural racism, there is also a tradition dating back to the nineteenth century of narratives depicting France as especially welcoming to blacks, especially compared with the United States. The French have long asserted their cultural superiority by portraying themselves as a haven for African Americans. This racial one-upmanship was seen, for example, with a French ban on the overtly anti-black American film *Birth of a Nation* in 1916 and 1923 (Stokes 2010). African Americans have also contributed to the image of France as a respite from American racism (Fogarty 2008; Sharpley-Whiting 2015; Tillet 2009). "How fine a thing," W.E.B. Du Bois remarked, "to be a black Frenchman in 1919!" (Lewis 2000: 45). Writing on the expatriate community, the historian Tyler Stovall suggests that African Americans in Paris were able to "recreate a black cultural presence abroad *freed from racism*" (Stovall 1997: n.p.; emphasis added).

Obfuscation of White Supremacy

A third concern with the literature on race in France is its general failure to acknowledge white supremacy as a continuing feature of French society. By neglecting to address white supremacy directly, scholars mask the systematic dominance of white people in societies built on colonialism and transatlantic slavery. In *The French Encounter with Africans*, William Cohen (1980: 292) observes that "the French, like other Europeans, established a racial society based on the claims of white supremacy." Although he acknowledges white supremacy, Cohen does not center the concept in his analysis. This is not particularly surprising, given that critical race theory was still incipient at the time. More difficult to explain, however, is the lack of attention to white supremacy in recent scholarship on French people of African and Caribbean descent. Important volumes, including *Black France* (Thomas 2007), *La condition noire* (Ndiaye 2008), and *The Anatomy of Blackness* (Curran 2011) inquire into the construction of blackness and whiteness without describing white supremacy as a feature of French society today. The compelling essays gathered in *Black France/France Noire* (Keaton, Sharpley-Whiting, and Stovall 2012) mention white supremacy only once. It is undoubtedly true that work on the subjective and objective experiences of black French people serves as an important corrective to race-avoidant research, as well as to analyses that trivialize anti-black racism. However, linking anti-blackness to white supremacy would strengthen scholarship in this area.[20] Analyses of whiteness, blackness, and racial construction that neglect the concept of white supremacy risk obscuring the sociopolitical dominance of people socially recognized as "white" today. The irony, as I show below, is that white supremacy actually *depends* on this very obfuscation (Mills 2015).[21]

Toward a Critical Approach to French Racism

Critical race theory (CRT) offers an alternative approach for studying race and racism in France. It is an intellectual movement explicitly oriented toward social justice that emerged in the 1980s from legal scholars in the United States who were struggling to make sense of (and address) the continuing legacies of racial inequality in post–Civil Rights Movement era. Critical race theorists found themselves increasingly faced with "color-blind" discourse from the judicial bench, despite the ongoing social realities of systematic racism and bias. As a result, they devised legal theory, grounded in narratives and story-telling, to unveil the role of the law in perpetuating racial oppression. In this way, critical race theorists frame present-day race relations temporally, within a historical context. The effort of legal theorists to respond to color-blindness is one of the main reasons CRT is a useful literature for those interested in race in France. Social scientists influenced by CRT have drawn attention to the systematic and global nature of white supremacy as well as its interrelation with the transnational history of European colonialism.

While it may seem surprising to talk about white supremacy in relation to France, a society that is often viewed as post-racial, the persistence of white domination is key to understanding how matters of race, colonialism, and slavery are represented in French society today. Color-blind discourse (which is hegemonic in France) not only denies the existence of racial groups (especially whites) generally; it also asserts a specific temporal representation of race. As critical race theorists have shown, color-blindness involves an attempt to erase race from representations of society and often entails a denial of various aspects of race in the past and present. At times, people are able to challenge this erasure by constructing what I call *racial temporality*—making connections among racial categories, relations, and processes across time. Such temporal labor, I argue, is both a key component of racial cognition and an important tool of antiracism.

Clearly identifying white supremacy in France, as well as in other nations with histories of white-supremacist domination, provides a better framework for understanding racism than other, less specific ways to describe racial conflict. This specificity is important for at least three reasons. First, the concept of white supremacy highlights the existence of the politically and socioeconomically dominant population, whereas vague references to "racism" tend to obscure the dominant group. Second, naming white supremacy powerfully contests the color-blind denial of politicians and others who insist that race has no political existence in France. Finally, scholarship on white supremacy by critical race scholars unveils the role of knowledge production in the maintenance of the racial status quo. Charles Mills (1997) argues that white supremacy involves an *epistemology of ignorance* in which whiteness and white dominance persist as unmarked racial projects. In Mills's view, white dominance involves and requires "cognitive dysfunctions" that are "psychologically and socially functional." These functional dysfunctions, in turn, yield "the ironic outcome that Whites will in general be unable to understand the world they themselves have made" (Mills 1997: 18).[22] Mills theorizes that the epistemology of ignorance produces a social reality in which "white misunderstandings, misrepresentation, evasion, and self-deception on matters related to race are among the most pervasive mental phenomena of the past few hundred years, a cognitive and moral economy physically required for conquest, colonization, and enslavement" (Mills 1997: 19). From this perspective, French efforts to downplay or deny processes of racialization in the past or the present can be understood as a result of epistemic ignorance produced by white supremacy itself.

Features of French White Supremacy

While white supremacy is global (Mills 2015; Pierre 2013), it also manifests uniquely in various national contexts. How does white supremacy function in France, a nation that officially bans racial categories, including whiteness, from the census? I argue that French white supremacy involves at least three key features: anti-racism, asymmetric racialization, and anticommunitarianism. Anti-racism (Goldberg 2009; Weiner 2014b), which is closely connected to color-blind ideology, refers to the denial of race as an extant phenomenon (and a legitimate category of analysis). In the French case, anti-racism is used, at times, to deny the biological existence of race and the social reality of racialization. Further, anti-racism involves the stigmatization and moral censure of people who use racial categories in the public sphere. The existence of white supremacy means, however, that minorities are more frequently racialized than the majority population, a phenomenon I refer to as asymmetric racialization. Finally, French white supremacy is distinguished by anticommunitarianism, which refers to the idea that French people should not emphasize their group membership in civil society—that they should subordinate their collective identities to their French national identity. In France, it is typical for minorities trying to organize and fight for their group's interests to be branded *communitauriste*, a word that translates roughly as "divisive." People (or organizations) that are labeled *communitauriste* are often portrayed as insufficiently French or poorly assimilated. For example, some of the activist groups that emerged in the 2000s to address the discrimination faced by black and brown people in France have been accused of communitarianism—a charge that aims to undermine the legitimacy of antiracist movements in the eyes of the dominant group.

These particularities of French white supremacy have consequences for the way slavery and colonialism are depicted today, as I show later. The existence of anti-racialism means that commemorators and activists who use racial categories to discuss the history and legacies of slavery are violating a pervasive taboo—namely, the topic of race itself. Patterns of asymmetric racialization mean that commemorators who break this taboo by racializing history or historicizing race may find it easier to refer to minorities (e.g., Africans and black or "colored" slaves) rather than whites. Finally, the stigmatization of groups viewed as communitarian suggests that those involved in commemorating slavery risk being seen as "divisive" or even anti-French. Together, these features of white-supremacist oppression severely limit the range of slavery narratives and representations that can be viewed as appropriate and compatible with French Republicanism.

Collective Memory and Temporality

So far, this chapter has examined the history of French involvement in transatlantic slavery, as well as different approaches to the study of race in France. Now, I turn my attention to the topic of how that history is represented today. In sociology, students of collective memory (Barthel-Bouchier 1996; Griffin 2004; May 2000; Olick 1999a; Olick and Levy 1997; Schwartz 1996; Zerubavel 1996) seek to explain how social contexts shape the way we interpret historical figures, events, and processes. Collective memory has referred alternatively to "a set of ideas, images [and] feelings about the past" (Irwin-Zarecka 1994: 4), a "cultural system" that has a generative capacity to shape society by providing both a "language and a map" for understanding the present (Schwartz 1996: 910), and "a sensitizing term of a wide variety of mnemonic processes, practices, and outcomes, neurological, cognitive, personal, aggregated, and collective" (Olick 1999a: 346). Commemorations make use of symbols, texts, and rites to recall the past in collective settings (Schwartz 2001). Émile Durkheim ([1912] 1965: 420) theorized that commemorative rites function to "revivify the most essential elements of the collective consciousness." By recalling the group's ancestral past, the tribe "periodically renews the sentiment which it has of itself and of its unity" (Durkheim [1912] 1965: 420). As in other studies of commemoration, my work draws on the concept of "narrative" (Eyerman 2001; Irwin-Zarecka 1994; Wertsch 2002). Narratives are stories that selectively identify past occurrences and protagonists and explain how actors and events are related to one another (Ewick and Silbey 1995). Such stories provide "cultural tools for remembering" through emplotment—that is, linking "settings, characters and events" and making the past comprehensible (Wertsch 2002: 58–59).

More generally, commemorative activities use narratives to furnish audiences with "meanings, worldviews [and] perceptions" (Vinitzky-Seroussi 2009: 11–12). The brand of cultural sociology advanced by Jeffrey Alexander and his colleagues (2004) applies the concept of narrative to the study of "trauma" and collective identity. From this perspective, collective memory traumas are past events or epochs that are characterized as negative, portrayed as permanent and immutable, and represented as a threat to a society's moral and cultural "presuppositions" (Smelser 2004: 44). Thus, culturally traumatic events affect individuals and groups indirectly through *mediated* representations and collective memories. Work in this area has focused on three dimensions of cultural trauma: (1) the identification of victims, (2) the nature of the suffering, and (3) the attribution of blame (Alexander et al. 2004).

Race-Based Movements and Collective Memories

While many sociologists trace the genealogy of collective memory studies back to Durkheim ([1912] 1965) and Maurice Halbwachs ([1925] 1952), W.E.B. Du Bois was in fact in the vanguard of theorizing about the dynamics of history, memory, and African American culture. As Ron Eyerman (2001: 75) notes, "Du Bois was one of the first and few intellectuals of his generation to argue for a distinctive African basis of slave culture and to call this up to memory." Scholars of collective memory also tend to overlook the contributions of non-white historians such as Carter G. Woodson (1933), who emphasized the importance of countering denigrating representations of the racial past to correct the historical record and bolster African American identity. Non-white scholars, activists, and educators have long recognized the need to challenge racist collective memories and historiography. Because members of minority groups have a margin of agency, they are capable of "creating a culture and, consequently, a memory separate from that which exists in the dominant society," thereby producing "ethnic commemorative activity" (Bodnar 1992: 42).[23] In the United States, W. Fitzhugh Brundage (2005) demonstrated that the meanings associated with the slaveholding past of the American South have been fiercely contested by blacks and whites. Commemorative practices were literally "segregated" in the American South until the Civil Rights Movement.

The role social activism and mobilization play in reframing the past (racial and otherwise) is a vibrant area of scholarship (Fleming and Morris 2015; Gongaware 2011; McAdam 1982; Olick and Robbins 1998). Social movements are organized mobilizations in which members of marginalized groups "promote or resist changes in the structure of society" (McAdam 1982: 25). Such activism and protest generally involves face-to-face meetings, consciousness-raising, and intellectual exchange—all of which I observed while attending slavery commemorations in France. Despite external constraints, members of minority groups can organize to reimagine their past in ways that run counter to dominant representations. Along these lines, Patterson (1971) discusses the interpretive frames that "New World Blacks" have at their disposal for imagining their historical heritage. These include *catastrophic*, *survivalist*, and *contributionist* frames. Catastrophism depicts what blacks have lost (e.g., indigenous cultural practices that were disrupted during the Middle Passage), survivalism emphasizes what blacks have retained, and contributionism celebrates blacks' role in constructing civilization (e.g., through the appropriation and glorification of Egyptian civilization as "black" or through reference to the efforts that blacks have made in their respective nations).

In a similar vein, the sociologist Ron Eyerman (2001) examines the traumatic memory of slavery and the formation of divergent perspectives on African American identity, focusing on cultural representations and elite discourse of activist leaders, intellectuals, and cultural producers. He shows that freed blacks and their descendants came to define African American identity retrospectively following the abolition of slavery. Eyerman identifies two distinct narrative frames that African Americans constructed to make sense of enslavement. The *progressive* narrative represented slavery as a cultural resource and emphasized how far African Americans had come, whereas the *tragic/redemptive* narrative framed slavery as a source of permanent trauma and urged African Americans to reclaim lost glory by returning to their African roots.[24] These alternative perspectives on slavery—optimistic and pessimistic—exist in much of the commemorative activism I encountered in France.

It is important to emphasize that representations of the racial past not only are the production of collectivities and movements; they can also shape the formation of ethnic and racial identities and attitudes (Griffin and Bollen 2009). Debates about the past contribute to the production of ideas about ethnicity and race (Lecouteur and Augoustinos 2001), as well as present and past race relations (May 2000). Mnemonic activity related to historical ethnic conflict such as slavery and genocide helps structure contemporary attitudes and policies relevant to immigrant groups and racial minorities (Foner and Alba 2010). In the United States, scholars have shown that collective memory contributes to the formation of alternative understandings of African American identity (Eyerman 2001), and micro-communities of memory function to circulate African Americans' stories of encounters with (and triumph over) racial incidents (May 2000). Collective memory also provides people with social knowledge (Swidler and Arditi 1994) about the groups to which they feel attached. The availability (or scarcity) of cultural knowledge about the past helps determine whether individuals perceive contemporary group relations in a historical context. In her comparative work on antiracism, Philomena Essed (1991) found that the history and memory of racialized oppression are less institutionalized in the Netherlands than in the United States; as a result, Surinamese women see their contemporary encounters with racism as largely ahistorical compared with African American women, who more frequently perceive connections between the slavery past and the present. Minorities can use the past as a resource for understanding contemporary racism, but this mnemonic and temporal work is more difficult to do when racial and colonial histories are minimized and erased.

From Racial Memories to Racial Temporality

While collective representations of the slavery past are certainly at stake in this book, I seek to move beyond the memory literature by highlighting the concept of something more fundamental—that is, *temporality*. My conceptualization of racial temporality owes much to the work of Gerda Lerner, a prolific scholar who founded the field of feminist historical studies in the United States. In her seminal text *The Creation of Feminist Consciousness* (1993), Lerner identifies key features of social awareness that facilitated women's resistance to patriarchal oppression. They include

> the awareness of women that they belong to a subordinate group; that they have suffered wrongs as a group; that their condition of subordination is not natural, but is societally determined; that they must join with other women to remedy these wrongs; and finally, that they must and can provide an alternate vision of societal organization in which women as well as men will enjoy autonomy and self-determination. (Lerner 1993: 14)

Although she does not use the term "temporality" here, Lerner's definition of feminist consciousness certainly underscores the importance of understanding domination as a force of history that extends through time. The use of the present perfect tense—the claim that women *have suffered* as a group—indicates a stream of action (i.e., oppression) that began in the past and continues into the contemporary moment. Influenced by Marxist theory, Lerner portrays feminist consciousness as a kind of social knowledge that is grounded in not only awareness of one's belonging to a group but also recognition of one's *ongoing* subordination within a system of power relations.

Racial temporality is not only a matter of representing the racial past, present, or future; it also involves *making connections* across time. Crucially, some scholars (Phillips 2010) argue that the ability to conceptualize race as a temporal phenomenon—to see that race relations today are shaped by the past—is *required* for understanding and fighting racism. Catherine Phillips (2010) makes this point in her critique of antiracist social work, arguing in favor of conceptualizations of race that foster temporal understandings of racialization. I contend that activists and educators involved in bringing attention to slavery and colonialism construct racial temporality by *historicizing race* and *racializing history.* Historicizing race involves situating present-day racial categories, group dynamics, and patterns within a historical framework. Racializing history, however, involves uncovering and recovering the history of race within societies shaped by the institutionalization of racial categories and the oppression of racialized others. Thus, I am interested in the extent to which commemorators and ordinary people alike make temporal connections, implicitly and explicitly, in how they frame and represent chattel slavery. I understand these temporal connections as cognitive tools that are necessary for challenging racism today. Without the time labor involved in linking slavery and colonialism to present-day inequalities among racialized groups, commemorations of slavery are unlikely to aid in the fight against present-day racism.

Conclusion

One of the most important consequences of transatlantic slavery and colonization was the emergence of whiteness as a social category and white supremacy as a system of social dominance. Neither the abolitions of slavery nor the adoption of "color-blindness" by the French government dismantled white supremacy. To the contrary, whiteness and white supremacy have continued to shape French life and reduce the life chances of non-white minorities. But much of the scholarship on race in France does not depict this temporal framing of French race relations. Outside of scholarship, how do people on the ground view these issues? The chapters that follow examine how different segments of the French population imagine the history of slavery, its racial content, and its relationship to the present.

2

Blackwashing Slavery

THE RACIAL POLITICS OF
COMMEMORATION

In the summer of 2005, minority activists took legal action against the historian Olivier Pétré-Grenouilleau, one of the best-known French scholars of slavery. The author of a sweeping global history of enslavement, Pétré-Grenouilleau ignited controversy by emphasizing the differences between slavery and the Holocaust. Members of the Collectif des Filles et Fils d'Africains Déportés (Collective of Daughters and Sons of Deported Africans [COFFAD]) and the Fédération des Associations d'Outre-mer et d'Europe (Federation of Associations from Overseas and Europe [FOAME]) accused the scholar of violating the Taubira Law of 2001 that defines slavery as a crime against humanity and viewed themselves as defending the memory of slaves and the honor of their descendants. The activists who banded together against the historian represented a range of different black and diasporic groups, including people from overseas France, as well as French activists of African immigrant origin. *L'affaire Pétré-Grenouilleau*, as it is known in France, caused a major scandal in debates over the *guerres des mémoires* (memory wars) that have fractured the French public sphere in recent years. But why, exactly, did Pétré-Grenouilleau's remarks cause such an uproar? And how did the white French academic establishment respond?

This chapter uses the Pétré-Grenouilleau affair as a launching point to examine the politics of slavery commemoration in France. In retracing Pétré-Grenouilleau's comments—as well as the response on the part of the minority activists and the white academic community—I attempt to show how the racial politics of white supremacy shape the norms of political correctness that govern how slavery is being resurrected in the public sphere. Another objective of this chapter is to highlight the particularities of France's "memorial laws," as well as their relationship to race politics. France's laws pertaining to collective memory are unusual and set the nation apart from other societies grappling with unflattering pasts. Next, I examine how French politicians themselves have talked about slavery through a content analysis of speeches. Taken together, these analyses equip us to better understand how laws and political discourse produced by the white majority both enable and constrain minority mobilizations related to slavery and colonialism.

Pétré-Grenouilleau and Dieudonné: Controversies in the Commemoration of Slavery

Dieudonné, an infamous biracial comedian, emerged on the global stage in 2015 when he was convicted by French authorities for "defense of terrorism" following the *Charlie Hebdo* attacks. Dieudonné was accused of supporting terror on the basis of a post on his Facebook page in which he stated that he felt like "Charlie Coulibaly," a phrase that referred simultaneously to *Charlie Hebdo*, the newspaper that was targeted by the terror event, and Amedy Coulibaly, one of the men who carried out the assault. It is important to note that Coulibaly was black and French, of Malian immigrant origin. But long before the *Hebdo* attacks, Dieudonné was known in France as a controversial figure who was repeatedly condemned for making anti-Semitic statements. He has also played a central role in shaping public discourse on slavery.

In an interview with the *Journal du Dimanche* on June 12, 2005, Pétré-Grenouilleau shared his views on what he called "the anti-Semitism spread by Dieudonné in relation to slavery."[1] In particular, he responded to the claim that Jews had played an especially important role in the transatlantic slave trade:

> This accusation against the Jews was born in the Black American community in the 1970s. It's remerging today in France. This goes beyond the case of Dieudonné. It's also the problem of the Taubira Law that considers the Black trade by Europeans a "crime against humanity," including in this fact a comparison with the Holocaust. The Negro trade is not genocide. The trade did not have as its goal the extermination of a people. The slave was a good that had a market value that one wanted to make work as much as possible. The Jewish genocide and the slave trade are different processes. There is no Richter scale of suffering.[2]

There are several important elements in these claims that reveal the political climate in which slavery is being debated in France. The first point to underscore is that *the* leading French historian of enslavement is objecting to the Taubira Law's definition of transatlantic slavery as a "crime against humanity." He argues that labeling slavery a "crime against humanity" involves an implicit comparison to the Holocaust—a comparison that he views as illegitimate. In his view, which represents the dominant framing of white intellectuals in France, the Holocaust was a singular event that should not be described as analogous to other atrocities, including transatlantic slavery.[3] Because the motive of European enslavers was not the "extermination of a people," Pétré-Grenouilleau says, it is wrong to include slavery under the same rubric as genocide. In making this argument, he criticizes the notion of a hierarchy of suffering even as he imposes a hierarchy of his own in which the Holocaust was a crime against humanity while slavery was not. This argument is in line with what was once the hegemonic position that the Jewish Holocaust was *singularly incomparable* to other human tragedies. By describing transatlantic slavery as a crime against humanity, the Taubira Law managed to challenge, if not entirely upend, this dominant view.

A second aspect of his comments concerns anti-Semitism and Dieudonné. The reference to Dieudonné is telling, as it speaks to his surprising centrality in debates over the representation of slavery in France. Dieudonné M'bala, a French humorist of white European and African (Cameroonian) origin, gained notoriety during the 2000s following a successful career as an entertainer at the Théâtre de la Main d'Or in the 1990s. After making a series of controversial statements and performances, Dieudonné came to symbolize pro-black anti-Semitism in France. Multiple reports, and interviews from my fieldwork, suggest that Dieudonné's grievances stem, at least in part, from his failure to receive government funding for a movie he wanted to produce about slavery and the Code Noir (Black Code) that governed enslavement in the French overseas territories. According to an article published in *L'Express*, "conspiracy theories" are Dieudonné's "favorite pastime," and his paranoia extended to the Centre National du Cinéma (National Cinema Center), which rejected funding for his proposed film because it was too "simplistic." Dieudonné apparently took the center's decision personally, saying, "For me, they were nine Whites who didn't have the courage to deal with a dark episode in the history of France."[4]

According to Stéphanie Binet and Blandine Grosjean, Louis Sala-Molins, a law professor at the Université Toulouse II, was "the one and only academic who agreed to work directly with [Dieudonné]," providing crucial help in writing the script for the "still unfinanced" film about the Code Noir. Afro-Caribbeans' attitudes toward Dieudonné have been seen as a kind of litmus test for their feelings toward Jews. "While [some] recognize that Dieudonné brought the history of slavery out of the blind spot in which it was stagnating,"

Binet and Grosjean continue, "other researchers believe that he 'perverted' the subject. 'Working on slavery exposes Black researchers to suspicions of anti-Semitism. Now we have to position ourselves for or against Dieudonné,'" a sociologist quoted by the journalists explained.[5]

For years, Dieudonné has been portrayed as a kind of "menace to society," a source of dangerous and increasingly incoherent rhetoric targeted mainly against Jews and Israel. In this way, Dieudonné occupies roughly the same discursive space as Louis Farrakhan in the United States. In some respects, his hostility toward Jews is even more outrageous and extreme than Farrakhan's. Take, for example, Dieudonné's appearance on December 1, 2003, on the live evening talk show "You Can't Please Everyone."[6] Dieudonné had been invited to roast Jamel Debbouze, a fellow comedian. Instead, he performed a short sketch dressed as an Orthodox Jew in which he declared, "I encourage all of the young people looking at us today in the ghettos to . . . convert to be like me, try to get yourselves together, join the Axis of Good, the American-Zionist axis."[7] He ended his routine with the phrase "Hail Israel!" and raised his right arm in a Nazi salute. The show's host, Marc-Olivier Fogiel, who comes from a Jewish family and identifies as atheist, laughed throughout the sketch but appeared visibly uncomfortable toward the end. The following week, the show displayed text messages said to have come from viewers who were angered and offended by Dieudonné's appearance, including one that read, "Would it make you laugh if someone did routines about Black people's odor?"[8] Shortly thereafter, Dieudonné filed a lawsuit accusing Fogiel and the show's producers charging that they had fabricated the message, a claim that was later validated in court.

Dieudonné's escalating attacks against Zionism and supporters of Israel include statements such as "Zionism is the AIDS of Judaism."[9] *Le Monde* published an article on February 22, 2005, claiming to present the comedian's "verbatim" response to a question about anti-Semitism during a press conference in Algiers:

> I simply need [to say], even if only to explain to my children, "[Y]our ancestors weren't necessarily the Gauls. You are a descendant of slaves, and this is how it happened." . . . [That] was taken away from us by the Zionist lobby, which cultivates a unitary suffering as if they're the only ones who have suffered on this planet. [To them,] the suffering of Blacks is shit; it doesn't exist. I won't even talk about Arabs. . . . [T]oday there is a real tension between communities that doesn't make any sense, because the values of the Republic should prevent that from happening to us. But there is a mafia controlling the French Republic: the CRIF [Conseil Representatif des Institutions Juives de France (Representative Council of Jewish

Institutions of France)], this organ of inquisition. . . . [S]eventeen government ministers and [Prime Minister Jean-Pierre] Raffarin himself were
with CRIF last weekend. . . . When I work to make a film about the Negro
slave trade and the Zionist authorities . . . respond, "This isn't a subject for
a film," that's a declaration of war . . . against the Black world and 400
years of slavery, and I won't even talk to you about decolonization. . . .
Let's be reasonable . . . share everything, [and] say, "It's the suffering of
humanity," and talk about it each time there's a problem. . . . Today I'm
talking about memorial pornography. It's getting to be intolerable. . . .
[I]t's becoming twisted. . . . I understand that certain people who experienced [the Holocaust] in their flesh and blood have a hard time hearing
this. But they should understand that it's in my flesh and blood. And if we
have to go back, it's even more ancient. The Antillean population was born
from the fruit of rape over the course of four hundred years, . . . so I don't
think there are any [moral] lessons to teach us.

Dieudonné also denied the severity of anti-Semitism, saying, "They speak of
the rise of anti-Semitism. . . . It's a vast fraud. Those who undergo racism
aren't mainly Jews, [because Jews] are a community who are more or less well
integrated and . . . particularly well taken care of financially. The Black community [is] the poorest, and the Arab community [is] the most vulnerable
[*sensible*]."

Dieudonné's reference to "memorial pornography" earned the condemnation of French Jewish activists and intellectuals, as well as of antiracist organizations such as the Movement against Racism and for Friendship between
People (MRAP), the International League against Racism and Anti-Semitism
(LICRA), SOS-Racisme, and the Union of French Jewish Students (UEJF).[10]

Taken together, these incidents reveal why Pétré-Grenouilleau, a noted
scholar, would refer to Dieudonné, a comedian, in his remarks about slavery.
Dieudonné has come to represent the dark side of emergent "black" movements. Although parallels between the history of slavery and the Holocaust
were drawn in French political discourse before Dieudonné's diatribes (notably,
in debates leading up to the passage of the Taubira Law in 2001), his polemics
functioned to polarize the debate over the uniqueness of the Holocaust and the
legitimacy of groups seeking recognition for slavery. His dual status as a public
anti-Semite and self-ordained spokesperson for the memory of slavery makes it
difficult for other minorities to mobilize for the recognition of slavery without
being accused of anti-Jewish sentiment. Indeed, some of Pétré-Grenouilleau's
comments mirror remarks by the historian David Brion Davis, who criticizes
"anti-Semitic mythologies that have . . . wrongly pictured Jews as the main
traders in slaves across medieval Europe and . . . as the dominant force behind

the transatlantic African slave trade to the New World" (Davis 2006: 67). Black Muslims in the United States are often associated with this "mythology," which explains Pétré-Grenouilleau's earlier reference to "black Americans" in the 1970s. Dieudonné and black Muslims in the United States alike are depicted as resurrecting slavery in ways that unfairly scapegoat Jewish people. In this way, Dieudonné has thrust minority activists under a cloud of moral suspicion. Are commemorators of slavery hostile (overtly or covertly) to Jews?

The Centrality of the Holocaust in French Commemorative Laws

The Holocaust broadly and French collaboration with the Nazi regime specifically occupy a special status in French collective memory and law. To understand why, we must consider France's peculiar *lois memorielles*—legislation pertaining to how certain atrocities of the past should be represented today. In the years following World War II, French society increasingly—and reluctantly—grappled with unflattering historical legacies. Under mounting pressure from French Jews and trailblazing historians such as Henry Rousso (1987), the history of collaboration with the Nazi regime increasingly came to light in the 1970s and 1980s. In a society that historically has emphasized cultural assimilation, the demands of Caribbean, Jewish, Armenian, and North African citizens to salvage uncomfortable memories pose a significant challenge to the universalism of the Republican tradition.

Under the presidencies of François Mitterrand and Jacques Chirac, the French government engaged in an unprecedented effort to legislate official pronouncements on the representation and commemoration of historical events. These "politics of memory" have been an active force on both the left and the right. In 1983, the French government established local commemorations of the 1848 abolition of slavery in the overseas departments. Four different dates celebrate this event: May 22, in Martinique; May 27, in Guadeloupe; June 10, in French Guiana; and December 20, in Réunion.[11] Beginning in 1990, the French government made several significant interventions into the representation of historical events, largely in response to the claims of ethnic minorities (Jews, most prominently). A series of policies referred to as memorial laws sought to legislate how certain historical events and periods should be remembered. These policy developments included the Gayssot Law of 1990, which prohibits denial of the Holocaust; a law enacted in 2001 recognizing the Armenian genocide; and the Taubira Law of 2001, which defines slavery as a crime against humanity.[12] In 2001, the French government also granted reparations to the families of the seventy-six thousand Jews who were deported to Nazi death camps during World War II. In each case, the role of the state in molding historical representations and repairing the past was both contested and celebrated by competing interest groups, including scholars, politicians, and representatives of ethnic and racial minorities.[13]

The march in memory of the victims of slavery of 1998 helped consolidate support for the legislation that eventually would become known as the Taubira Law. As of this writing, France remains the only nation in the world to have issued such a proclamation. The law called for the formation of an official body of scholars and experts to critically examine the collective memory of slavery in contemporary France. Chaired by Maryse Condé, the esteemed Guadeloupean writer, the Comité pour la Mémoire de l'Esclavage (Committee for the Memory and History of Slavery) was convened in 2004 and issued a report of its initial findings on April 12, 2005.[14] Of the many recommendations regarding the inclusion of slavery (both its persistence and eventual abolition) in the national imaginary, the committee sought to establish an official day of remembrance on May 10 of each year.

Despite these symbolic gains, the lack of consensus over how (and whether) the history of slavery should be commemorated has led to an ideological tug-of-war that has created significant confusion and inconsistency. Only four years after the Taubira Law was passed, the center-right Union pour un Mouvement Populaire (UMP) majority passed legislation requiring the educational curriculum to emphasize the "positive" dimensions of colonization.[15] After a general uproar from many actors in civil society, the law was eventually repealed by President Chirac. And despite the establishment of May 10 as a broadly conceived commemoration for the entire French national community, Prime Minister François Fillon signed a symbolic *circulaire* in 2008 that recognized May 23 as a distinct commemorative date set aside for *Français d'outre-mer* (French of overseas origin) in the metropole, a departure from previous efforts of the state to frame commemoration in universalist terms as a national endeavor. The declaration states, in part, that

> numerous associations for natives of the overseas organize a commemorative day in memory of the suffering of slaves on May 23. This date recalls, on the one hand, the abolition of slavery in 1848 and, on the other hand, the silent march of May 23, 1998, which contributed to the national debate, culminating in the vote for the law recognizing slavery as a crime against humanity. The date of May 23 will be, for associations bringing together French from the overseas in the Hexagon, the day of commemorating the painful past of their ancestors, who should not be forgotten.[16]

In addition to generating complications (and confusion) by recognizing yet another commemorative date, the *circulaire* implicitly excludes French of sub-Saharan African origin and solidifies the "overseas French" as a group with particular claims on the memory of slavery. Far from representing a coherent, consistent policy of symbolic integration for its postcolonial migrant and immigrant populations, French officials' pronouncements about the colonial past resemble the "circular reasoning" and short-term logic (Lewis 2007: 153) that pervaded France's governance of its foreign workers in the interwar period. Some have emphasized the role of Jewish activism in providing a cultural template for people of French Afro-descended people to demand the recognition of slavery as a crime against humanity. Thus, Jean-Yves Camus suggests that the Jewish movement around the 1990 law functioned as a model for blacks in France, even as they noted how difficult it was to gain the recognition given to French Jews: "For many Black activists, this form of lobbying set an example for what needed to be done. There was also widespread resentment within their ranks that what had been granted to one minority, the Jews, was denied to another, the Black community" (Camus 2006: 649). It is, of course, no mistake that the Comité des Filles et des Fils d'Africains Déportés (Committee of Sons and Daughters of Deported Africans) bears a striking resemblance to the Association des Fils et Filles des Déportés Juifs de France (Association of Sons and Daughters of Jews Deported from France). It is certainly the case that discourse about the memory of slavery frequently refers to both Jews and the Holocaust.[17] Yet it also bears underlining, as Johann Michel (2010) points out, that early efforts to remember the history of French Atlantic slavery predate the commemoration of World War II.

Returning once again to the Pétré-Grenouilleau affair, we can now assess several consequences of the controversy. The first pertains to the response on the part of minority activists, including groups representing the overseas French, as well as people of African origin. After filing suit against the historian for his suggestion that slavery was not a crime against humanity, these same groups were ultimately persuaded to drop their case in February 2006, less than a year later. Their decision to halt legal action against the historian must be read in the context of the pressure they faced from white elites, including academics who rushed to defend Pétré-Grenouilleau. In addition to impugning the legitimacy of the activists' attempt to challenge slavery's equivalent to Holocaust denial (which, as we have seen, is illegal in France), intellectuals attacked the legitimacy of *all* of the *lois memorielles*, including the Taubira Law itself.[18]

In sum, the controversies surrounding Dieudonné and Pétré-Grenouilleau illustrate several features of the political landscape that commemorators of slavery must confront. First, commemorative activists must deal with the risk of being accused of anti-Semitism. The result is that French minorities seeking recognition for slavery must appease powerful French Jewish groups or risk marginalization. As later chapters demonstrate, some minority groups involved in commemorating slavery take great pains to signal that they are not competing with the Holocaust. Conversely, French Jews did not have to deal with being accused by powerful people of being "anti-black" when depicting the Shoah as a singularly tragic event. Second, Afro-descended people and organizations involved in commemorating slavery operate in a context in which making denigrating statements about the Holocaust actually violates French law, yet they have not been able to gain similar legal recognition for the denial of slavery as a crime against humanity.

How French Politicians Talk about Slavery

Having explored some of the factors that shape norms of political correctness with regard to slavery, I now explore how French politicians themselves discuss transatlantic enslavement. Representatives of the government, political parties, and public institutions help shape collective memory by contributing to the construction of official (or elite) memory (Bodnar 1992: 248; Gillis 1994). My intervention here is to underscore how the memory work of political officials influences how collective identities are represented in relation to transatlantic enslavement. Through close attention to officials' discourse about colonial slavery over a thirty-year period (1980–2010), I show that political speech shapes the commemoration of slavery in at least two ways. First, officials provide the public with interpretive frameworks for understanding French involvement in the slave trade and the place of colonial slavery in French national identity. Many officials highlight tensions between French values of *freedom, equality,* and *brotherhood* and the brutal history of French Atlantic slavery and racialized oppression. Yet they also provide cultural tools for both European-descended groups and African-descended groups to imagine some dimensions of the slavery past with a sense of pride. On the one hand, officials typically frame the Republic as the architect of abolition, implicitly allowing the predominantly white majority to view themselves as inheritors of the fight against slavery. On the other hand, officials appease people from the overseas departments by portraying the enslaved in glorious terms, emphasizing their dignity and resistance against slavery and downplaying African involvement in the slave trade. In so doing, public figures try to provide discursive pathways for both whites and non-whites to relate to slavery with a sense of pride.

Second, officials influence the commemorative public sphere through their references to ethnic and racial categories. I find that, by and large, public figures use terms for African-descended groups (e.g., Africans, Antilleans, and blacks) far more frequently than they single out "Europeans" and "whites."

Such asymmetrical racialization is important because it suggests that political speech confers visibility to "blacks" as a group while maintaining the white majority's invisibility. Another asymmetry in officials' memory work is the divergent manner in which public statements constructed overseas populations and black populations. National figures in French politics portrayed DOM groups, and Caribbeans in particular, as historical and contemporary actors with a special claim on the memory of slavery. Yet references to "blacks" and "Africans" were largely restricted to historical representations, while contemporary blacks in France (and French of African immigrant extraction) were not usually mentioned. Thus, officials typically overlooked "blackness" as a contemporary group category but provided ample memorial discourse about blacks as figures in French history. The conclusion to this chapter explores the contradictory implications of these findings.

The analysis developed here is drawn from a database of more than 100,000 texts compiled by the Direction de l'Information Légale et Administrative (Office of Legal and Administrative Information) and published on its website.[19] I used this electronic resource to construct a data set of speeches, statements, and public interviews delivered by public figures that mention the word "slavery" (*esclavage*). An initial search identified 487 such texts. After excluding references unrelated to transatlantic slavery, I subsequently identified and analyzed 225 speeches and statements made by 61 public figures between 1980 and 2010.[20] I read and coded each text to identify (1) the geographic context (where the speech took place), (2) the speaker and his or her public role, (3) historical narratives (specific temporal stories told about the history of transatlantic slavery), (4) characterizations of slavery and the slave trade, (5) characterizations of historical protagonists (practitioners of slavery, the enslaved, other historical figures), (6) references to contemporary social groups, (7) references to ethnic and racial categories, (8) references to historical dates, (9) moral discourse about the commemoration of transatlantic slavery, (10) discourse about the consequences of slavery, and (11) whether the reference to transatlantic slavery was a primary or secondary subject.

With regard to the patterns of racialization I found in these data, I want to draw attention to two major findings. First, as mentioned above, officials engaged in the racialization of the victims and generally avoided using racial terms to refer to the enslavers themselves. This is what I refer to as the "blackwashing" of slavery, one of the key features of asymmetric racialization. Second, they engaged in the nonracial stigmatization of slavery without saying much explicitly about the institution's racial component. What this means is that even in cases where politicians were directly addressing the history or legacies of transatlantic slavery, they did not generally represent enslavement as racial history. As a result, their discourse did not directly facilitate racial temporality or the capacity to make connections between racial phenomena across different time periods.

Officials often described themselves as "honoring" and "restoring dignity" to slaves who were dishonored during their lifetimes and subjected to physical and moral indignities. Sometimes this honorific memory work was done explicitly, by highlighting slaves' efforts to resist and overthrow slavery or to affirm their humanity through cultural production. But they also sought to highlight the innocence and worthiness of the enslaved by conveying the straightforward notion that slavery was simply wrong. As a rule, French officials were very specific in their condemnations of the practice of slavery but were ambiguous with regard to how they portrayed the responsible parties. These findings corroborate work by Doris Garraway (2008) showing that the Taubira Law and related public debates generally failed to identify the individuals or groups that were culpable for slavery. Thus, public officials almost never stigmatized the practitioners of slavery themselves. At times, they referred to enslavers' racial prejudices, but rarely were the practitioners directly criticized. References to the passage of the Taubira Law of 2001 were almost always used as occasions to celebrate France as the only nation in the world to have defined the colonial slavery and the slave trade as a crime against humanity. The abolition of slavery in 1848 was often depicted as a source of pride and the proof of the moral superiority of the French Republic. Discourse about the short-lived abolition in 1794 was less celebratory, for obvious reasons. While some officials also framed 1794 as an example of the triumph of revolutionary (and therefore Republican) values, others pointed to 1794 as a moral failure, given the reinstatement of slavery by Napoleon only eight years later.

Nonracial Stigmatization of Slavery

Public officials used a vast lexicon to convey the immorality and depravity of transatlantic slavery, yet they did so in terms that generally avoided mentioning race. In part, this moral dimension of officials' memory work can be understood as broadly representative of the "politics of regret" (Kammen 1995; Olick 2007) in which public officials increasingly have expressed recognition for the moral wrongs of their nation's past. Thus, 39 percent of the texts (88 of 225) explicitly brand the slavery system morally reprehensible. Political leaders used a staggering 44 different words and expressions to characterize slavery negatively (see Table 2.1).

Yet for all of these condemnations of slavery, officials mostly avoided the thorny issue of condemning enslavers themselves. I interpret this as an effort

TABLE 2.1. OFFICIALS' DESCRIPTION OF SLAVERY	
Characterization	Number of texts (*N* = 225)
Criminal/crime	62
Barbaric/barbarism	15
Inhuman/dehumanizing	10
Tragic/tragedy	9
Atrocious/atrocities	6
Horror/horrific	6
Drama	4
Infamous/infamy	4
Injustice	4
Shameful/shame	4
Cruel/cruelty	3
Ignoble/ignominy	3
Intolerable	3
Trauma/traumatizing	3
Monstrous	2
Odious	2
Terrible	2

to save face: framing slavery as immoral without explicitly castigating particular individuals or groups is the easiest (and least controversial) moral stance for public figures to take, thus explaining the prevalence and diversity of this claim in political speech. Moreover, one of the ironies of officials' discourse about slavery is the way in which the stigmatization of slavery as a "crime" was often coupled with assertions of pride in French values. For example, on January 30, 2006, Chirac framed commemoration as an occasion to glorify France for having the courage to face its slavery past, saying, "Slavery and the slave trade were an indelible stain (*tache*) for humanity. The Republic can be proud of the battle that she won against this ignominy. In commemorating this history, France is showing the way. This is her honor, her grandeur, and her strength." In the same speech, he went on to say:

> Ladies and gentlemen, the greatness of a country is taking responsibility . . . for all of its history, with its glorious pages but also with its dark parts. Our history is that of a great nation. Let us look at it with pride. Let us look at it as it was. This is how a people draws itself together, becoming more united and stronger. This is what is at stake in questions of memory:

unity and national cohesion, love of one's country, and confidence in what we are.

Two years later, during the national commemoration, Nicolas Sarkozy echoed these calls for unity and solidarity in the face of what could easily be interpreted as a divisive history:

> We come together, this May 10, 2008, to celebrate the day of National Commemoration for the Memories of the Negro Trade, of Slavery, and Their Abolition. On this day of the nation's solemn homage, we should all have in mind the values that our Republic incarnates, values of which we should be proud. It is in the name of these values of liberty, freedom, and brotherhood that women and men fought to have slavery abolished. Let us look at this history as it was. Let us look at it clearly, because it is the history of France.

Like Chirac and Sarkozy, many French officials framed the purpose of talking about French Atlantic history as "looking at" (*regarder*) the slavery past and "taking responsibility for it" (*assumer*). Yet the gaze they advocated was largely nonracial, and the responsibility they ostensibly embraced was tempered by their celebration of French values.

Ethnic and Racial Categories in Commemorative Speech

In principle, French officials could avoid discussing racial categories (terms such as "black," "white," and "mulatto') and anti-black racism altogether in their narratives about slavery by omitting group labels or limiting their discussion of collective identities to safer ethnic categories (e.g., "African," "European"). Yet, as I explained in the Introduction, completely avoiding race talk in relation to slavery would be difficult, given that many of the phrases related to transatlantic history racialize the victims. In fact, I found that many public officials chose to embed in their narratives about colonial slavery explicit references to historical and contemporary ethnic and racial groups, ranging from broad continental categories (e.g., "African" or "European") to specific collective identities based on phenotype or presumed racial mixture (e.g., "black," "white," "mulatto"). At stake in their use of group categories are the norms for talking about ethnic and racial groups in the French public sphere. In the post–World War II period, antiracist movements (e.g., MRAP, SOS-Racisme) and antiracist legislation have traditionally framed the concept of race itself as anathema to Republican values of universalism and inclusion (Bleich 2004; Keaton 2010: 108). References to *racial differences*—particularly discourses that depict essential differences between groups on the basis of race or national origin—are still considered taboo and constitute a violation of public norms (Tin 2008).

Of the political texts that featured historical narratives about slavery, 40 percent (61 of 152) invoked ethnic or racial categories. Examining how (and under what circumstances) officials talked about race and ethnicity when discussing slavery provides a lens into understanding what kind of understandings of ethnoracial groupness and difference were present (and therefore perceived as authorized) in public officials' representations of the colonial past. One hypothesis might be that public officials mention ethnoracial categories more often during their speeches in overseas departments and territories, where ideas about ethnoracial difference and groupness are more salient and were historically institutionalized. This turns out not to be the case. Most statements about ethnicity or race were actually made in mainland France (42 of 61). One might also expect officials with responsibilities in the overseas departments and territories to invoke ethnicity and race more frequently than other public figures, regardless of the geographic context of their speech. Overseas officials were, in fact, responsible for a disproportionately high percentage (41 percent) of speeches referring to ethnic and racial categories.

Blackness in Political Discourse about Slavery

From the time of the colonial period, French authors writing on the slave trade have used a range of racialized terms. The terms *nègre* (Negro) and *négresse* (Negro woman) date back to 1516 and were derived from Spanish or Portuguese terms for *noir* (black).[21] The *Grand Robert de la langue française* tells us that *nègre* indicates "a person belonging to the Black race." Beginning in 1704, the word *nègre* became explicitly associated with the Atlantic slave trade. Thus, references to the Negro trade (*la traite des nègres*) emerged at this time, with *nègre* denoting both blackness and slave status.[22] The expression *la traite négrière* emerged later (in 1829) to refer to the Negro trade.[23] The French noun *négrier* has no direct equivalent in English. In principle, it refers to the captain of a slave ship involved in the Atlantic trade, yet unlike the more neutral English term "slave ship captain," *négrier* rather explicitly highlights the notion of black enslavement.

The existence of these well-established racialized terms for black enslavement helps explain why blacks were featured as historical protagonists in political speech about chattel slavery. For example, in 1998, the 150th anniversary of the second abolition, Minister of Culture and Communication Catherine Trautmann remarked, "All slavery is a crime . . . but the slavery of Blacks in the Americas was a crime against humanity."[24] Speakers often associated the concepts of "blackness" and "enslavement" with African origin. As President Jacques Chirac proclaimed, "Europe has too often incarnated unhappiness and desolation in the Americas, as well as in Africa. It is because the Native American people (*peuples amérindiens*) were decimated that a systematic mechanism of the black African trade (*traite des noirs africains*) was put into place."[25] That same year, André Rossinot, then the president of the Radical Party, also underscored the African origins of enslaved blacks, saying, "For the first time, France recognizes its responsibility and its participation in the human trade of Black slaves from Africa to the Americas and the Antilles. The French Antilles have been too often forgotten in our history books."[26]

Two observations stand out with regard to the racial classification of the enslaved population. First, it is important to highlight the unproblematic way in which speakers often used "black" as a commonsense label, without further explanation. When categorizing individuals as black, officials did not explain what they meant or imply that the category was in any way unnatural or socially constructed. Second, there was a persistent asymmetry in how groups (historical and contemporary) were described in terms of their ethnic or racial belonging. Thus, public officials reinforced the legitimacy of blackness as a racial category even as they remained mostly silent about whiteness.

The Invisibility of Whiteness

While the enslaved were frequently referred to as "black" or "African," the practitioners of slavery (e.g., slave traders, ship captains, colonial officials, slave masters) were rarely described as members of ethnoracial groups.[27] Only four public figures (Mitterrand, Lionel Jospin, Jean-Jack Queyranne, and Bernard Thibault) mentioned "white" historical agents. Jospin spoke of whites in a positive light by portraying them as partners (with blacks) in the abolition of slavery. In 1998, he proclaimed:

> The commemoration of the 150th anniversary of the abolition of slavery should also constitute an occasion for proclaiming our desire and our capacity to live together and build a model of society founded on mutual respect and tolerance. Because it is the common work of Blacks and Whites—first, of the rebel slaves, the fugitives that they call "maroons" [*marrons*], and of the abolitionists of the revolutions of 1789 and 1848— abolition is the illustration of the capacity that men have, when they want it in a determined fashion, to attain great ideals.[28]

On two occasions, speakers mentioned whites by using the words of other historical or contemporary figures. For example, at a commemoration of the

150th anniversary of the abolition of slavery in 1998, Queyranne referred to white historical actors by ventriloquizing Jacques-Henri Bernardin de Saint-Pierre, a writer and botanist who visited the French colonies in the Caribbean and the Indian Ocean in the eighteenth century:

> The celebration of the 150th anniversary of the definitive abolition of slavery . . . is an occasion to remind the entire nation of its duty to remember. The reality of what, over three centuries, was the enslavement of Blacks in what they called the New World . . . constitutes one of the darkest chapters in our history. Bernardin de Saint-Pierre described this reality in his "Voyage à l'Isle de France" in April 1768 with these terrible words: "I do not know whether coffee and sugar are necessary for the happiness of Europe, but I definitely know that [they] caused the unhappiness of two parts of the world. They depopulated the Americas to have . . . land for crops; they depopulated Africa to have a nation to cultivate them." [In] Africa, . . . men and women were traded "like beasts in order for the Whites to be able to live like men," [according to] Bernardin de Saint-Pierre.[29]

Unlike Jospin, Queyranne associates whites with the practice of slavery, a stigmatizing portrayal. Queyranne also referred to white complicity in slavery through the voice of another speaker during an event honoring the Guadeloupean writer Gisèle Pineau. In his homage to her work, he referred to enslaved women (often the subject of her writing) and drew on her own words, describing "these women who knew how to put into place these subtle strategies of subversion or resistance," disrupting the "fixed order of the master-slave relation by a presence which troubled the white world."[30]

Thibault, former secretary-general of the Confédération Générale du Travail (General Confederation of Labor [CGT]), was the only speaker in the data set to explicitly connect whiteness with racism. In March 2000, he said:

> It is necessary to identify the crimes of the past, to make known the cynicism that accompanied the slave trade—the cynicism of the colonists, the ship owners, and those who trafficked, and that of the States. But let us guard against the useless concept of collective responsibility and the temptation of retrospective justice. For the descendants of whomever, there is nothing to gain from the victimization of some and the guilt tripping of others. To the contrary, we have a duty to be clear about the historical realities and the longevity of their consequences. . . . The colonial expansions were first driven by more or less unadulterated versions of Christian proselytism. They were next driven by the feeling or, more

so, the conviction, that with Science (with a capital "S"), the white european [*sic*] had definitively proved his racial and cultural superiority, and
by enlightening the world, he was authorized to lead it.[31]

Crucially, Thibault connects whiteness to the racialized ideology of supremacy. Yet he is able to do so only by prefacing his comments with the warning
that one should "guard against the useless concept of collective responsibility
and the temptation of retrospective justice." I interpret this as suggesting that
the memory of slavery should not be used to imply white guilt or make any
demands on justice today. It is also noteworthy that Thibault's reference to
whiteness here is entirely in the past: present-day whites are sort of recognized
implicitly when he mentions "the guilt tripping of others," but again, present-
day whiteness is not explicitly acknowledged. And, of course, without acknowledging white people today, it is impossible to understand white-supremacist racism as a temporal phenomenon that stretches through time.

Conclusion

In this chapter, I have examined the political context in which activists and
officials are attempting to bring the slavery past back to life. This work of
commemoration is fraught with political complications for non-white
minorities, who not only must deal with French taboos on discussing race
and colonialism but also risk being accused of competing with the memory
of the Holocaust. To revisit Pétré-Grenouilleau's interview with the *Journal
du Dimanche* of 2005, it is worth noting that he explicitly associated a black
racial group—"African Americans"—as well as black and mixed-race people
with the specter of anti-Semitism while remaining mute on anti-Semitism
among French whites. This is particularly odd, given the sad, brutal reality that the overwhelmingly white French state—not French blacks or Maghrebis—was responsible for sending seventy-six thousand French Jews (as
well as black people, Romani people, and homosexuals) to Nazi gas cham-
bers. The racialization of anti-Semitism as a threat emanating from non-
whites in this case functions as a political constraint faced by those involved
in resurrecting slavery. Later chapters show how activists navigate this challenge.

What does it mean for French public officials to commemorate slavery
without remembering whiteness? In other words, what kinds of racial temporalities and constructions are both made possible and obscured in political
discourse about slavery? In answering this question, I intentionally probed
the silences and absences in the data that I gathered on commemorations of
slavery. I concur with the sociologist Melissa Weiner (2012), who studies

representations of slavery in the Netherlands, that what *is not* said and what *is not* represented in depictions of transatlantic slavery must be brought into the light. This is particularly the case in a society such as France, where so much related to race and racism is not said—and, to the contrary, is actually denied or simply is not addressed at all. In their commemorative speech, French officials erase whiteness from their temporal representations of slavery and race. Crucially, this erasure of whiteness does not reflect a complete avoidance of race altogether. Rather, it represents a selective suppression of whiteness from the national imaginary.

3

Activist Groups and Ethnoracial Boundaries

W hat does slavery commemoration have to do with black politics in France? In this chapter, I delve into the complications and cleavages that exist among the Afro-descended groups involved in crafting representations of transatlantic slavery. Using content analysis, ethnographic observations, and insights gleaned from interviews, this chapter explores the extent to which commemorators understand slavery as "black history" in France. The chapter is divided into four sections. First, I explore racial representations and temporalities in one of France's first slavery expositions to show the particular salience of blackness. Next, I unpack the racial and ethnic politics of the major cultural organizations involved in commemorating slavery. I show that most groups fall into two categories: Caribbean-centered commemorators and African-centered commemorators. The third section highlights differences between these approaches by focusing on the practices and politics of two activist groups. Finally, I show how Caribbean-centered and African-centered groups diverge in their descriptions of memories of the 1998 march, the turning point in recent commemorations of slavery in metropolitan France.

Setting the Scene: Representations of Blackness in a Slavery Exposition

L'Ombre du Silence (The Shadow of Silence) was a traveling exposition that circulated throughout overseas and mainland France in the late 1990s. I learned about the exposition when I took a short trip to the port city of Nantes, on the western coast of France. I had been in contact with the organization Les Anneaux de la Mémoire (The Chains of Memory), which was responsible for producing the first large-scale commemorative exhibition related to colonial slavery in mainland France. Through conversations with the organization's staff in Nantes, I eventually identified some of the first contacts for my research in Paris. One of those informants was Odile Lantier, the president of the small Les Anneaux de la Mémoire, which had organized the exposition "Slavery throughout History."

Unlike many of the commemorators I met who felt emotionally tied to the history of slavery because of their own ethnic or racial identities, Lantier described her connection to the commemorative project as primarily professional. A white woman without any family lineage in overseas France, she came to work on the expo because her experience in bookbinding was instrumental in helping to produce the graphic design. Lantier worked with a small team to bring the project to fruition. Two Caribbean historians were responsible for researching and writing the text, while Lantier and two other designers provided the technical expertise needed to create the panels. The final exposition consisted of thirty-six richly illustrated panels divided into three sections, focusing on France, Africa, and the Antilles, and covering a time period from 1625 until 1848.[1] After our first meeting, Lantier generously allowed me to photocopy and scan miniature reproductions of the panels, which I analyzed to gain insight into the historical narratives and racial politics of metropolitan commemorative movements related to slavery.

The Regional Council of Guadeloupe originally commissioned *The Shadow of Silence* for the bicentennial of the French Revolution in 1989, but a political shake-up resulted in the panels' not being shown on the archipelago until 2000. In the interim, they were lost and subsequently found in a series of unlikely events. Over tea, Lantier told me that the panels had been put on a cargo ship of abandoned goods and were later featured at a flea market in Paris, where one of her collaborators happened to see them and bought them back. After the chance recovery of the panels, the expo traveled throughout metropolitan France. The first showing occurred in September 1994 in Montreuil, just outside Paris. The panels went on to appear in at least twelve other cities in mainland France, including Chateauroux, Yzeure, Roubaix, Bourget, Paris, Bourges, and Colombes. They were also featured in an official installation sponsored by the Overseas Ministry in the Great Hall of La Villette in Paris during the 1998 commemorations.

Lantier confessed that she had felt some rivalry from Caribbean organizations that were upset they had not put the show together themselves. While Caribbeans were very "passionate" about the exposition, she said, "Africans" became even more interested over the course of its traveling itinerary in mainland France. At one point, she touched on the emotional reactions the exposition provoked in whites, including complaints she heard, such as "This is nonsense! Why are you doing this? It's just blaming us again!" She also learned, by contrast, that some Caribbeans saw the exposition as a source of healing. An introduction to the panels emphasizes the particular importance of the French Caribbean islands, the Antilles: "In choosing to illustrate the three centers of concern—France, Africa, and the Antilles—in a parallel manner, we wanted to plunge the visitor into their political, economic, and social realities. Through this mirror effect, we allude to the identity crisis that the Antilles is currently experiencing." In this case, foregrounding Caribbean (Antillean) identity is the straightforward consequence of the panels' being commissioned by local Guadeloupean officials (with historical research provided by French Caribbean historians). Yet using the Antilles as a kind of imaginative anchor to bring coherence and meaning to French Atlantic slavery was a reoccurring pattern in many metropolitan commemorations and functioned to portray Africans largely as historical characters rather than as contemporary populations.

Examining the discourse and images in the panels foreshadowed many of the findings I would encounter later in the field. For example, the exposition's panels used racial categories in an asymmetrical manner, signaling the existence of "blacks" and "blackness" but remaining relatively mute about "whites" and "whiteness." I found that the word *noir/noire* was used about four times as often as *blanc/blanche*. In general, the panels invoked blackness as a category when describing (1) the Code Noir, (2) Africans broadly, (3) the enslaved in particular, and (4) African Americans. Representations of blacks are at the center of two panels entitled "France" that open the exposition, including blacks in the historical narrative of French history and collective memory.[2] The caption of a 1767 illustration of the Black Code invokes blackness this way: "The Black Code appeared in the general indifference of French philosophical thinking and unleashed the furor of the masters. The timid recognition of a 'soul and a bit of dignity' in Blacks by Montesquieu in 1748 marked the beginning of a polemic over the merits of slavery." A reproduction of Marie-Guillemine Benoist's *Portrait d'une Négresse* (1800) shows a dark brown woman in a seated position, her head draped with a white head wrap, with white fabric cascading down her torso, exposing her naked breast. The accompanying text seems to have no direct link to the painting beyond its aim to uncover the representation of "blacks" during the time of slavery:

> Since time immemorial, literature has provided men with a justification for slavery. [The notion] that Blacks were a "cursed people" [*peuple maudit*], brutes by nature, a people led by the basest instincts and the vilest appetites are ideas profoundly anchored in mentalities. Even [Nicolas de]

CHAPTER 3

Condorcet, a fervent abolitionist, would say regarding Blacks: "One cannot deny that they have, in general, considerable stupidity" [*On ne peut dissimuler qu'ils n'aient en general une grande stupidité*].

These references to anti-blackness (e.g., stereotypes regarding their supposed moral or mental inferiority) were used to uncover the basis upon which the practice of slavery was justified during the transatlantic trade, as demonstrated in the "Black Code."

An explicit concern with the portrayal of blackness also motivates another panel, entitled "The Image of Blacks" in the section on France. Sculptures and paintings from eighteenth- and nineteenth-century French artists are featured and contextualized with reflections on their historical meaning and aesthetic qualities. Frédéric Bazille's *Négresse aux Pivoines*, showing a young black girl arranging flowers, is juxtaposed against this text:

In Europe, Blacks (men and women) could be perceived as simple models without the moral, social and political considerations that one attributes to them across the Atlantic. . . . The physiognomy here is treated attentively, although the face and hands have more or less the same importance as the flowers in the play of colors.

Throughout the panel, the word "negro" (*nègre*) was attached to images of black men as shown in busts and paintings produced by Charles Cordier and Eugene Delacroix. A caption beneath Delacroix's *Nègre au Turban* reads, "This darkly beautiful negro has a stern forehead that commands respect." A "mixed-race" woman, with bare shoulders and a black necklace fills the canvas of Eugene Delacroix's *Aspasie la Mulâtresse*, shown in the lower left-hand corner of the panel. Her image is used to illustrate the artist's efforts to challenge Eurocentric ideals of beauty:

Delacroix broke with the conventional notion in Europe of the feminine ideal. At the beginning of the 19th century, the seduction of dark beauty was a solely literary theme. One sees, through [his work,] a new image of femininity taking shape.

The inclusion of a mulatto woman under the banner of "black" images reinforces (without explicitly problematizing) a definition of blackness drawn from the one-drop rule of hypodescent, in which a single drop of "black" blood categorizes the individual as black.

Against the politics of color-blind racial denial, the exposition made an effort to unpack the historical construction of blackness by showing how the meaning of the category changed over time. One slide entitled "Before the Slave Traders," in a section on Africa, shows that blacks were not always associated with enslavement:

> In ancient societies, the connotation between "Black" and "slave" had not yet imposed itself. [The slave] exists and is more frequently [associated with] White slaves. Any foreigner in the city or prisoner of war can be enslaved. In Greece, as in Rome, the African slave is an article of luxury that is much costlier than a Syrian or a Gaul. When Egypt established itself in Nubia during the Middle Empire, a path to penetrating Black Africa was opened.

To illustrate transformations in the portrayal of slaves and blacks, the panel features photographs of Michelangelo's *The Slave*, a statue of a nude white man in bondage, and "The Black Musician," an unattributed statue of a nude black man that dates to the Gallic-Roman era.

Importantly, the exposition also invokes African Americans as blacks with relevance to the French Atlantic slave trade in a section of the dossier that pertains to cultural production in Guadeloupe and the United States. The text refers to the work of Guy Konket, a Guadeloupean artist, and Jalal Mansur Nuriddin, a founding member of the Last Poets, an African American performance group that emerged in the 1960s. Konket's music of choice, *gro'ka* (also known as gwoka),[3] is portrayed as "the symbol . . . of Guadeloupean identity . . . of African essence [and was] banned during slavery" for being perceived by slave masters as a form of rebellion. In our meetings, Lantier indicated that she and the other organizers of the exposition had become acquainted with Jalal during his travels in France, which sparked their interest in his work and its connection to their commemorative project. The influence of American "blackness" is evident in a section of the exposition's dossier on the Last Poets. An interview about the group's album *Scatterrap/Home* (1994) highlights U.S. racial politics:

> 1970: Black America rumbles like never before. They do not want their sons going to die for The Man, the White [man (*le blanc*)]. Two global bloodbaths taught them a lesson. They knew from experience that after the victory marches, the lynching would start again. Here, they said "no." This new war against other "people of color" [*gens de couleur*], others who were the "wretched of the earth," is even less their own than the others. They scream "Black Power!" The ghettos rustle with rumors of revolution, of armed battle. The summers were hot, burning. "Burn, Baby Burn." In '67, Detroit, Newark burned. . . . [T]he Black Panthers took back the flame that Malcolm X, assassinated on a cold and clear Sunday afternoon, February 21, 1965, had put down. Soon, the FBI

would strike and begin to demolish the Black Panthers. 1970: It was also the year that an unforgettable and first, eponymous album appeared from an unknown Black group—the Last Poets—who would become the mouthpiece of insurrection in the ghettos, inventing the passage to modern rap, heir to an oral tradition as old as Africa.

Unlike the profile of Konket (which emphasized the slavery roots of *gro'ka*), the music and rhymes of the Last Poets are never explicitly tied to the cultural production of slavery in the exposition. But inclusion of this text strongly implies that the problem of racism and the assertion of a black identity ("Black Power") are both relevant to the commemoration of slavery. In addition, references to African Americans illustrate an imagined community (Anderson 2006) of descendants of slaves, tied together by their African origins, as well as by their shared experience with historical and contemporary racism. In this way, *The Shadow of Silence* uses musical expression by descendants of slaves in Guadeloupe and the United States to highlight the contemporary relevance of the slavery past and to construct a transnational black identity. However, it also bears underlining that the recognition provided to whiteness in this instance—the "white [man]"—is restricted to the United States. The panels did not, by and large, produce representations of French white people, thus masking the historical and contemporary presence of the white majority. As a result, the racial temporality displayed in the exposition explicitly and implicitly framed slavery as "black history" while largely avoiding whiteness.

The Racial Politics of Commemorative Groups

If hegemonic representations of slavery minimize whiteness and emphasize blackness, how do commemorative groups on the ground construct race? One of the most interesting and unusual features of French commemorations of slavery is the lack of consensus—among Afro-descended people themselves—as to whether slavery should be framed as black history. The dispute over the racial and ethnic framing of slavery reflects, in part, the influence of Caribbean activists who at times have sought to distance themselves from contemporary black movements. I also observed firsthand that the opposing race politics of commemorative groups are compounded by continual drama, gossip, and conflict among and within organizations involved in resurrecting the slavery past.

I began to get a sense of these cleavages when I attended Chanté Nwèl, a French Caribbean Christmas celebration, in December 2007, with the hope of gaining entrée into the networks of "overseas" activists who play a central role in making claims about the slavery past. I had been invited by Daniel Dalin, co-president of the Collectif-DOM, a lobby for overseas French (*ultramarins*) living in the Paris region. The festivities were being held at the Overseas Ministry at 27 Rue Oudinot in the Seventh Arrondissement, under the auspices of Christian Estrosi, Deputy Minister of Overseas France, and Patrick Karam, the Inter-ministerial Delegate for Equal Opportunities for Overseas French. This would be the first of many visits to the ministry during my fieldwork, and I had yet to find my bearings in Paris, having arrived only two months earlier.

That evening, I took the subway to the Sevres-Babylone subway and walked about five minutes past the well-known shop Le Bon Marché. After asking a few police officers, then a shopkeeper, for directions, I finally came upon an imposing administrative building with guards at the entry and a few well-dressed, brown-skinned people standing near the entrance. Daniel met me outside with my invitation in hand. It was printed with my name and enclosed in an official, sealed envelope from the ministry. Almost everyone who walked by us greeted him by name and with *la bise*, the familiar kiss on the cheeks given to friends and family. Despite the festive atmosphere of the occasion, I knew conflict was brewing in the French Caribbean community. On the phone earlier that day, Daniel had told me that Charles Dagnet, his co-president at Collectif-DOM, was no longer affiliated with the organization. This had surprised me, as Charles had mentioned nothing about problems with Collectif-DOM when we had met a few days before the Chanté Nwèl event. As we stood outside the ministry, Daniel quickly filled me in on related political gossip: Patrick Karam, former founding president of Collectif-DOM, had resigned from his inter-ministerial position that evening. Everyone seemed surprised by the news, and most people in attendance were unaware of the political drama that was unfolding. I listened as Daniel explained to a few others that Patrick had been blocked politically from carrying out his agenda, part of which included efforts to fight discrimination and to teach Creole in metropolitan schools. Before we headed in, Patrick made his way out of the ministry, shaking hands and greeting people. Daniel introduced us briefly and asked me to explain what I was doing in Paris. I told Patrick that I was working on a thesis regarding Caribbeans. Looking slightly annoyed and rushed, he politely responded, "Well, you're in good hands. Daniel's definitely the one to talk to."

Denise, a fifty-year-old Martinican woman, took me inside.[4] She was quite a bit taller than I, with a dark brown complexion, and she wore her hair relaxed and styled in a bun.[5] Denise was a friend of Daniel's and, as I found out later, she worked as a high-level civil servant at one of the ministries. Although she seemed hesitant and cold at first, she warmed up when she found out I was a student at Sciences Po (a prestigious French university) and studying at Harvard. The event was being held in the Salle Félix Eboué, named for the famous French Guianese politician and colonial administrator who had served in

French territories in Africa and the Caribbean in the early 1900s, including as governor of Guadeloupe. I had expected a somewhat reserved Christmas show in a large auditorium, with performances. Instead, I found a festive concert filled with French Caribbeans, most of them from Martinique and Guadeloupe, with banquet food, an open bar, disco lights, and dancing. Later that evening, over the din of the crowd, Daniel told me that this was the first time the ministry had ever organized such an event. "Why is it only happening now?" I asked. "The crazy thing," he said, "is that this was pushed by Patrick." It was strange seeing everyone dancing and having a good time while knowing that political turmoil was not far under the surface. Cameramen and reporters from Radio France Outre-Mer crowded near the center of the room, where Overseas Minister Michèle Alliot-Marie stood with an entourage.

Over Antillean cocktails—most notably, the rum-and-fruit juice concoction known as *punch*)—and hors d'oeuvres such as *boudin* and *accras*,[6] Denise began to tell me about her life. She was born in Martinique but had been in the metropole for about thirty years. She told me that she had traveled to the United States, mostly in New York and Miami, to visit friends from Haiti. She admitted that she did not have a great opinion of African Americans when she first went to the United States, particularly given the bad neighborhoods she had seen. Unlike some other Caribbeans I had met who seemed to identify with African Americans, Denise was critical of them for speaking only English and being too focused on themselves as a group. Denise had also been to Africa, including the island of Gorée off the coast of Senegal, where she had seen the "door of no return," now a veritable shrine to the enslaved Africans who began their forced sojourn in the Middle Passage. She had imagined that she would feel some connection to Africa, but in fact, she did not.

Denise told me that her family in Martinique had wanted her to bring a "blond-haired, blue-eyed" man home so she would have mixed children. Although she did not end up doing so, she was now dating a Jewish man. Another Caribbean at the party told me that he was married to a woman whom he described as *metropolitain*. This was one of the first contexts in which I learned that "metropolitan" was often used as a euphemism for "white" (*blanc/blanche*). Denise used the word "black" (*noir/noire*) to describe herself and other people of African descent in France. I asked her whether she identified as the descendent of slaves, and she said, "Absolutely." When I asked her whether it was normal for Caribbeans to identify that way, she said, "In the past, no. They didn't teach the history [of it] at all. But now things are starting to change." I asked her, given her travel experiences, whether she thought black people were better off in France or the United States. After thinking about it, she said she thought that blacks were better off in the United States. She said she faced discrimination in France and that discrimination was, in fact, the reason she had gotten involved with Collectif-DOM two years earlier. She had worked for France Telecom before it became a private company, and when it was reorganized, she lost her position. With the help of the association, she was able to get back on her feet and find a new job. She said that many people had a hard time accepting a "black woman" in her high-profile role. Often, she said, they would assume that she held a lower position in the ministry or that she was a cleaning lady. Denise said that being black and female made it doubly difficult for her; she was the only *noire* in her division at work.

Midway through the evening, I stepped out of the room to make my way to one of the other banquet areas. I encountered Daniel in the hall, who was dripping sweat. He said that he had just given the overseas minister a piece of his mind. In particular, he had admonished her to stop "trying to distract the Caribbean community with music and dancing" and, instead, to do something about the real problems they faced (including discrimination). "This is how it is with the French Caribbean community: we dance, we sing, we drink, have a good time—but we don't get anything done," he said. When I returned home, well past midnight, my feet were numb from dancing, and I found myself struggling to sort out the tales of political intrigue I had witnessed that night. My conversation with Denise (who would later become a friend) would also play an important role in shaping my insight into Caribbean identity and historical consciousness. Her migration experience, racial identity, and experience with discrimination foreshadowed many of the themes that would emerge later in my interviews. Most important, the discourse of commemorative activists and ordinary people would echo her observation that Antilleans had been loath to identify as "descendants of slaves" because the history of slavery had not been taught. I would also come to understand better just how and why things were "changing," as she had said, in a period of unprecedented attention to the history and memory of colonial slavery in mainland France.

Although the Chanté Nwèl was not itself a commemoration of slavery, many of the people present were key players in the field. Moreover, several features of the evening would reemerge at other events I attended during my two years of fieldwork. Music, singing, dancing, and the consumption of Antillean food and drink were often integrated into commemorations, as were moments of political confrontation, such as Patrick Karam's sudden resignation and Daniel Dalin's confrontation with the overseas minister. The conflict surrounding the leadership of Collectif-DOM was also an early indication of the ongoing personality clashes I would observe in the shifting politics of "overseas" associations. The feelings of uneasiness I experienced that night hearing unflattering comments from group leaders about their "enemies" would also become a familiar dilemma for me during my fieldwork. Gaining access to commemorative organizations required me to foster collegial relationships with quarreling factions, to be on the receiving end of rumors and privy to the insults and ill will that commemorative leaders frequently hurled at each other. In many instances, I found myself awkwardly in the middle of these conflicts, constrained by the need to understand the political and personal divisions that both generated and circumscribed commemorations of slavery.

While the vast majority of commemorative groups I encountered during my fieldwork either explicitly or implicitly embrace black identification, there were notable exceptions. In fact, fractures around identity politics among ethnic associations frequently appeared in the field of slavery commemorations in Paris. One of my goals in recruiting commemorative organizers was to include participants from the most visible groups. A second consideration was ensuring variation in the groups' collective identities and racial politics. Yet classifying organizations in the highly complex, shifting field of slavery commemorations was a difficult task. As fieldwork progressed and I began to tease out

Figure 3.1. *Activists, administrative officials, and employees of the city of Paris at an annual commemoration of the abolition of slavery at City Hall on April 27, 2009. The day-long event included the laying of a wreath, a minute of silence, music and dance performances, speeches by city officials (including former Mayor Bertrand Delanoë), an exposition entitled "Antillais d'Ici" (Antilleans from Here), and panels (produced by CM98) showing the names given to enslaved people in the French Caribbean. For an account from a French Caribbean website, see "Delanoë commémore le décret d'abolition de l'esclavage," available at http://www.fxgpariscaraibe.com/article-30754507.html.*

Figures 3.2 and 3.3. *Musicians and singers perform at the annual commemoration of the abolition of slavery at City Hall in Paris, April 27, 2009.*

patterns in how the groups were connected relationally, I would inevitably come upon new evidence or developments that muddied the waters. One source of difficulty was the frequent—and vicious—conflict that regularly erupted among leaders of the various organizations. Group leaders bickered with one another in private and in public. Power struggles were frequent both within and among organizations. Candidates for positions within associations contested election results. Presidents of groups would resign one week and create a new group the next. The constant upheaval, controversy, and shifting allegiances made situating the commemorators a formidable enterprise. A second challenge was making sense of the groups' boundary work when the names of the organizations were rarely accurate indicators. To take just one example, while the groups Black Passage and Conseil Representatif des Associations Noires (Representative Council of Black Associations [CRAN]) both incorporate the word "black" in their names, the two organizations do not assert the same representation of their collective identity. Black Passage is, in fact, an organization that frames its collective identity in ethnoracial terms by embracing the concept of an African diaspora that links blacks in Africa and the West. By contrast, CRAN is an organization that rejects the concepts of race and ethnicity, framing itself as an antiracist coalition in defense of people who are socially categorized as black.

Faced with these complexities, I developed a provisional typology based on what I call *group framing* and *boundary orientation*. An organization's "group framing" is the primary representation of its collective identity. I use *boundary orientation* here to indicate the extent to which an organization's collective identity is exclusive (highly bounded) or inclusive (porous). In Table 3.1, I identify two main types of group framing: (1) regional/ethnoracial and (2) coalition. The regional and ethnoracial category includes groups that portrayed themselves as representatives of the Antillo-Guianese and those that portrayed themselves as representative of a broadly defined African diaspora. I found that while most of the "regional" groups claimed to represent overseas migrants in mainland France, many were, in fact, geared toward Caribbeans, with very few members from overseas departments such as Guiana (in South America) and Réunion (in the Indian Ocean). It is for this reason that most of the "overseas" groups can, in fact, be understood broadly as Caribbean-centered.

Coalition groups did not include ethnic or racial criteria in their projected identity. These included some national commissions (e.g., the Committee for the Memory and History of Slavery) and CRAN (which, although it includes the word "black" in its name, actually rejects the concepts of race and ethnicity). I also distinguish between organizations whose identities were exclusive and those whose identities were inclusive. Groups were categorized on the basis of my evaluation of interviews with respondents, organizational publications (including mission statements), and relevant supporting documents (media coverage, websites, commemorative discourses, and so on). This typology should be viewed as a rough guide for understanding some of the similarities and differences among organizations involved in the commemoration of slavery in metropolitan Paris. While evidence is drawn from the overall sample of commemorative organizers, throughout my fieldwork I focused on the claims making and group boundaries of one group in particular—the Comité Marche du 23 Mai 1998 (1998 March Committee [CM98])—to deepen my understanding of the most visible Caribbean commemorative group in mainland France.[7]

The first observation that stands out about these commemorators is the considerable variation in their form. The commemorative groups I encountered included associations, nationally appointed commissions, media outlets, and transnational organizations and offices. Commemorative groups in metropolitan France include memorial work from above (e.g., state-appointed bodies such as the Committee for the Memory and History of Slavery and elite-driven organizations such as CM98, CRAN, and the Collectif des Filles et Fils d'Africains Deportés [Collective of Sons and Daughters of Deported Africans (COFFAD)]) and from below (e.g., labor unions such as the

TABLE 3.1. TYPOLOGY OF COMMEMORATIVE GROUPS		
Regional/ethnoracial	Exclusive	Inclusive
Caribbean-centered	Association of Régie Autonome des Transports Parisiens Agents from the overseas departments and territories Collective of Antilleans, Guianese, Réunionese, and Mahorans Inter-ministerial Delegation for Equal Opportunities for Overseas French March 23, 1998, March Committee Municipal DOM-TOM Welcome and Information Center National Antillean and Guianese Chaplaincy	Tropiques FM Confederal Protest Collective of Overseas Natives for the General Confederation of Labor Overseas Delegation for the City of Paris Study and Research Center for French from the Overseas
African-centered	Acting for Reparations Now for Africans and Descendants of Africans Collective of the Daughters and Sons of Deported Africans	African Diaspora Black Passage International Caribbean Club May 10 Organization Committee Orig'in Association
Coalition		
Committees and offices	–	Committee for the Memory and History of Slavery Inter-ministerial Mission for the 1998 National Celebration of the 150th Anniversary of the Abolition of Slavery Cultural Affairs, City of Brunoy
Associations	–	Representative Council of Black Associations Associations of Descendants of Black Slaves and Their Friends L'Ombre du Silence

Confédération Générale du Travail and fledgling grassroots organizations such as the May 10 Coordinating Committee).

Yet across the board, commemorators I interviewed agreed that the activism of Afro-Caribbeans in particular was the central force pushing the commemorative agenda ahead. Although groups such as CM98, CRAN, and COFFAD have highly educated leaders who belong to the middle or upper-middle class, they are nonetheless elite members of marginal groups who historically were excluded from French citizenship during the colonial period and face contemporary stigma and exclusion in French society. An outgrowth of this historical marginalization is the suppression of French colonial history from French collective memory, historiography, and the national educational curriculum. All of these factors taken together explain why the legitimation work of slavery commemorators is particularly fraught in France.

The second important observation is the role of political context in constraining the visibility of slavery commemorations in general, especially for groups whose messages are considered controversial or combative (e.g., pro-reparations groups). Commemorative groups generally depended on government resources to provide funding and venues for their events, and private resources were nearly nonexistent. One consequence of this dependence was the pressure some groups' leaders felt to package their commemorative activities in the most politically correct way.

Yannick Meyo collaborated with the Orig'in Association to produce a festival (including concerts, film screenings, and debates about slavery) called *Africaphonie*. Orig'in received funding for *Africaphonie* from a number of sources, including the National Agency for Social Cohesion and Equal Opportunities in part because the group framed the event as a celebration of diversity and solidarity. Support from the business community was more difficult to obtain. Yannick complained that nearly all of the businesses the group approached for funding turned them down, describing situations in which Caribbean employees of large firms assured him that they understood and supported the project, but they knew they would be unable to obtain funding from their superiors. In this revealing exchange, Yannick explained the challenges Orig'in faced in framing *Africaphonie* in a way that could not be construed as divisive (communitarian):

> *Yannick:* You're obligated to pay a lot of attention to your intonation, to show that you're not impassioned, because passion, you know—we're in a country where when a Jew talks about the problems of Jews, he's [called] a Zionist, and when a black talks about the problems of blacks, he's pro-black, you see? It's very easy in France to directly paint you as extreme. The problem is that it

never bothered anyone to have a Breton talk about an international inter-Celtic concert . . . you see? That's not communitarian. . . .

C.F.: And in France, what does it mean to be communitarian?

Yannick: Concretely . . . it doesn't have at all the same sense as in the United States. . . . Being communitarian in France means being an extremist. That's what it means—no more, no less.

C.F.: So you have to avoid, at all costs, being categorized as communitarian?

Yannick: Oh, yes. Yes. Whether it's you or your event, anything you do should not be associated with communitarianism, that's for sure. [And] it's quite difficult, when you talk about slavery, to not be communitarian.

C.F.: So how do you present your objectives in the dossier?

Yannick: [*Laughs.*] Well, in fact, you're forced to present the event as a kind of opening [*ouverture*]. That's what's funny—the fact that you have to present the event as an event, like a celebration, a party.

C.F.: Why do you have to do that?

Yannick: You have to . . . because, actually, if you don't do a party, then it means you're serious. And if you're serious, then you have something against them.

C.F.: It has to be light?

Yannick: There you go. *Light. Light.* Because otherwise, it won't work. I met people who told me frankly, "I support your cause, but it won't get approval from my boss." The director of public relations [at a firm] told me that.

C.F.: Why did he say that?

Yannick: Because he knows that there won't be money for it.

C.F.: Even if you presented it in a "light" way?

Yannick: Because it's always sensitive associating with a thing like [slavery]. . . . [I]t's always perilous. You don't know how journalists are going to present it, and . . . you don't know if there will be communitarian connotations or not. . . . Businesses are afraid of giving money. . . . [W]hen I tell you which [businesses] turned me down, it's going to drive you crazy as an American. . . . For example, Soft Sheen Carson said "no" . . . you see?

Soft Sheen Carson is well known for its line of specialized beauty products for African-descended populations, including the chemical relaxer Dark and Lovely and Weave Care. In Yannick's view, the company's refusal to support the *Africaphonie* event ran counter to its own business interests (because the event would draw large crowds of blacks). "It's beyond . . . business," he said. "We're into politics . . . an entrepreneur who for political reasons won't seize an opportunity to make money." In the current political climate, even *Africaphonie*, a consensus-building, inclusive event, risked being perceived as "communitarian" because of the fraught subject matter (the memory of slavery). From Yannick's perspective, blacks and Jews are both portrayed as "extremists" when defending the interests of their group. In this way, anticommunitarianism, a staple of the French ethnoracial and political status quo, stigmatizes certain forms of minority mobilization.

Comparing Caribbean-Centered and African-Centered Diasporic Groups

In this section, I compare the memory work of two contrasting groups to demonstrate some of the patterns in the data more clearly. Through analysis of activists' discourse and ethnographic observation of events about the history and memory of slavery, I show how groups with contrasting ethnic and racial politics—that is, CM98 and COFFAD) temporally frame the oppression of slaves and their descendants. Because it represents "Africa as the homeland of Africans and persons of African origin" and affirms "solidarity among people of African descent," as well as "belief in a distinct African personality [and] rehabilitation of Africa's past pride in African culture," COFFAD fits P. Olisanwuche Esedebe's (1994: 4) definition of Pan-Africanism. In contrast, CM98 typically asserts a Caribbean (*Antillais*) or overseas French (*Français d'outre-mer*) identity, framing the historical experience of slavery as the foundational myth for the group's social and cultural formation. Audrey Célestine (2010) characterizes CM98's identity work as a strategy of "differentiation," an effort to distinguish the specific concerns of French Caribbeans from those of the larger population of French Afro-descendants. Although informally its leaders generally describe themselves as representing Antillean migrants, CM98 claims to address the "identity and memory issues of Antilleans, Guianese and Réunionese for the purpose of ameliorating their integration within the Republic" (Rolle-Romana 2010).

CM98 and State-Focused Stigma Reversal

Founded in 1999, a year after the march, CM98 uses "race-blind" language of citizenship (Keaton 2010) to blame the French government for slavery. Serge Romana, a geneticist from Guadeloupe and the president of CM98, views the group's action as motivated by present-day concerns: "Slavery is far from being a question about memory. It's our foundational period. It's this construction [*fabrication*] in and by slavery that generates the major difficulties of our societies" (Hopquin 2005).[8] Over the years, CM98 partnered with other organizations representing victims of "crimes against humanity," including the Conseil Représentatif des Institutions Juives de France (Representative Council of French Jewish Institutions) and the Conseil de Coordination des Organisations Arméniens de France (Coordinating Council of French Armenian Organizations).

As mentioned previously, the 1998 march was a watershed moment in the commemoration of slavery in France, as it signaled broad support among Afro-Caribbeans for recognition of their historical presence in the nation. However, it was not universally understood as a "black" movement as the question of race emerged as a divisive topic among some activists. According to Romana, COFFAD wanted to use "black" as an umbrella term for the marchers:

> We had some problems with [COFFAD] because [our] flyers for the march said, "Who better than Guadeloupeans and Guianese? . . . [W]ho else could honor the memory [of our ancestors]?" [COFFAD] said we had to take out "Guadeloupean" and "Guianese." They wanted us to put in "black." . . . I said no. . . . I couldn't even imagine that we would do it any other way, because . . . it's the 150th anniversary of the abolition of the slavery of Negroes in the French colonies. . . . [The president of COFFAD] is not a descendant of slaves. So for me, it didn't make any sense.

Romana felt that descendants of slaves from the overseas departments (e.g., Guadeloupeans and Guianese) were the most appropriate bearers of the memory of slavery. For that reason, he rejected a racially defined "black" identity that would include French of sub-Saharan African origin (such as COFFAD's president). Romana emphasized the inadequacy of "blackness" as a criterion for group membership, saying, "Black French are defined by . . . the problem of racism. It is a social category, not an identity. . . . Descendants of slaves aren't a single color—there are all sorts of skin colors, and that's something that comes from our particular history."

Despite acknowledging anti-black racism, Romana (who identifies as mixed) argued that people from the islands could not be categorized as black because of their cultural and racial mixture, as well as their wide-ranging phenotypes. These arguments mirror developments in French Caribbean literature. Over the course of the 1980s, Antillean activists and writers reacted against the Negritude movement of Aimé Césaire and Léopold Senghor by proposing the concepts of *Creolité* (Creole-ness) and *Antillanité* (Antilleanness) to reflect a transnational Antillean identity (Beriss 2004: 68; Smith 2006)—a position incompatible with the U.S. rule of hypodescent, which defines anyone who has one drop of African blood as "black."[9] The ethnic framing of Caribbean identity by CM98 emphasizes French citizenship, slave ancestry, and shared historical heritage of plantation culture and colonization.

As a result of this narrow definition of identity, CM98 privileges ethnic terms (e.g., "Martinicans," "Guadeloupeans") to describe the victims of slavery and their descendants over broad racial terms such as "black," which includes sub-Saharan Africans. It is also important to note that many Caribbeans both within and outside CM98 understand Martinican and Guadeloupean identity in quasi-nationalist terms, often referring to the islands as their "country" (*pays*). Thus, while these activists emphasize Frenchness and citizenship, CM98's representations of group belonging are also fundamentally transnational, framing Caribbeans as an ethnic group whose history and present-day problems span the Atlantic. The boundaries that CM98 draws against Africans, in distinguishing their ethnic identity, does not mean the group excludes Afro-French from their events. As one staff member explained:

> We are different. We are French from the Antilles. We were constructed [*fabriqués*] differently. . . . That's precisely what's nice about CM98. . . . CM98 does conferences and invites people. . . . [W]e invited some Africans, some professors. . . . [T]here was a man who came who is Yoruban, and he talked to us about the construction of his ethnic group. There was a foundational myth . . . and this myth is followed by the entire ethnic group and there are rites that are perpetuated . . . whereas the Antillean—why do we say that we are no longer African? It's that the Antillean has been cut off from his rites. They cut him off from his foundational myths and put him in the position of making another myth, you see, to rebuild himself, because he had nothing—no culture, no language. There was nothing left. So he was forced to rebuild himself in slavery. That is why we are not African at all.

Drawing on catastrophic discourse that frames slavery as cultural loss (Patterson 1971), this temporal claim emphasizes discontinuity between Antillean culture and African roots. In this way, the inclusion of some African guest speakers at CM98 activities may actually reflect perceived distinctions between French people of Caribbean and African origin rather than the construction of a "shared" memory.

Nonracial Normative Inversion

When CM98 blames the French state for slavery, it has tried to avoid framing these issues primarily in terms of race. One CM98 leader revealed that the group eschews racial discourse because it can be construed as racist. He criticized COFFAD's leader, Assani Fassassi, for creating racial divisions:

> Fassassi's . . . dream is to become the French Farrakhan because he's Muslim and he identifies as black. Since he's African, he's not a descendant of slaves. The only thing he could hold on to was the idea of being black, and as soon as you say "black," they take over the entire movement. . . . [W]e had to prevent [CM98] from becoming a pro-Negro movement, a racist movement. . . . From the moment you emphasize the color of your skin, it's a racist movement—or, at least, a racial movement. And racist madness can develop very quickly, because if there are "blacks," then there are "whites," so there's a war between blacks and whites. . . . We were dealing with a simple thing: slavery happened. [If] the French state wants to commemorate slavery, we should honor the memory of the victims of slavery. It's a completely different concept.

Like many French Caribbeans, CM98 members are predominantly Catholic, and they sometimes distance themselves from COFFAD because of that group's ties to Muslim activism in France. Although in this interview the respondent called himself and other Antilleans "black," he used blackness to refer to skin color, not identity.

Moreover, he explained that CM98 was not interested in *racialized* stigma reversal—that is, defining whites as "bad" and blacks as "good." Instead, CM89 condemned the crimes of the French government (under slavery) and demanded symbolic and cultural recognition from the state today. Romana explained the importance of blaming the perpetrators of slavery, saying:

> We want . . . the Republic to recognize that our ancestors were victims of slavery. . . . But they can't do it . . . because doing so means the Republic has to face its guilt. They'll tell you that slavery was a crime against humanity, . . . [but] it's the first crime against humanity without a guilty party. When the French government talks about the Armenian genocide, they say it was the Turks. When they talk about the Holocaust, it was the Germans. . . . But here, there's nothing.

Highlighting African Complicity

Another point of divergence between CM98 and COFFAD is CM98's emphasis on African participation in colonial slavery. A section of the group's website, titled "European and African Complicity in the Trade," reads:

At the beginning of the slave trade, the Portuguese raided Africans on the coast to make them work in the Iberian Peninsula. But this technique quickly revealed itself to be inefficient. . . . In 1445, King Henry of Portugal commanded his subjects to renounce the raids and to establish durable commercial relations with the Africans. The other European nations adopted this tactic and engaged in commerce with those African kingdoms that agreed to provide them with captives.

For CM98, questions of blame go beyond "black and white." Europeans found African leaders who were willing to sell other Africans into slavery. Framing African complicity in this way may also reflect the group's rejection of a "black" or Pan-African identity.

Following the passage of the Taubira Law, Jacques Chirac convened the Committee for the Memory and History of Slavery in 2004, an official body of scholars and representatives of ethnic associations, to examine the collective memory of slavery in France. Originally chaired by the Guadeloupean writer Maryse Condé, with Romana's participation, the committee deliberated over possible dates for a national day of memory for slavery and its abolition. Romana staunchly supported May 23 in honor of the 1998 march he helped organize, as the date was associated with Caribbeans' efforts to memorialize the victims of slavery. When other committee members favored the more "universal" date of May 10 (the date the Taubira bill became law), Romana resigned from the committee and vowed to fight for the recognition of May 23 (Romana 2005).

COFFAD and Ethnoracial Stigma Reversal

Established in the early 1990s, COFFAD holds debates, conferences, and marches on the history and legacies of the transatlantic slave trade.[10] It has also sued individuals for making disparaging remarks against Afro-Caribbeans and the memory of slavery (including the French historian Olivier Petré-Grenouilleau) and organizations that have attempted to auction off objects and documents related to the slave trade. Unlike CM98, COFFAD explicitly includes French people of sub-Saharan African origin, as well French Caribbeans. For example, COFFAD helped organize a march in 2008 where I observed black French activists displaying a banner that read, "1454–2008: 554 Years of Plunder, Pillage, Deportations and Genocides for Africans and Descendants of Africans. Justice and Reparations!" Fassassi, COFFAD's founder and president, is an academic from Benin and a member of the executive committee of the French Council of the Muslim Faith. Caribbeans also play a key role in the group's activities: its vice-president, Joby Valente, a

TABLE 3.2. COMPARISON OF HISTORICAL NARRATIVES					
Group	Ethnic identity	Victim frame	Responsible party	Legacies	Destigmatization strategies
CM98	French descendants of slaves, Caribbeans	Slaves	France, Africans	Cultural, psychological, and social dysfunctions among present-day Caribbeans, exclusion from cultural membership in France	Nonracial normative inversion
COFFAD	Africans/ blacks	Deported Africans	Whites, Western nations, and institutions that benefited from the slave trade	Racism, generation of wealth in the West, exploitation of Africa	Ethnoracial normative inversion

singer and activist, and Frédéric, the group's spokesperson, are both from Guadeloupe.[11] (For a comparison of the historical narratives of the two organizations, see Table 3.2.)

Asserting a Transnational "Black" Identity

COFFAD grounds its ethnic identity in African ancestry, yet the group also affirms a racial identity based on shared phenotype (e.g., being categorized as having "black" skin). This broad, ethnoracial framing of its group membership explains why COFFAD refers to both the victims of slavery and the present-day bearers of their memory interchangeably as "black" and "African." In addition to emphasizing African ancestry, COFFAD's name bears similarity to the Association of Sons and Daughters of Jews Deported from France. When CM98 has also drawn parallels between slavery and the Holocaust, it has done so in partnership with Jewish organizations. COFFAD, by contrast, has been criticized for creating "competition" between the two historical traumas.[12] In particular, COFFAD refers to slavery as "the most monstrous crime against humanity," suggesting a comparative hierarchy among atrocities (COFFAD 2000). The group's public discourse portrays Jewish activism as an example for (black) Africans to follow, particularly with regard to obtaining material reparations. For example, a flyer for a debate on reparations held on January 8, 2000, states:

The compensation of the JEWS opens the door for AFRICANS. This noble . . . approach of the Jews, which imposed material, financial and moral reparations as well as acts of repentance from Western institutions and governments, should encourage the BLACK PEOPLES, victims of the slave trade, of slavery and forced labor. (COFFAD 2000)

While COFFAD seeks recognition of the transatlantic slave trade as a crime against humanity (a strategy of normative inversion that blames the perpetrators of slavery rather than the enslaved), the group also wants Europeans, whom it alternately refers to as "whites" and "Westerners," to pay individual financial reparations to "Africans and descendants of deported Africans." COFFAD's focus on material repair reflects its temporal claims about the racial and economic consequences of slavery, a narrative that depicts blacks as both subjected to racial oppression in the past and potential recipients of compensation in the future.

Victim Framing and Denial of Slave Status

Instead of referring to "slaves," COFFAD materials generally use the terms "enslaved Africans" or "deported Africans." Frédéric explained:

> We would never say that we are daughters and sons of slaves [because] our ancestors weren't slaves when they arrived in America, in the Caribbean. Before they arrived, they were normal people. . . . [Then] they were captured, deported, and enslaved. . . . We don't want to . . . define ourselves by a situation that we denounce.

I attended a "Unity Commemoration" in the suburb of Saint-Denis in May 2008. Organized by Club Caraibe, a small association, the event was an intellectual and cultural exchange among members of the African diaspora. Fassassi and Frédéric were present. During the debate, members of the audience used the word "slave." Fassassi intervened, suggesting that "descendant of deported Africans" was the appropriate term. Toward the end, I was asked to discuss my research and my perspective. I tried to answer honestly, but broadly, as I recorded in my field notes:

> The issue of how to present my identity at these events is a thorny one. At CM98 events, I regularly introduced myself as a black American and descendant of slaves. At the Club Caraibe event, I knew this would be a problem. I decided to say that I was all of those things—"I'm an African

American, a black American, descendant of slaves, descendant of deported Africans." Several audience members shook their heads [and] said, "*No!*" . . . [E]ven [the organizer], sitting next to me, whispered, "You're a descendant of deported Africans."

This tense episode reveals the extent to which COFFAD and similar groups stake their historical claims on rigidly defined collective identities.

Racialized Normative Inversion

Frédéric, the COFFAD spokesperson, met with me at a café near the Opera subway station in Paris. Wearing tan khaki pants, a white striped shirt, and glasses, he led me to a seat in the very back, in a corner where no one could see us. When asked about the consequences of slavery, Frédéric pointed to present-day racism:

[W]hen there is a calamity in Africa . . . if five thousand people are threatened, humanitarian groups will organize to save ten of them. And when they've saved ten, they're happy: they've reached their objective. And when *one* French man or woman is held somewhere, the president of the Republic will go. . . . We're still considered the same way we were during the trade—below others. There's no equality. . . . [T]he slave trade institutionalized racism. Black and white didn't exist before.

As it is for CM98, blaming those responsible for slavery is an important strategy of reverse stigmatization for COFFAD. On May 7–8, 1998, the group helped organize a UNESCO colloquium entitled "The Slave Trade: A Crime against Humanity." The meetings culminated with the adoption of twelve "resolutions," including one that calls for the replacement of the term "slavery" with *Yovodah*. In the Fon dialect of Benin, *Yovo* means "European" or "white," and *dah* connotes evil or cruelty. *Yovodah*, then, can be understood as "white cruelty." By signifying "cruelty," *Yovodah* represents a moral transfer of stigma from the deported and enslaved Africans to white individuals and institutions:

The word "slavery" . . . obscures the atrocious, cruel and racial particularities of the transatlantic slave trade. . . . Historians will also acknowledge . . . that this . . . human tragedy was executed and put into practice during more than four centuries by Europeans and Westerners (the whites), to the detriment of Africa and the Africans. It is for this reason that we have found it just and correct to designate the phenomenon of the transatlantic slave trade by a word that expresses at once the identity of the perpetrator and the nature of his enterprise. The perpetrator is the White European, and his enterprise is pure cruelty. (COFFAD 1998)

Not all of COFFAD's discourse about whites and Europeans take the form of reverse stigmatization. One of the resolutions adopted by COFFAD in 1998 recognized "courageous and dignified Europeans" who "have given their lives for the Black cause" (COFFAD 1998).

Remembering 1998: A Black March?

Having explored the major differences in how CM98 and COFFAD frame their collective identities and racial temporalities, I now examine the question of whether the 1998 march that polarized the two groups was, in fact, viewed as a "black" mobilization. The representation of the 1998 march continues to weigh heavily on contemporary debates over the appropriate way to commemorate slavery in France. The enduring stamp of past memorial practices on present-day commemorations is what Jeffrey Olick (1999b: 383) refers to as the "memory of commemoration." One critical difference in how commemorative activists remember the 1998 march is the degree to which they represent it as a racial movement. One of the founding members of CM98, a Guadeloupean activist,[13] downplayed race in his account of the march but remembered the event as a moment in which he and other Caribbeans affirmed their citizenship:

> I led the fight for May 23 very actively. . . . I wanted the whole political fabric of France to understand the necessity of having this date, so I addressed [them]. I wrote thirty thousand letters saying, "Here's the situation. There was this march [on May 23, 1998] where forty thousand people marched, all of the Republic." For me, it was a step toward citizenship. The fact, contrary to what I was saying earlier, is that when we do a demonstration and we ask people to come, they don't come because they're afraid. The skin color, you see that from a distance. But this time, for once, there weren't forty thousand Blacks. There were forty thousand people. . . . So there were politicians from the left; there were labor unions; there were African associations; there were a lot of people. . . . For me, it was a gathering for a new citizenship so that they could say that these people are capable of going into the streets, capable of claiming their rights, capable of demanding to be less discriminated against. They are capable of saying, especially, "I can be the mayor of Paris, the mayor of Lyon, or even the president of the Republic."

It is worth noting that some activists who belonged to other, "restrictive" Antillo-Guianese groups did not describe the march primarily in racial terms. Thus, Daniel Dalin, president of Collectif-DOM, which frequently partners with Romana's CM98, described the march using frames similar to those used by CM98 members:

> *C.F.:* Were you in the march in 1998?
>
> *D.D.:* Yes.
>
> *C.F.:* In what capacity?
>
> *D.D.:* Simply as an individual . . . as an Antillean, if you will. I felt concerned.
>
> *C.F.:* How was the march?
>
> *D.D.:* It was impressive. First of all, they did not think that it was going to gather that many people. And second—no, it went really well. There were—but, really, there was an enormous amount of people. . . . I would say [there were] thirty-five thousand. . . . There was a very strong common desire—very, very strong—for the French government to take its responsibility with regard to slavery.
>
> *C.F.:* And what is this responsibility?
>
> *D.D.:* It was first of all to recognize—it was done by May 10. To teach—and this still hasn't been done—teaching in schools, and then that they conduct public policies. You should, in fact, fight against the phenomenon of forgetting, the phenomena of—the duty of remembering, the realms of memory [*devoir de mémoire, les lieux de mémoire*], Nantes, Bordeaux, and do an important event that takes account of this period of French history, because we're talking about four centuries. Four centuries. It's not insignificant.

Along with members of CM98 and its immediate allies (such as Collectif-DOM), Françoise Vergès, former president of the Committee for the Memory and History of Slavery and a migrant from Réunion Island, did not frame the march as black.[14] She also remembered it as a statement about citizenship:

> *F.G.:* I went around. I went to meetings, to associations, to debates. I was at the march, the demonstration of May 23. . . . It was an important expression . . . because for the first time, really, there was demonstration around that issue of being descended from slaves. [It was] the first time that the question of slavery was raised in France. It was not in the university; it was not in school or

whatever. It was in the streets. . . . And that was the first time, and I think that was extremely important. . . . [T]he government had this ad, this big big ad in the streets of Paris. It was with kids of different colors, kind of like a Benetton ad or something. And it was like, "We were all born in 1848." And I was like, "Excuse me?" that's not possible! For me—

C.F.: So tell me, why does that bother you?

F.G.: Because we were not born. It was not the decree that gave us life. Life comes from our ancestors, from our resistance, from our struggles, not from that amendment. That amendment gave us citizenship, not life. The march was in reaction to . . . against this discourse, which was really incredible. . . . [W]e are in 1998, and they are still not understanding that slaves were the first abolitionists, the first captive rebel was a slave abolitionist, the first captured in Africa. That was the first abolitionist. Please stop with that, you know? So I was there, and I started to write this book on [slavery (see Vergès 2006)]. I was analyzing the discourse on French abolitionism and its complicity with post-abolition colonial conquest. The big, deep ambiguity and ambivalence of the discourse that remain on the moral grounds—that this is bad, slavery is bad—never really connected with economic interests, with the question of racism. So let's put this aside [by saying], "This is bad, this is not good, we are all European and should be civilized," but never addressing the question of race, the question of economic interest, the question of incredible inequality in the colony, and the question of colonizing.[15]

Given the involvement of Vergès in a nationally appointed commission (a coalition organization), it is not surprising that she would privilege citizenship over race in her description of the march. Yet many other commemorators explicitly or implicitly sided with COFFAD's position by framing the mobilization as a black movement. One French Caribbean who works on commemorations for the city of Paris described the march as

the beginning [of a] realization [*prise de conscience*] in the streets. It was a silent march. . . . It didn't happen all at once. . . . [B]efore, there was a desire to be recognized, a desire to know that Antilleans were present and that the Antilleans were in France, that it was necessary to become aware [*prendre conscience*] and . . . that their history was not known in the Antilles even by Antilleans. It was not known by the French, and it was forgotten in the history of France. It was all this realization. . . . [The march] was enjoyable [*ca faisait plaisir*] . . . because we weren't used to seeing so many blacks together [*qu'on n'était pas habitué à voir autant de noirs rassemblés*].

Marie-Georges Peria, vice-president of the Centre d'Étude et de Recherche des Français d'Outre-Mer (Study and Research Center for French from Overseas [CERFOM]), also viewed the march as a black mobilization and was critical of CM98's restrictive group boundaries:

> *M.P.:* It was very dignified . . . a silent march. It was the first time that . . . there was a large black march.
>
> *CF.:* Who really organized the march?
>
> *M.P.:* Well, there were several people. There was the famous [Serge] Romana, who is actually rather criticized [*qui est quand même critiqué*]; it's true that I do not always agree with him. . . . I was in the march, and I saw that it was really good. . . . [B]ut afterward, in the following years, with his wife, who is a psychologist and all that, they organized a . . . kind of event with—
>
> *C.F.:* Chemins de Fer?
>
> *M.P.:* Yes, Chemins de Fer. . . . It took a turn that strongly displeased me . . . because it was rather racist, saying, "We want this to be only us, Antilleans, and Guadeloupe and Martinique, and all the others—"
>
> *C.F.:* Not the others?
>
> *M.P.:* Not the others, not the French, not Africans—it's not about you. So, overall, that's what it was. . . .
>
> *C.F.:* He said that openly?
>
> *M.P.:* Well, that's what came out in [his] speeches: "Listen, it's us. It's for us." . . . That's what I dislike, because I don't have that mind-set. And then also there [were some] who took on a kind of crazy mysticism—you know, "They were our ancestors," as if they spoke to the ancestors; "The ancestors are happy now." But what do they know about it? I wanted to tell him . . . and those around him, "It's not just [you], you know." . . . I asked him the question, and he didn't respond.
>
> *C.F.:* You asked him, "How do you know?"
>
> *M.P.:* Yes. Afterward I met him on several occasions . . . and I asked him, "[W]hen you say this, what do you know about it—when you say that now our ancestors are happy?" What does he know? Has he had particular communication [with them]?
>
> *C.F.:* And he didn't respond?

M.P.: He did not respond. I also find this dishonest, because it is a way to destabilize people. There are people who leave in tears and all that, who have experienced, who have actually suffered. But let's say that you should take people and destabilize them like this, and that was his plan. . . . There's something wrong with that [*il y a quelque chose qui va pas quoi*].

Peria felt that Romana and his wife were manipulating CM98 members by pretending that they spoke not only for but also somehow spoke with their ancestors. She was also critical of the group's boundaries against Africans.

Théo Lubin, president of the May 10 Coordinating Committee, is of Martinican origin and self-identifies as an "Afro-Ethiopian." Over the years, he has partnered with COFFAD on commemorative marches and other activities.[16] In his view, CM98 and COFFAD were polarized primarily because of COFFAD's denial of Antilleans' African roots:

T.L.: So CM98 and COFFAD are totally divided. Why? Because CM98 is a group of Antilleans . . . who say that they do not recognize their African ancestry. . . . Their slogan is "We don't come from Africa. We come from the sea, because it was in the boats that we [formed our group]. . . . The sea produced [us]."
C.F.: It's not Africa. That's the idea?
T.L.: That's the idea, so that's what made the break . . . and that's why COFFAD positioned itself each year in République, waiting for CM98 to show up. But they never came. They never marched. . . . I mean, they never marched again. . . . They call themselves the 1998 March Committee, but they marched only once—in 1998. We never saw them again in Paris. . . . [CM98] doesn't recognize all of the groups that participated in and contributed to the march. . . . I'm Antillean but . . . if you listen to the speech of Mr. Romana, it's the non-recognition of our African origins [*c'est de la non-reconnaissance de nos origines africaines*] under the pretext that Africans sold us [into slavery], under the pretext of things that are not historically true.
T.L.: Do you think that it's a minority point of view, or is it representative?
T.L.: It's a minority point of view because a black remains a black [*un noir reste noir*]; in whatever country he lives, he will always be thought of as an African. So now not recognizing one's African origins, it's as if one doesn't recognize that we're earthlings. It means we don't exist.

Joss Rovelas, president of Agir pour les Réparations Maintenant pour les Africains et Descendants d'Africains (Acting for Reparations Now for Africans and Descendants of Africans [ARMADA]), is another Antillean at the helm of an African diasporic organization. Like Lubin, Rovelas was critical of CM98, describing Romana as essentially anti-African:

C.F.: You were in the march?

J.R.: Yes. A lot of people helped. We even helped. We provided essential . . . coordination for sending materials, because there weren't any materials circulating. . . . We had to . . . distribute [the flyers]. Mr. Romana did not have a network [*réseau informatique*]. We had a network at [the French trade union] Sud PTT because all of this was happening around Sud PTT, you know? We provided the coordination, and Mr. Romana used everyone, manipulated everyone. There were actually 350 organizations. Mr. Romana didn't represent any organization. He didn't have [one]. The [1998] March Committee didn't exist. . . . He created his organization afterward . . . only in 1999, you see?

C.F.: Yeah.

J.R.: So . . . Mr. Romana's organization was driven—was managed, if you will—by Tobie Nathan, who is a member of CRIF [the Representative Council of Jewish Institutions in France].[17] [Dr.] Nathan, who is a psychiatrist, was the director over [Serge Romana's] wife, who was studying psychiatry. Thus, Nathan, who is part of the Jewish community, managed Mr. Romana and his wife [to gain] a hold on the black community. That's why Mr. Romana said, "No reparations." He was against reparations from the beginning, when he created his thing. He asked that we get ourselves crying; he said we were the victims, that we should ask for apologies, because that's what happened at the Chemin de Fer events he was doing every year, where they make people march on their knees, burn incense, and put candles in the street. People beat their chests. It's like the Catholic religion. I won't say more—you know what I mean. That always inclined us to accept the executioner's abuses and to think we'll be better in the great beyond, in the next life, and the whole nonsense of Catholic religion. . . . So Mr. Romana, [using] this Catholic religion, is doing a real takeover of the community so that it accepts its situation. So he says, "We don't have anything to do with Africa." [That is] the discourse of Mr. Romana and his association. "We were born in the holds of the ships . . . and in the sugarcane fields."

C.F.: They created that expression?

J.R.: That's what it is, you see? It means that we were born there. . . .
[W]e don't come from the same tree; we don't come from that
tree. There is a tree with two branches: one branch is for those
who are still there [in Africa], and one branch is for those who
were deported. So from there, that does not mean that we have
the same identity; it means that we are the children of the same
family. Some of us were dispersed, but we are still from the same
family, and we still have the same ancestors. We have cultural and
historical bases, spiritual bases, for liberating ourselves that are
the same. We cannot make an abstraction of our past under the
pretext that we were forcibly mixed.

Conclusion: Fractured Memories and Racial Politics

Both CM98 and COFFAD portray slavery as a morally reprehensible institution, but they differ sharply in their collective identities and politics. CM98
has largely avoided framing its commemorative work in terms of race, especially in public. As a result, the collective memories and temporalities they
construct revolve mainly around ethnic categories rather than racial identities. By contrast, COFFAD, along with a wide variety of other groups I
encountered, generally discusses slavery as a racial history with relevance to
a racialized present. This representation of slavery (and the racial temporality
it entails) is more transgressive and controversial in France, as it violates the
hegemonic norms of color-blind ideology and anti-racialism.

As organizations, COFFAD and CM98 use divergent strategies to trans-
form the representation of chattel slavery and construct present-day ethnic
and racial identities. Activists with COFFAD use commemorations to express a transnational black identity rooted in Africa and emphasize the cultural survivals binding people of African descent across time. By contrast,
CM98 draws on a catastrophic framing of slavery, rejects racial categories, and
emphasizes what Caribbeans lost through the historical process of displacement and oppression. Differences can also be seen in the temporal labor the
two groups employ. While CM98 typically underscores discontinuities between Africa and the formation of French Antillean identities, COFFAD
represents Afro-descended people as bound together through time.

French Afro-descendants' lack of consensus over how to frame their ethnoracial identity is sometimes obscured in the literature on recent black
movements in France. Jean-Yves Camus (2006) and Géraldine Faes and Stephen Smith (2006) have argued that slavery commemorations reflect the
emergence of a collective black identity in France. The data presented in this

chapter complicate this simplistic portrait by demonstrating that activists use historical narratives in ways that both assert black identification (e.g., COFFAD) and undermine it (e.g., CM98). As Pap Ndiaye (2008) and Audrey Célestine (2009b) suggest, individuals who are categorized as black in France make up *multiple* communities, with distinctions not only *among* people of African and Caribbean origin but also *within* these broader groups.[18] The next chapter takes a closer look at how racial and ethnic categories are mobilized in commemorative events and provides insight into the role of organizers and educators in helping ordinary people understand slavery and race as temporal phenomena.

4

Racial Temporality in Action

As dusk settled over the outdoor pavilion in Saint-Denis where the Comité Marche du 23 Mai 1998 (1998 March Committee [CM98]) held its annual commemoration on May 23, 2010, I stood with the crowd in front of a stage in the shadows of the famous cathedral. The technical sophistication of the mise-en-scène was impressive. The stage glowed with colorful lighting, and an elaborate sound system amplified the voices of the many singers and artists who had been invited to perform. As usual, I was far from the only person recording the event with a handheld video camera. I noticed many others in the crowd making their own digital mementos, along with CM98 staff members producing professional footage of the event. At this moment, a young rapper and reggae artist from Guadeloupe named Krys walked up to the microphone. Known for hits such as "Bootyshake," he also made music inflected with socially conscious lyrics and antiracism. As the rhythm of an infectious dancehall beat began to thump over the large speakers, he addressed the crowd:

> We've got to teach them to respect people in this country, right? [*with "right" said in English*]. Because there are the rich on one side and the poor on the other, and the rich don't respect the poor. Nobody, nobody is worth more than anyone else. We're all humans made of flesh and bone, right? [*with "right" again said in English*]. Scream "More fiyah!" [*Applause.*] . . . Put your hands in the air! . . . [This is for] all the French from the DOM-TOM who have had it up to here with discrimination!

After this energetic prelude, Krys launched into "Français des DOM-TOM" (French from the overseas departments and territories), a track from his 2010 album *Step Out*. In the song, he embraces a black identity, acknowledges racial discrimination, and describes the difficulties of feeling respected in France. Later, he rapped, "We're French but we're victims of racial discrimination," complaining about identity controls and harassment from police. The group identities he claimed—Antillean, black, and Overseas French— were multifaceted, not monolithic. Krys also invoked Frenchness as a justification for not expecting unequal treatment. That is, like many of the Antilleans I interviewed, he framed being Caribbean and French as an entitlement to equal treatment. Yet when Krys threw his fist in the air and spoke on behalf of black people (not just Antilleans), no one from the audience seemed to protest or show displeasure. Instead, they threw their fists in the air along with him. Members and leaders of CM98 did not intervene to stop Krys or to insist that "French descendants of slaves" was the more appropriate collective identity. Despite the rigid identity discourse of the group—and the political motivations that shape its narrow ethnic claims—CM98 was either uninterested in policing black identity in this setting or simply unable to fully control the boundary work of the many individuals (e.g., invited speakers, politicians, cultural performers) invited to participate in its events. In either case, the result was clear: even the Caribbean-centered May 23 commemoration, organized by a group with documented hostility to black French movements, gave space for the expression of collective black identity.

Thus far we have seen that commemorators, officials, and politicians attempt to produce various kinds of temporal representations and experiences, all with the intention of highlighting the relevance of slavery to the present moment. Yet as I have argued, resurrecting France's history of slavery does not always involve consistent constructions of race. French politicians manage to discuss slavery in ways that divorce the racial past from the present, often by avoiding any acknowledgment of whiteness. But race *is* being linked to slavery in other arenas in France, including commemorative events at which members of the public are invited, implicitly and explicitly, to understand slavery and colonialism as racial phenomena with relevance to the present.

This chapter explores the subtle and explicit ways in which constructions of race and racial temporality were signaled through symbolic gestures in ceremonies, speeches, cultural performances and in the display of cultural objects related to slavery. It also examines how discursive exchanges between commemorators (e.g., organization leaders, activists, historians, elected officials, journalists) and audience members in public debates produce opportunities for the French to racialize history and historicize race. Throughout, I aim to build on prior scholarship on the reemergence of black mobilizations in France by providing insight into the range of collective identities being constructed in contemporary mobilizations as well as the mechanisms that shape expressions of group belonging in commemorative practices (e.g., verbal and nonverbal cues in cultural production, consumption, and discursive exchange).

As I attended commemorative events, I witnessed racial temporality emerge through discursive practices involving ascriptive categorizations and pedagogical storytelling. By *ascriptive categorization*, I mean instances in which speakers attached ethnic and racial categories to groups, sometimes associating characteristics with these groups. On occasion, ascriptive categorization and claims making were met with "color-blind" moral policing on the part of other participants, who warned against reifying or creating divisions among racial groups. *Pedagogical storytelling* most often involved the recounting of stories based on current events related to group members (e.g., current racial controversies); accounts of the (recent) history of slavery commemorations in France; and historical narratives about slavery, colonization, abolition, and departmentalization. In practice, speakers almost always combined ascriptive categorization with pedagogical storytelling. Indeed, it was the mutual imbrication of narratives with ethnoracial categories that *facilitated* the construction of racial temporality in these settings.

The chapter proceeds as follows: First, I revisit prior research on constructions of blackness in France and specify my contributions. Second, I share ethnographic observations from a range of commemorative events to explore the role of visual representations and consumptive practices in signaling temporality and group belonging. Third, I focus on verbal cues of group categorization and belonging in formal and informal speech. Here, I pay particular attention to discursive practices in panel discussions and debates that were often incorporated into commemorative events. Fourth, I clarify how commemorative events contribute to the production of knowledge about race and slavery. The conclusion explores the relevance of these findings for our exploration of racial temporality in France.

Black Activism in France

Prior studies have pointed out that recent "black" mobilizations in France represent a variety of Antillean and African organizations that claim to speak for different conceptions of the black community (Célestine 2009b: 8; Wuhl-

Ebguy 2006: 513). Audrey Célestine (2009: 10) refers to the appellation "blacks" in France as "an entity of ambiguous contours" (*une entité aux contours flous*). The growing—yet still sparse—literature on French black activism is largely historical and qualitative due to significant constraints on the collection of ethnic and racial data in France and the absence of an equivalent to black studies (or even postcolonial studies) in France (Gueye 2010: 83). Abdoulaye Gueye's work (2001, 2006) has focused in particular on the activism of African intellectuals and community leaders in France. Postcolonial African protest movements in France include efforts to defend residents' rights in *foyers* in the 1970s, as well as more recent and publicized mobilizations on behalf of the *sans-papiers* (undocumented residents) in the 1990s (Gueye 2006). Gueye (2006: 228) characterizes black mobilizations of the 2000s as "the reemergence of a '*pan-nègre*' (black and African) dynamic in postcolonial France involving Afro-Caribbeans and Africans who stress a common Black destiny."

More recently, Gueye has argued that, in mainland France, transformations in French society that occurred from the 1960s to the 1990s have made a "black collective voice" possible. Using data from interviews with "mobilization entrepreneurs" (i.e., Afro-Caribbean activists and intellectuals) and media reports of their activities, he points to five factors that have played a role in equipping the French Afro-Caribbean population with cognitive, social and cultural tools necessary for mobilization: (1) increased postcolonial migration and immigration of Africans and Caribbeans to the metropole, (2) rising educational attainment on the part of African-descended populations, (3) the transition from a settler population to a population that includes many native-born French of African origin, (4) Afro-Caribbeans' increased familiarity with French society, and (5) the establishment of forums that contribute to "consciousness-raising." Of particular interest is Gueye's emphasis on "consciousness-raising" venues of dialogue and exchange. Moreover, unlike other scholars who have generally overlooked slavery commemorations as venues of ethnoracial identity construction, Gueye underscores the role of these events in building awareness and disseminating knowledge about the colonial past:

> The annual commemoration of the abolition of slavery begun in 2006 is also contributing to this dynamic of group consciousness-making, although the various organizations involved have yet to combine their efforts. Slogans such as "slaves yesterday, discriminated today because of skin color," invoke in the public mind a French historical continuity and confers [*sic*] common meaning on different historical experiences of Af-

rican-descended people within France, laying the foundations for an ideology of difference which . . . fuels and legitimizes the sense of group identity. (Gueye 2010: 88)

Building on Gueye's insights, I suggest that the efforts of commemorative activists to highlight continuities related to racism and slavery can be understood as time work that empowers racialized minorities to push back against the historical erasure of French color-blind ideology.

Audrey Célestine's comparative study of Caribbeans in France and Puerto Ricans in the United States documents the "strategies of differentiation" used by French Antillean activists to distinguish their collective identities from those of groups defined as black. In particular, she argues that Antilleans have been increasingly faced with "pressure" that stems from "the emergence of all-encompassing ethnic or racial labels [such as] 'Blacks' in a way similar to how Puerto Ricans have had to confront the prevalence of 'Hispanic/Latino' categories in the United States" (Célestine 2009b: 21).[1] The most recent and salient source of pressure in asserting black categorization in France has come from the Conseil Representatif des Associations Noires (Representative Council of Black Associations [CRAN]). Since its establishment in 2006, CRAN has sought to represent blacks as minorities defined not by a common culture but by group members' shared experience of being externally labeled as black and being vulnerable to anti-black racism and discrimination. This description of blackness was described as inclusive and compatible with Republicanism by the group's former president, Patrick Lozès; prominent members, including Pap Ndiaye, a historian and professor at the École des Hautes Études en Sciences Sociales; and its current president, the Martinican intellectual Louis-Georges Tin.[2] Trica Keaton (2010) also argues that CRAN appropriates black categorization while also rejecting the notion of race. In so doing, she argues that the group obscures France's historical and contemporary role in constructing racialized categories. Ironically, CRAN's restricted black activism nonetheless serves as a basis (and inspiration) for people who consider themselves black to produce racial identification and collective solidarity (Keaton 2010: 177).

As Célestine (2009) notes, several Antillean groups (including CM98 and Collectif-DOM) spoke out vehemently against CRAN's creation, portraying the group as racist and divisive (for making "racial" distinctions) and unrepresentative of the identities and concerns of the Antillean community. I also confirmed this finding in numerous interviews conducted with activists who claimed to represent French Caribbeans. These individuals mainly perceived CRAN as a threat to Antillean groups' access to political and material resources (Célestine 2009b; Wuhl-Ebguy 2006), and despite its public insistence on Republican values, integration, and inter-group solidarity, CRAN regularly has been demonized by some Antillean activists and put in the same category as the explicitly "anti-white" group Tribu Ka. In contrast with CRAN, some Antillean activists shift between representational strategies "emphasizing an ethnic or racial identity that renders the group specific" and reminders of the group's "French citizenship as [its] primary identity marker" (Célestine 2010: 152). Moreover, Célestine (2009: 152) argues that CM98's and Collectif-DOM's boundaries against black identity reflect their leaderships' resistance to being perceived as similar to Africans.

My work builds on these studies by clarifying the role of commemorative events in building awareness of race and racial oppression as temporal phenomena. As I illustrate here, commemorations of slavery contribute to the construction of racial temporality by inviting audience members to imaginatively identify with a racialized past, to draw connections to present-day society, and, at times, to discuss and debate how the racial future might yet take shape.

Nonverbal Signals of Group Belonging

During commemorative events such as the May 23 commemoration described earlier, I observed a range of nonverbal cues that were used to depict ethnic and racial belonging. Generally, they included visual representations in posters, artwork, and film, as well as objects of cultural consumption and entertainment. Materials related to commemorations often incorporated images of people who appeared to be of African or Caribbean origin on posters, in pamphlets, and in art displayed at events. This was the case for commemorative events produced by ethnic associations, as well as for those organized by media outlets, such as Tropiques FM and Radio France Internationale, and by public officials (e.g., the General Overseas Delegation for the City of Paris). For example, an invitation to *Africaphonie*, the name of the commemorative event and documentary film produced by the Orig'in Association, shows men and women of varying shades of brown surrounding a microphone at the center of the image. The idea of a transnational diaspora is conveyed by a map of the globe onto which images of people of color are superimposed. In my interview with Alain Bidjeck, then the president of Orig'in, he confirmed his group's desire to build a cosmopolitan, diasporic identity. As a first-generation migrant from Cameroon and a naturalized French citizen, Bidjeck had lived on two different continents and experienced his own identity as a mixture of cultural influences stemming from Europe, the United States, and Africa. He brought this cosmopolitan perspective to the conceptualization of *Africaphonie*:

> C.F.: What does "*Africaphonie*" mean?
> A.B.: "*Africaphonie*"? It could be exemplified by Africa speaking—the voice of Africa, or the polyphonies born in Africa. . . . [It's] simply a festival with the idea of reuniting the Caribbean, the Indian Ocean, the Americas, Africa, and France.

Orig'in's visual depictions of group belonging were unusual in their explicit display of Africa (as the center of the map shown in the invitation).

With few exceptions, representations of whites were rarely included in printed commemorative materials I collected at commemorative events. This pattern mirrors the asymmetric racialization and "blackwashing" of slavery mentioned earlier. On the few occasions when I saw whites visually represented, they were usually depicted as historical protagonists (rather than in photographs of contemporary white people). For example, the flyer for a film screening of *La marche des esclaves* (The Slaves' March) features a drawing of two men—one white, one black—staring each other down across a thick chain. In general, however, whites were visually absent from flyers and event documents.

Ethnoracial belonging (especially for minorities) was also signaled through the display and consumption of cultural objects. Markers of Antillean or "overseas" culture and identity were especially salient. Many of the events I attended followed a set format that included speeches, cultural performances, and entertainment, as well as a place to partake of (typically Antillean) food and drink. Indeed, eating admittedly delicious French Caribbean cuisine and having one or two small servings of traditional rum punch was part of the informal ritual that took place during or after many commemorations. Because these events often last for several hours (or an entire day), food and drink served the practical function of providing participants with much-needed refreshment. Yet they also served as cultural markers of leisure and belonging—markers that typically included French Caribbeans while excluding other Afro-descended groups.

During the three consecutive years I attended CM98's May 23 commemoration, opportunities to consume Antillean cultural products were interwoven throughout the day-long ceremony. Consider, for example, the commodification of Caribbean culture I observed and recorded over the course of nearly eight hours of fieldwork at the 2010 commemoration held in and around the Saint-Denis cathedral:

There were three sets of stands set up in the pavilion. The "village" was towards the back of the pavilion, across from the stage, in the shape of an "L." Here, there were tables lined with information (flyers and publications) done by CM98, including their new book, *Non à nou* (Creole for "Our Names"), which they were selling for 50 euros. There were also CDs on sale from some of the artists who performed, as well as tables set up for the genealogical service, with computers that attendees could use to look up family names that were not included in the exposition. . . . The second major group of stands was the *restauration* to the right of the stage. Here, people lined up to buy Caribbean food, including *bokits* (codfish and chicken sandwiches), *colombo*, [and] rice, as well as desserts (cakes), handmade coconut sorbet, and a very strong punch (made with rum, sugar, spice, and limes), which they served in tiny white plastic cups. (I had two.) The third set of stands was across from the *restauration* and had a few tables for Help Center for Single Parent and Matrifocal Families, a Haitian association, and a few other groups handing out flyers and information about their activities.

CM98's genealogical work, mentioned above, stands out as an extraordinary example of temporal labor framed in ethnic, rather than racial, terms. Through archival research, publications, workshops, expositions, and individual consultations, CM98 staff assist French Caribbeans in identifying the names given to their enslaved ancestors. As Eviatar Zerubavel (2003) explains, social practices and environments shape how individuals imaginatively connect to their ancestors. For CM98 activists, helping Antilleans construct mental links to the specific names of their enslaved ancestors was important for their identity and well-being. In the words of Emmanuel Gordien (2013), then vice-president of the group and director of its Workshop on Genealogy and French Caribbean Family Histories, the problem for CM98 was this: "Did we know our ancestors, who we claimed and who we said we were proud of during [the 1998] march?" Finding this knowledge lacking (a familiar problem for descendants of slaves), the group published two books featuring the names of nearly fifty thousand enslaved people in Martinique and Guadeloupe (Comité Marche du 23 Mai 1998 2011, 2012).

At one of the tables, I took note of the wide range of books and CDs that were for sale, including several titles related specifically to Guadeloupe (e.g., *Mai 1967, Pour savoir l'histoire de la memoire guadeloupeenne,* and *Gwo-ka modern*), one book about Martinique (Guillaume Durand's *Les noms de famille d'origine africaine de la population martiniquaise d'ascendance servile*), titles related to the history of French colonial slavery (e.g., *France et ses esclaves*

Figure 4.1. *Genealogical panels on display at a CM98 commemoration on May 23, 2015, in Place de la République.*

and *Esclavage, métissage, liberté*, both by the Guadeloupean historian Frédéric Régent), one book about Olaudah Equiano, several books related to Haiti (e.g., *Un siècle de relations financiers entre Haiti et la France*, by François Blancpain, and *La chute de la maison Duvallier*, by Martin-Luc Bonnardot and Giles Danroc), and one book on slavery in Africa (*Les traites négrières en Afrique*). I saw one title that explicitly mentioned the word "black": *Mémoire du monde noir*, by David Gakunzi.

I also noted the presence of Harmattan, a Parisian publishing house founded in 1975 that focuses on the African diaspora. The inclusion of Harmattan at a CM98 event illustrated one of the main findings that emerged during my fieldwork—namely, the inconsistency between activists' identity discourse and the forms of group belonging constructed through cultural production and consumption at the organization's events. Leaders of CM98 have long decried the use of "black" as a collective identity for French Caribbeans and frequently have drawn boundaries to distinguish Guadeloupeans and Martinicans from Africans in France. Yet despite these rigid and very specific identity claims regarding the particularity of Antilleanness, attendees at CM98's hallmark event, the May 23 ceremony, could obtain books and information pertaining to "blacks" and "Africans," even if these cultural objects were subsumed in a sea of materials marked "Antillean," "Martinican," or "Guadeloupean." In this way, Antillean and overseas identities had primacy

Figures 4.2 and 4.3.
A clothing booth in a tent at a CM98 commemoration on May 23, 2015. A "Black Wear" sign announces merchandise representing ethnic and racial discourse, including one shirt that reads, "Mixed and Proud of It."

Figures 4.4 and 4.5. *Intellectual exchange and distribution of historical and textual resources at a CW98 commemorative event on slavery in Paris on May 23, 2015. Many such events feature tables where publishers display books on topics such as history, race, ethnicity, colonialism, and slavery throughout the Afro-descended diaspora, including Malcom X's autobiography; works by the noted historian Cheikh Anta Diop; and recent books on white racism, including Rosa Amelia Plumelle-Uribe's* La ferocité blanche *(2001). Publications related to black identity and Afro-centricity contrast sharply with some of the CM98 discourse that distances French Caribbeans from black movements and people of sub-Saharan African descent in France.*

over other identity constructions (such as "Pan-African" or "black"), but these alternative conceptions of diaspora and group belonging were not entirely excluded. They were minimized.

This pattern was also evident at a commemoration I attended on May 9, 2010, at the headquarters of the Confédération Générale du Travail (General Confederation of Labor [CGT]) in Montreuil, a suburb just north of Paris. The annual event, established in 2006, is principally organized for the CGT by the Collectif Revendicatif Confédéral des Originaires de l'Outre-Mer (Confederal Protest Collective of People of Overseas Origin), a group of workers of "overseas" origin and allies who bear no ethnic ties to the DOM-TOM. The large-scale and professionally produced event ran from noon until 1:00 A.M. and included ample opportunities for attendees to partake of Antillean food and consume a range of other products, such as clothing, music, books, and other odds and ends. Participants could even pay for the services of a hair stylist, who was stationed in the middle of the massive indoor pavilion.

Near the entry, I perused several tables full of merchandise, including black thong underwear adorned with "971," the administrative department number for the island of Guadeloupe. I also came across a box of small cell phone holders that were distinctive mainly because they bore images representing the overseas departments (Guadeloupe and Réunion Island were especially prominent). In the lower right corner was a single product bearing the image of Africa. Once again, while images of "overseas" belonging dominated the frame, images of Africa were nonetheless available for cultural consumption. These kinds of clothing items, emblazoned with ethnic and racial identities, were common at commemorative events organized by people of African and Caribbean descent. When I returned to see CM98's May 23 commemoration in 2015, years after I completed my fieldwork, there was an entire section of clothing called "Black Wear" that featured, among other items, a shirt that read, "Métisse et Fier de l'Etre" (Mixed and Proud of It).

Racial Temporalities in Discursive Exchanges

Aside from visual representations of ethnoracial belonging, participants in commemorations regularly signaled ideas about group membership and temporal processes through verbal expression. Of the thirty-two commemorative events I observed, nearly all of them (thirty-one) incorporated speeches, panel discussions, or debates.[3] Public speeches are a standard feature in the French commemorative repertoire, providing commemorative entrepreneurs with an opportunity to describe their interpretation of the past. As seen in Chapter 2, political speeches about slavery contribute to the construction of group boundaries by attaching ethnoracial labels to collectivities. But focusing on speeches obscures the other kinds of "group talk" that go on in commemorative events, particularly interactive discourse between two or more speakers. Because commemorators generally see their role as both "breaking the silence" around slavery and promoting consciousness-raising about its present-day relevance, they often orchestrate occasions for dialogue and debate between panel speakers and audience members. This was especially the case for events I attended that included film screenings or cultural performances, where audience members were often seated for long periods of time. Within these spaces, I observed many discursive exchanges in which participants made temporal claims about the relationship between slavery and race relations in France.

Below I analyze how commemorators and audience members talked about slavery in public events I observed in the Paris region to unpack how racial belonging and temporality were constructed on the ground. I focus on speech utterances during six events that I attended and videotaped between 2008 and 2010. For each event (see Appendix C for full descriptions), I wrote an analytical summary and partial transcription that I translated directly into English. Below, I provide insight into temporality and racialization in France by examining moments in which commemorative discussions turned to issues of race and ethnicity.

Commemorative Events, Ethnoracial Talk, and Taboo

While public talk about race remains fraught, especially for minorities, my fieldwork shows that speakers in public forums routinely used ethnic and racial categories. This finding counters the widespread perception that France's official discourse of "color-blindness" actually reflects how people live and interact at the micro-level. On the few occasions that references to racial distinctions were criticized, these criticisms did not result in the suppression of racial categories and racial identities in public discussions. Overall, I found that context and timing both played a crucial role in transforming commemorations into forums where participants felt they could address ethnicity and race. Questions and comments from the audience were preceded, and partially determined, by the discourse and images to which the audience members had been exposed. Thus, film screenings functioned to provide audience members with explicit or implicit references to race and ethnicity through representations of transatlantic slavery, as well as discourse about contemporary racism and discrimination. In this way, they can be understood as contributing to time work and perceptions of temporality. Moreover, event organizers saw films as a particularly important mechanism for producing emotional reactions on the part of viewers and promoting identification with the plight of the enslaved and those who fought against slavery. The desire to provoke audience response, was, of course, deliberate on the part of organizers: that is why the question-and-answer periods typically followed film screenings.

Thus primed, audience members were able to legitimately talk about race and ethnicity because the film screenings and introductory comments made by the events' organizers and panelists had already implicitly or explicitly framed such questions and comments as "relevant." Color-blind taboos over public talk about race were also eroded by a process I call *ethnoracial cascading* during public debates and discussions. Ethnoracial cascading occurs when speakers' references to ethnoracial categories build on one another. As soon as one audience member invoked race or ethnicity, the legitimacy and relevancy of the topic was asserted. Subsequent claims (either of agreement or disagreement) in response to prior ethnoracial discourse further solidified the "appropriateness" of talking about ethnic and racial difference, despite the occasional concerns expressed by speakers who were wary of drawing distinctions among ethnoracial groups. In many cases, audience members were able to provide direct feedback to the cultural producers and commemorators themselves, not only contributing to the production of ideas about race and ethnicity in the immediate environs of the public debate but also potentially influencing the future cultural production of elites.

Ethnoracial claims about group categories and temporal processes served a variety of interrelated functions at the events I observed. First, they allowed speakers to redefine national identity by asserting that history of slavery and colonization should be included in French history. Second, these opportunities served to depict the victimization and agency of the enslaved by highlighting the historical mistreatment of the group, as well as resistance. Dramatic and heroic tales of resistance were often framed as sources of pride for descendants of slaves and other African-descended groups. Third, claims about race, ethnicity, and time were used to assert the de-stigmatization of present-day groups by promoting identification with (and de-stigmatization of) the enslaved and stigmatization of those implicated in slavery. Fourth, speakers mobilized ethnoracial narratives to historicize the symbolic construction of groups. In these cases, speakers sought to explain the construction of ethnoracial categories and transformations in their meaning over time. Fifth, commemorative participants used ethnoracial categories and claims to discuss present-day legacies. This temporal labor typically involved asserting the continuing significance of the slavery and colonial past, especially with regard to anti-black racism and discrimination, the white minority's economic domination in the Antilles, the impoverishment of African nations, and France's continued political and economic subjugation of Haiti.

In the examples that follow, I show how participants in commemorative events mobilized discursive practices to racialize history, historicize race, and engage in time work.

Constructions of Whiteness

While whites were often visually absent in representations of slavery, whiteness was verbally acknowledged in all six of the public debates analyzed here, although the same general asymmetry persisted (i.e., most racial discourse was about "blacks," "Negroes," "Africans," "Antilleans," and so on). Discourse about French whites fell into these categories: (1) descriptions of historical figures and groups, (2) statements regarding the historical construction of "whiteness" as a group category, and (3) claims about present-day whites' attitudes and perceptions of blacks. In general, historical references to whites were usually employed to describe colonists, and in a few cases, "white" was used to indicate specific historical figures (such as Napoleon or Victor Schoelcher). Notably, speakers almost never referred to whites as slave masters. When masters were described, they were not explicitly racialized.

Occasionally speakers told more complex stories about whites and their historical roles in slavery. For example, at an event organized by the CGT, Suzanne Dracius, a Martinican writer who self-identified as racially mixed, shared several historical narratives about whites who had supported the abolition of slavery, as well as those who had fought to maintain the slavery system. She began by explaining why the first abolition of slavery in 1794 was not applied in Martinique:

> The *békés*, the [*pause*] white French colonists, sold Martinique to the British so they would not have to apply the law abolishing slavery. The French colonists thus were royalists. That, by the way, is why in our history the . . . monarchy power, whether it was Napoleon or the king . . . , was always pro-slavery [*esclavagistes*].[4] The Black Code . . . written by [Jean-Baptiste] Colbert in 1685, which was intended to establish the rules and life conditions of the slaves throughout the Antilles, including in Saint-Domingue, was signed by King Louis XIV. Of course, King Louis XIV did not write [the Black Code], but he signed it, and [this] shows that slavery was a sacred desire, because this king of France, you will recall, was the king of divine law [*droit divin*]. . . . That's a very important notion. The French colonists made people believe that being a slave was divine law and it was something normal. The slave and everyone belonging to the black race was inferior. But now we have to be careful, because—and I'm making a big aside here—there were whites and mulattos who served the black cause and opposed slavery. That's why it

would be very sad today to continue to make racial distinctions. Why? Because Haiti was made to pay . . . the debt of independence, beginning in
1825. In 1848, the first consequence for us in Martinique and Guadeloupe
was . . . , the colonists were compensated [*indemnisé*]. . . . [T]he pretext for
the debt Haiti was made to pay from 1825 on was the compensation of
whites for having lost their slaves. . . . In 1849 and the years that followed,
France gave an enormous amount of money to white colonists; the proof is
the opening of the Crédit Martiniquais bank. The white colonists lent
money among themselves, over decades, on the heads of Negroes, on the
heads of slaves, and practically no one in Martinique knew it.

In this portrait, whites are described as "colonists" and *békés* who received
compensation for the losses *they* experienced after slavery was abolished and
who also colluded to use the Crédit Martiniquais bank to lend money to one
another, excluding "Negroes." But Dracius made sure to clarify that whites'
historical behavior was not entirely negative, by noting that "there were whites
and mulattos who served the black cause and opposed slavery." Yet despite her
effort to point out that some whites were in solidarity with blacks, she later
described some whites as enslavers and implied that their participation in the
slave trade was a source of dishonor for their group:

> In my parents' library, I saw Césaire, who had written, "Haiti is the coun-
> try where *négritude* stood up for the first time." For a little girl, an adoles-
> cent, that really brought up some questions and represented for me a kind
> of beacon, a kind of torchlight [for] my mixed blood [*sang mêlé*], mixed
> [*métisse*] side. [I am a] descendant of both Africans deported from Africa
> and white enslavers. [I do] not feel shame for the slave ancestry, but I feel
> shame for that of the others, the enslavers.

Like many French Caribbeans I interviewed, Dracius did not express pride
in her white European ancestry.

Moreover, in contrast to the political speeches (which appropriated racial
categories without problematizing them), the public debates I attended were
venues in which the social construction of racial categories was historicized
and explained. For example, during the debate that followed the screening of
The Slaves' March, Émile Batamack, of the organization Passerelle Noire,
emphasized that racial categories, including whiteness, are neither absolute
nor timeless:

> The categories that were created—black and white—the world [already]
> existed [and] preceded them [*le monde les a précède telle qu'il existait*].

When they say, "Africa" today . . . there was indeed a black world, [but] it wasn't called Africa [before]. There was a world that existed, that had its customs, its traditions.

Similarly, at the *Africaphonie* event, Christiane Taubira discussed the invention (and function) of racial categories such as "white" and "black" during the slavery period:

> For the system to last, it had to be justified. There is no ambiguity. There is the Black Code [Code Noir], the "black race." Even the abolitionary decree of 1794, it's the abolition of the slavery of Negroes and [it says] that, without distinction of color, all men are French citizens. Schoelcher's decree is the same, because during this period the world was projected in a binary manner—as black and white—[to enable] the exploitation of this slavery system. When Napoleon reestablished slavery . . . in the Civil Code [of] 1805, [he said] that the color distinctions still existed in the colonies and was necessary for the management of slaveholding countries.

Later during that same event, Françoise Vergès, then president of the Committee for the Memory and History of Slavery, also underlined the social construction of whiteness:

> This question of color: it's necessary to understand that it was entirely invented. And it's necessary to understand that white is a color [*le blanc est une couleur*]. [*She smiles broadly and pauses.*] White is a social and cultural color that claims to be universal and so has become invisible [*Le blanc est une couleur, le blanc est une couleur sociale et culturelle mais qui se veut universelle donc qui est devenue invisible*].

By unveiling whiteness as the product of social invention, Vergès engaged in subversive and antiracist time work.

Sometimes speakers discussed the historical basis of white privilege, as when a historian noted during the CGT debate that in 1789, France supported "the equality of men . . . except [for] slaves" and claimed that the revolutionaries distinguished between "two categories of men, which I would say were blacks—the slaves—and whites." In addition to rendering "whiteness" a visible category, this statement also contextualized its historical construction. This pedagogical work, in turn, depicted whiteness as a temporal phenomenon—a group category that was created in the past and has relevance to understanding France today.

On a few occasions, speakers shared anecdotes and observations from personal experience to discuss how they thought whites viewed blacks or felt about the history of slavery. For example, during *The Slaves' March* event, an audience member recounted his experience taking a tour of a fourteenth-century chateau near Nantes. He said that he had been pleasantly surprised to find that the château contained two rooms that displayed information about the slave trade. He noted that a white woman (*une blanche*) led the tour:

> I think that she explained things to us without any hang-ups [*sans complexe*]. I was expecting—there are people who are white-skinned [*de couleur blanche*] who, faced with slavery, are not well in their minds [*ils sont mals dans leurs têtes*] because they think, "Oh, my slave-trading ancestors did terrible things [*saloperies*] like this, and now [that] I'm seeing this . . . Black history, how do I feel about it?" But some have succeeded in getting over it and have come to terms with [*assumer*] this history. I think that's wonderful . . . because [when] we asked questions, I didn't feel [that there were] a lot of taboos . . . and I thought that, maybe twenty years ago, this kind of reaction wouldn't have been possible.

This exchange is important, as it involves a racial minority violating hegemonic norms of color-blinding by labeling whites a *present-day* racial group in France. Later, the same audience member described himself as a descendant of slaves and expressed support for Passerelle Noire's efforts as he felt that "blacks and whites" should "defend this history together." This comment drew an annoyed response from Guylène Brunet, the white director of *The Slaves' March*, who insisted that "the conclusion of [the] film is that . . . there weren't good blacks and bad whites or good whites and bad blacks."

During this debate, discourse about whites' racial attitudes emerged again when audience members began discussing how blacks should view themselves and define their identity. At one point, a black male audience member with a thick salt-and-pepper beard brought up a conversation he had had with a white friend:

> What I mean is . . . [we should develop] the maximum amount of competence and dignity in ourselves, not with regard to the other, [but] dignity in who we are. . . . I'll give you a simple example. . . . [T]here was a show . . . about Soweto, [Nelson] Mandela. . . . I went with a friend to see the show. When she went to the bathroom, there were two women of color . . . who were washing their hands at the sinks. Then they left [without] turning off the faucets. . . . My friend said, "I was shocked, so I turned off the faucets, and I didn't say anything because, since I'm white,

I didn't dare make a remark because they could say it was racism." There you go. It could seem like a small thing, but there is plenty of behavior that we don't appropriately own up to . . . because there are a lot of people who [say,] "I'm black, [so] I'm the victim." When I speak of dignity and competence, it's having the temper of the sword [*la trempe de l'épée*] that [Aimé] Césaire speaks of . . . because Césaire said things that are very profound, very important. It's this type of dignity, this kind of vigilance. . . . [I]t's facing yourself with as much dignity as possible, not with regard to others, but with regard to yourself.[5]

A female audience member wearing a colorful head wrap spoke next. She appeared to be white and in her thirties. "When your friend says that they would have called her racist, I find that absurd," she said. "We don't have to justify ourselves anyway." The woman's friend, another apparently white woman also wearing a head wrap, added:

> People who use racism like that to victimize themselves . . . [i]t's a pretext. . . . I think the [things] that will advance, in fact, [the efforts to] break these barriers are the things that will help make these prejudices disappear on both sides. Of course, there are people who will accuse others of racism . . . [but] everything that can allow for an understanding of the other . . . will help.

The original anecdote about the black audience member's white friend served as a springboard for a broader discussion of race—in this case, accusations of racism directed toward whites. These comments also illustrate another general pattern regarding references to whites: in most cases, speakers made an effort to emphasize solidarity with whites rather than boundaries against them. Indeed, comments that were perceived as anti-white were generally treated as taboo during commemorative events I attended. Consider this revealing exchange that took place at the beginning of *The Slaves' March* debate when a male audience member asked Batamack whether Passerelle Noire's commemorative events were being well publicized:

> *Batamack:* The other day, I told the General Overseas Delegation that when Carnival takes place in Paris, it's the only time—I live two seconds from Place de la Nation. I've never seen as many Negroes in France, in my entire life, as during Carnival.
> *Male Audience Member:* But on May 10, Place de la Nation is a desert.
> *Batamack:* There you go.
> *Male Audience Member:* It's terrible.

Batamack: It's also a way for us to understand that things . . . I think that things are getting better [*ça avance*], because you're here [*pointing to the audience*]. And there aren't just a few of you. You are, in fact, here—before, if we did something like this, there might not have been anybody. Today there are—you are here, like messengers. . . . [T]hose who want to come to Nantes can come to Nantes to see the play in person. . . . [O]ur goal, and I think it's an objective that we should always be aware of, is that we cannot stop taking action [*poser des actes*]. Let's make the most of what we have [*Soyons dans l'économie de moyen*]. If someone is Negro and an actor, let him say that his contribution is to go and be an actor, without being paid. If someone is a Negro and a producer, let him say that he will go and produce [a film] without being paid.

Male Audience Member: And if someone is white?

[*Guylène Brunet, the film's white director, smiles and leans back. Laughter from the audience.*]

Batamack: I'm not excluding whites—

Brunet: Hmmm! That's a bit worrisome! [*Ça craint!*]

[*Several people speak at once.*]

Batamack: I mean, I mean, we have to—we have to. . . . [Guylène] knows quite well [what I mean] because she talks to me about it a lot. . . . The real problem we have, and I'm not the first person to say it, is first a Negro problem [*un problème des nègres*] . . . and when I see Negro, it's not a color; it's a *consciousness* of a reality, and this reality concerns, increasingly, those who have dark color [*la couleur foncée*] like mine [*pointing to his hand*].

Male Audience Member: I don't agree. I *don't* agree!

[*Several people speak at once.*]

Batamack: But I'm not making a separation. I'm saying that—

Male Audience Member: Wait, wait, wait [*putting up his hand*].

Batamack: I'm saying that it's blacks and whites, and, and, let me finish. . . . [I]t's not a problem. One more time I'm going to say, you do not know me personally, and I don't want to talk about my personal life, but I would be the last person to imagine that for a debate like this one here, [there would be only] blacks and no one but blacks, for blacks. That would seem absurd to me, because all of the realities that blacks have had . . . were always struggles shared by blacks and whites. I'll give you an example: . . . the creation and invention of [the publishing house] Présence Africaine, which was first a coming together . . . of blacks.[6] [*Pause.*] . . . [But if] you ask, "Who was the white man who was always in the background at Présence Africaine so that works like Césaire's could exist?" no one can give you his name. . . . [H]e was an anthropologist . . . and an ethnologue, [but no one] knows about this man. [*Several audience members object.*] . . . We've often seen that Negro artists have had a lot of white collaborators [who] were in a position to help them to get their message across [*tapping his fist on the table*] to the white majority. . . . [S]o that's why . . . I think that it's not about blacks being on one side and whites on the other. But we've got to see at least the desire on the part of blacks to [do] *something.*

The tension in the room was palpable as Batamack fought off the perception that his comments were anti-white or divisive. Brunet's response ("Hmmm! That's a bit worrisome!") was as an effort to sanction discourse that she perceived as exclusionary toward white people. Batamack took this charge seriously and spoke forcefully when he insisted, "I'm not making a separation." As the audience member interjected his disagreement, Batamack launched into a defense of his call for blacks to take the initiative in spearheading their own concerns (e.g., anti-blackness) while working in partnership with whites. In his view, black mobilization is the necessary condition for achieving the group's goal, while collaboration with white allies is an additional (and complementary) factor. Drawing distinctions between whites and blacks in this way allowed Batamack to make a case for black collective action. Yet in so doing, he violated French norms of anticommunitarianism and was forced to perform interracial politeness by taking great pains to show that his views were not hostile toward whites.

Critical discourse about the ideology of white superiority regularly emerged in these settings. Speakers pointed to both historical and contemporary examples of whites being viewed as (or viewing themselves as) superior to non-whites. During the CGT debate, Monique Vatonne, a white woman, explained why it was important to fight for symbolic reparations for slavery, including a paid holiday for all French citizens to reflect on the continuing legacies of racism:

What we demand in the CGT . . . is, in fact, that recognition. The memory work continues in schools, but [it is] also [needed for] adults, because . . . it's complicated to learn this history. . . . When we demand a paid holiday [*chomé, payé*], we demand it for the entire French population so they can ask themselves questions. . . . [T]hat would perhaps allow a lot of mainland French to pose questions to themselves, to reflect. The second thing that is also important is that we obtain official and public apologies from the president of the Republic, because without that we'll never be able to get rid of racism and discrimination. For a lot of people, there is still a conception in the collective unconscious [*l'inconscient collectif*] of white superiority with regard to blacks [*un conception de superiorité du blanc par rapport au noir*]. . . . Of course, there is the "crime against humanity" law, but it is incomplete because it doesn't target the criminals. There can be no crime without a criminal . . . and without punishment. The punishment is reparations. France should face it. The government should open discussions, and we should be able to debate together over reparations so that, finally, everyone can be well in the French society [and] so that we can get along well with one another.

Vatonne's intervention here discussed whiteness as an actually existing social category and explicitly acknowledged the lingering imprint of white supremacy and anti-blackness in France. Significantly, she paired this discourse with strong advocacy for reparations. This explicit temporal link—between slavery and white dominance today—is quite different from the commemorative discourse expressed by French politicians.

Constructions of Blackness

What do participants mean when they talk about blackness in commemorative forums? One might think that the obvious answer is "slaves," but, in fact, most references to blacks in the public debates I observed were descriptions of contemporary populations rather than historical references to the enslaved. This is important, as it suggests that certain kinds of commemorative events (particularly those that involve interactive speech rather than purely ceremonial or symbolic gestures) are venues in which temporal connections between the history of slavery and present-day black populations are negotiated and debated. Below, I present examples of the black representations I observed in commemorative events.

The Boundaries of Black Identity

In *We Who Are Dark*, Tommie Shelby (2005) distinguishes between *thin* and *thick* forms of black solidarity. Thin blackness connotes a "vague and socially imposed category of 'racial' difference that serves to distinguish groups on the basis of their members having certain visible, inherited physical characteristics and a particular biological ancestry" (Shelby 2005: 207). Thick blackness, by contrast, "requires something more, or something other, than a common physical appearance and African ancestry. Here the social category 'Black' has a narrower social meaning, with specific and sometimes quite austere criteria for who qualifies as black" (Shelby 2005: 209). From this perspective, thin blackness derives from recognizing a social condition: being externally categorized as black. Thick blackness, by contrast, is an acquisition, a set of ideas, beliefs, or behavior that can establish whether an individual is "authentically" black.[7] Shelby (2005: 212–213) further notes:

> A person who satisfies the thin social criteria for being classified as black may nevertheless choose, with varying degrees of social pressure, not to define his or her self-conception in terms of "blackness" at all. That is, such a person may choose not to subjectively identify with the label "black" or to conform to its associated behavioral norms. . . . It should be clear, however, that the choice not to self-identify as black, whatever its rationale, does *not* dissolve the often constraining social realities that are created by the fact that *others* may insist on ascribing such an identity to one and consequently may treat one accordingly, whether for good or ill.

In my fieldwork, I found that at different junctures within the same debates, the black category was imagined broadly (e.g., as skin tone or as an inclusive category for all African-descended people) and narrowly (e.g., as pertaining specifically to African immigrants or Antillean migrants). Discourses about black groups generally fell into two categories: (1) African-centered blackness and (2) Caribbean-centered blackness. Both African-centered and Caribbean-centered notions of blackness can be understood as transnational. For many speakers, the concept of an "African diaspora" referred to blacks throughout the world (especially in Africa, Europe, and the Americas). Less often, speakers talked about blackness as pertaining primarily to descendants of slaves or as a part of being Antillean. Some of the events occurred in contexts that implicitly or explicitly linked the concept of blackness with the idea of an African diaspora. Issues of the magazine called *Diaspora Africaine* (African Diaspora) were for sale at the entrance of the Cinéma Images d'Ailleurs during the screening of *The Slaves' March* and follow-up debate. Curators and staff of the Musée Dapper, the venue for Radio France Internationale's presentation of *Retour à Gorée* (Return to Gorée), wove references to Africa throughout the museum's exhibits and screened a film that specifically focused on the concept of an African cultural diaspora.

Finally, Africa was explicitly represented as a cultural homeland in the screening of *Africaphonie* at Paris City Hall. In these four cases, associations among blackness, Africa, and Africans were signaled prior to the follow-up debates, creating a context for the notion of an African diaspora to be understood as plausible and relevant. Such associations were also driven home by the presence of speakers who themselves were immigrants from Africa, including Alain Bidjeck for *Africaphonie* and Émile Batamack for *The Slaves' March*. The debates during CM98's event titled "French Descendants of Slaves" and during the CGT's annual commemoration were both primarily contextualized with representations of Antillean identity. Context, however, was not destiny: discourse during debates was not limited by the ethnoracial representations that preceded them. However, the ethnoracial framing of the events certainly served as an indicator of the kinds of group categories and ethnoracial themes that were understood as legitimate topics of discussion.

Overall, I found that discourses about black identity expressed in commemorative settings exceeded thin definitions (i.e., imposed black categorization or threat of anti-black racism) and drew heavily on thick cultural and historical elements. In part, this is to be expected, given that organizers of commemorations explicitly structure events to produce thick definitions of group membership (as Antilleans, descendants of slaves, blacks, or African-descended people). Yet attention to these historically and culturally grounded depictions of blackness suggests that, at least in the context of slavery commemorations, black identity was pervasively and persistently portrayed as meaning more than simply skin color. Blacks and whites expressed such thick descriptions of blackness. For example, during the *Return to Gorée* event, Catherine Ruelle defined blackness in terms of an African-centered cultural heritage:

> I think that here, with this film . . . , we're really touching the roots of all of these [forms of] black music, whose source is, in fact, Africa [*On touche vraiment les racines de toutes ces musiques noires, dont la source est, quand même, l'Afrique, quoi*].

She went on to argue that another film was about "leaving to find one's ancestors, those who went far away, those who are in fact . . . in new territories— that is, the Antilles, Africa, the Americas."

During *The Slaves' March* event, the relationship between Africa and members of the diaspora was a subject that highlighted differences in how participants of African and Antillean origin defined their identity and their understanding of blackness. The topic was prompted by an audience member from Martinique who wanted to know why Passerelle Noire, the association that produced the film, had chosen its name. In French, *passerelle* has multiple meanings. It can refer to a "footbridge" or "link" or to the gangway leading to a ship. Passerelle Noire, then, carries a general connotation of "Black Connection" or "Black Passage" between point A and point B. The audience member wanted to know precisely what that connection was. Brunet, the film's white director, and Batamack, a black representative of Passerelle Noire, tack-led the question:

> *Brunet: Passerelle*; it's a passage—
> *Batamack: Passerelle*, because—
> *Brunet:* It connects Africans with—
> *Batamack:* It's simply a link—
> [*Audience members begin speaking over the panelists.*]
> *Male Audience Member 1:* Let them respond, please, because if they chose a name, that's [important].
> *Batamack:* Yes . . . Passerelle Noire. If this name was chosen, I think I can speak about it—
> *Brunet:* Of course, of course.
> *Batamack:* I wanted to simply say that the idea of Passerelle Noire was—it's the only way that we could find [to convey] that there is a passage on both sides [*de part et d'autres*]. . . . [T]he idea was to exchange on both sides, because with a *passerelle*, you don't have a one-way street. You have a two-way street. A *passerelle*, in general, passes over. . . . [There's] something beneath it [*making a sweeping gesture with his hands*] . . . to make the link—
> *Male Audience Member 1:* Between what and what?
> *Batamack:* Between our two worlds.
> *Male Audience Member 1:* Which two worlds?
> *Batamack:* The worlds that confronted each other and that we know well and that [are learning to] live together. [*Silence in the room.*]
> *Male Audience Member 1:* Yes, but you spoke very explicitly about the black world. What worlds? Because I have a *passerelle* with three worlds: I'm Martinican, so I have a *passerelle* with Europe through France, and I have a *passerelle* with Africa. So what is the *passerelle* for you?
> *Batamack:* If you look closely at your *passerelle* between Africa and Martinique, . . . you could divide it, but it should really be one [*il faudrait bien qu'elle soit une*]. [*Pause.*] . . . When you say you have a *passerelle* with Africa . . . a *passerelle* with Martinique, me, in my mind—
> *Male Audience Member 1:* No, I *am* Martinican.
> *Batamack:* Yes, but Europe is the West [*c'est l'occident*]. [*Silence in the room.*] Europe is the West. . . . Earlier we spoke about black Americans and all the others—that's the West. That is to say that they called themselves in the simplest manner: the concept of the West, it's that everyone is European, including those who came

to share their world with them—they call that the West. Even in Japan, you have the West. . . . [Y]ou [could] have the West in China. That's why I say, the black world—I didn't invent it; it's Césaire [who] defined it. Césaire said the "*black world*," and he said "*the black man.*" I'm not the one who invented this expression. . . .

Male Audience Member 1: So it's the West and—

Female Audience Member 1: It's the *passerelle*, the point of departure . . . where the black world and the white world would meet each other. That's the idea.

[*Several people speak at once.*]

Male Audience Member 1: Yes, yes, I know. It's these two worlds—

Female Audience Member 1: That's the—

Male Audience Member 1: It's the West, and then it's—? [*Pauses and gestures with his hands.*]

Male Audience Member 2: In fact, I think that—the *passerelle*, as I conceive it, in its broadest sense . . . is to connect all of the values of this black culture that was scorned [*bafoué*], that they tried to completely annihilate, to permit the emergence of these values of this black culture, of all of the values. When I say "all," I mean *all* of the values of this black culture, [in] a type of Western society that first developed . . . from Europe, and then . . . in the United States and the Americas, and now in the extreme East . . . the states that have chosen this type of Western society. And now it's about figuring out how to reconcile the specificities of what we really are, to keep our cultural authenticity. . . . I believe that the goal of the *passerelle* is to reconcile the two values, not to place them in opposition. . . . What I would say is that the first preoccupation of all the people, of all the citizens [*resortissants*] of the Negro people [*peuple négroïde*], . . . is to develop competence in the *present*. In this regard, whatever the domain in which we're operating, [we need] to have a kind of dignity and pride. . . . [W]e are already victims of prejudice, so let's show that we're the best—that is, that we are as competent as we can be in all . . . domains. . . .

Batamack belongs to an organization that is intentionally invested in creating a *passerelle*, a cultural connection across racial lines between audience members and the history of transatlantic slavery. He understood the first audience member as having expressed a link with Africa and Martinique. In his view, the audience member should not see a division between Africa and Martinique ("If you look closely at your *passerelle* between Africa and Martinique, . . . you could divide it, but it should really be one"). This charge prompted the audience member to interject and affirm his ethnic identity ("I *am* Martinican"), thereby emphasizing Martinican identification as the *basis* of his group definition. This claim, in turn, prompted Batamack to try to clarify *his* ethnic stance, framing Europe (and France) as representative of "the West." At this point, he asserted a distinction between the "black world" and the "West." In so doing, Batamack pointed out that Césaire had already written about "black men" and "black worlds," thereby constructing a conceptual genealogy and using this genealogy to legitimate his understanding of blackness. Having introduced the concept of the West, Batamack rendered the idea of Western culture relevant. In this context, male audience member 1, female audience member 1, and male audience member 2 all contributed their own theorizing about the relationship between blackness and the West implied by the name Passerelle Noire and the history of transatlantic slavery at the heart of the debate. Male audience member 1 comes to agree with female audience member 1's suggestion that the "link" in question was in fact "the point of departure . . . where the black world and the white world would meet each other." Male audience member 2 further developed this conceptualization by calling for the de-stigmatization and diffusion of black culture in the West ("The *passerelle*, as I conceive it, in its broadest sense . . . is to connect all of the values of this black culture that . . . they tried to completely annihilate, to permit the emergence of these values of this black culture . . . [in] . . . Western society"). His defense of "cultural authenticity" underscores the *thickness* of his definition of blackness, which he portrays as grounded in certain unnamed values. Finally, the speaker goes on to suggest that affirming black cultural authenticity and black pride can be done without *opposing* "blackness" to "the West" and instead reconciling the two.

Valorizing Blackness

As seen in the Introduction to this book, when a young black Frenchman critiqued Larousse's definition of "Negro," perceptions of black inferiority were sometimes directly addressed at commemorative events. The notion that slavery resulted in the stigmatization of people racialized as black (and not only descendants of slaves) was the implicit assumption behind speakers' allusions to anti-black racism and internalized oppression (i.e., blacks' own feelings of shame and inferiority). One discursive strategy for valorizing blackness involved denaturalizing the present-day association between blackness and slave status. For example, Naissant Bernier, one of the Haitian historians featured at the CGT commemoration, told audience members that slavery, in historical terms, was not originally associated with black people:

> No little French kid in the metropole has studied the history of the Antilles in an academic curriculum. And if we're able to get this message through, it's already a [form of] reparation because reparation can be *mental*: someone may see you thinking that slavery was the [idea that] "Negro" goes along with . . . "slave," and this is *untrue*. The word "slave" comes from the word "Slav," so the Slav was a slave before the Negro.

Similarly, this contentious exchange between an audience member and the historian Myriam Cottias during an event organized for the film *1802: L'Épopée guadeloupéenne* (1802: The Guadeloupean Epic) centered on the historical encoding of "blackness" with "enslavement":

> *Female Audience Member:* It seems to me that this commemoration and this film especially are only a way of [*pause*] making a way for finding an identity [*se frayer un chemin pour trouver une identité*]. They refuse us an identity [*une identité, on nous la refuse*] because they only want to see us as black . . . and black is the color of the *slave*. There is a word in Arabic that means "black," and this "black" also means "slave." . . . What I would like to add is that freedom should work . . . in our minds and in our mentalities, not only in these events. *No one* can take away my liberty! No one can change my way of seeing other people [*personne ne peut enlever mon regard sur les autres*]. I'm here; I'm as proud of being black as I am of my slave past [*mon passé esclave*] because the resistance of my ancestors allowed me to be here. . . . [T]his is what we should hang on to the most. I prefer to say that freedom is *in our minds*. A commemoration? I don't know if it will change anything. I think involvement [*l'implication*] will change something. . . .
>
> *Cottias:* The equivalence between the terms "slave" and "Negro" constructed itself historically. . . . [I]t's a representation constructed in transatlantic slavery, really. That is to say . . . this equivalence of terms is centered in the eighteenth century. The representation travelers [*voyageurs*] say "slave" when they say "Negro," and they say "Negro" when they say "slave." So this equivalence existed from this moment here. It endured . . . with the experience of the second colonization, for inverse reasons, because Africa would

be colonized in the nineteenth century . . . to combat the slavery that persisted in African lands. So what was attached to the equivalence between slavery and "Negro" was all of the negative representations that were attached to all dominated populations. What is interesting to see is that when we speak of . . . delinquents, and all populations that are a bit marginal, we speak of them in the same terms: they're thieves; they're liars; they generally have unbridled sexuality—in fact, they have everything that afterward got attached to "Negro." These negative representations have endured, as I was saying to you, via the experience of the second colonization and with a return to the European metropole via immigration since the beginning of the twentieth century, immigration from the sub-Saharan region, with populations that come to work in under-the-table jobs [*emplois subalternes*]. . . . But, again, history isn't written for all eternity—that is, history is also made, and it's not because these equivalences have existed for centuries that we're going to be stuck like this. The combat and the rest of the history that should be written is precisely to break these equivalences and break down what Césaire said: turning the term "Negro" around to make it into a term of combat and triumph and opening to the world, participating in the world with . . . dignity. So, certainly, the history of slavery should be known, but in my view . . . , slavery should become an object that can be seen from a distance, because it seems to me that the young generation that's coming up should not remain bogged down in this history [*demeurer engluée dans cette histoire*].

The audience member was not convinced by Cottias's assertion that blacks were not always conceptualized as slaves. Indeed, she challenged Cottias's authority as an expert by interjecting, "I'm not a historian, but I know that . . . the first slaves that were taken were black—*because* they were black." At this point, the actor Jean-Michel Martial reasserted Cottias's historical authority and portrayed the association between blacks and slavery as a form of "propaganda." His claim was supported by Ruelle:

> *Martial:* It's possible that what you're saying is true. Me, I pose the question to a historian: "When we speak of the Egyptians, for example, . . . [were they] white? [Were they] black? [*Light laughter from the audience and Cottias. An audience member interjects, but Martial continues.*] I just want to talk about the relationship between the dominated and the dominant. From, generally, the

eighteenth century, or from a certain period, the dominated—we took it for granted that it was a black individual. . . . It's nothing but belief in a dominated-dominant relationship. If we take history before, we could be in another relationship, in another epoch in the history of humanity. . . . The dominated [person] was not necessarily the black. When we speak of Egyptians, when we speak of this period, the dominated was not only the black.

Female Audience Member: Yes, because there were several slaveries—

Martial: I would simply like to say that if—I understand the question that you asked earlier—if, today, the dominated person has this notion of the dominated, we encode the words "black," "Negro" and "slave." It's a manipulation of history, because if we had wanted to tell the story of humanity from a long time ago, we wouldn't arrive at this aberration. It's only a belief. It can be right, just as it can be false.

Ruelle: And it dates to the eighteenth century. Watch out [*pointing her finger to emphasize her words*]!

Martial: It can be false. But the fact that it's false is intentional. It's false so people will not question certain authority. It's only manipulation. It's propaganda.

Ruelle: By the—it was European, of course.

Female Audience Member: Not really.

Martial: Who wrote history, madam?

Ruelle: But of course, madam. Look at the great ancient texts, the Greeks, etc. They knew black populations [*on connaissaient les peuples noirs*]. I'm sorry, but if you look at the court of King Louis XIV, there were ambassadors from Africa and princes from Africa, black princes, and it posed no problem at all. There were also some in England. It was in the eighteenth century, really, . . . that the relationship between the European world and the black [world] began to change. It absolutely was not like this before. History was rewritten. When was Egyptian history written? The eighteenth and nineteenth [centuries]. What did Europeans go searching for in Egyptian history in the eighteenth century? . . . It's necessary now to see how the evolution of European societies created a situation in which [white Europeans] needed to deny blackness strength and power [*de nier le noir en tant que force et puissance*].

Martial: It's very perverse, and—I'll try to be brief for once—it goes very far. . . . [T]he West . . . proposed a model to the world that continues today. In another era, I was a dental surgeon. I learned about the implantation of teeth; I was taught . . . the reference points between bones [in the face], and we had to position the teeth . . . in a manner that would reproduce the average European model [*le modèle Européen moyen*]. [*Soft laughter from the audience.*] Do you see the perversity? This wasn't wrong; it was simply acceptance of the idea that the model should be the Western model. . . . Today, we say, "That's how it was," . . . but it shouldn't be like that anymore. It's our responsibility, equally, through the distribution of knowledge, to make it so that this stops and we move on to other things. We need to recognize everyone's beauty rather than saying that there is a model of beauty that we must impose.

A few dynamics of the interaction in this exchange are striking. First, the joint effort of Cottias, Martial, and Ruelle effectively shut down the controversy that the audience member had stimulated with her insistence that blacks were always viewed as slaves. Although she attempted to impose her view, the panelists talked over her, and, in her role as moderator, Ruelle closed the topic by calling on another audience member. Second, although Cottias, who is now the president of the Committee for the Memory and History of Slavery, did speak as an expert, the audience member who twice expressed disagreement nonetheless treated her claims with suspicion. While Cottias's authority was ultimately affirmed by the other panelists (e.g., Martial's comment that he would "pose the question to a historian"), other participants did not perceive her narratives as absolutely true. Finally, Ruelle's references to "African princes" in the court of King Louis XIV was an attempt to show that ideas about black inferiority were not timeless and immutable. The irony of her historical example, however, is that Louis XIV was also responsible for signing the "Black Code" that did, in fact, assert black inferiority—a point that was not made by any participant in the debate.

Anti-blackness in Commemorative Events

While the vast majority of speakers valorized some form of black identity, I observed a few instances in which participants in public debate either rejected or policed black identification. One of the starkest examples of boundaries *against* black identity occurred during the French Descendants of Slaves event organized by CM98. Dressed casually in a black fleece jacket, Serge Romana, the group's president, prepared to address a crowd that had gathered in the lower-level auditorium of Paris City Hall. There was no film screening or cultural performance to contextualize the event—only a carefully crafted and spirited lecture by Romana, who has undeniable charisma. His facility with language and his academic training allow him to speak extemporaneously for long periods of time, shifting at will between standard French and Guadeloupean Creole. He smiled and laughed often, cracking jokes—usually in Creole—to create a feeling of intimacy among the mostly Antillean audiences that came to see him. On this occasion, a debate on the "future of Antilleans in metropolitan France," he engaged in a kind of ethnic proselytization, spreading the gospel of CM98 and its normative views on how Antillean migrants should define their identity. The event occurred in the wake of the 2009 uprisings in the overseas departments, which had thrust the question of Antillean identity and citizenship—in overseas and mainland France—into the public sphere. He began by evaluating Antilleans' ethnic options and urging them to make a choice *against* black identity:

> A choice, is—my definition—the action of an adult. Not making a choice is the action of a child. . . . There is . . . an identity choice [*le choix identitaire*]. We've heard several identities expressed: the point of view that, for example, Guadeloupean men and women are the descendants . . . of Africans and Indians. . . . The question is "Are we capable of making choices?" And it's not easy making choices because, by definition, "choosing" is "renouncing." [*Pause.*] . . . [S]o that's the first thing. . . . [W]hat is our choice? What do we want to do? Where do we want to go? Tonight, I simply want to bring up points of view; I certainly don't see these as certainties—not at all. To begin with . . . , one of the things that the movements in Guadeloupe and Martinique brought to Antilleans who live in Hexagonal France is, indirectly, visibility. Before, well, we were among "blacks" [*on était dans des noirs*], and there were people who spoke for us [*il y avaient des gens qui parlaient à notre place*]. Often, it was CRAN that spoke for us. It was CRAN that was put on-stage. It was [Professor] Pap Ndiaye who explained BUMIDOM.[8] It was [Patrick] Lozès who explained slavery in our homelands. Frankly, it's rather annoying. [*He smiles and laughs softly.*] . . . [I]f I had to summarize the objective for the conference today, it's to say that . . . Antillean people are not visible and don't function as a human group. They don't function as a human group because there is no visibility . . . because, in the first place, [the Antillean] hasn't chosen what he is [*il n'a pas choisi ce qu'il est*].
>
> [*Pause.*]
>
> He could define himself as *ultramarin*, as *domien*,[9] as Guadeloupean, as Creole, as black, as anything you want. When you have a multifaceted identity, no one sees you [*on ne vous voit pas*]. You see people, fractured . . . so the Antillean world has a certain number of difficulties with defining

itself, with existing. I believe that it should choose. It should make an identity choice and a political choice, because today he lives in a world that, in fact, functions through networks. It's necessary to understand how French society functions. It functions through networks. There are several types of networks, of course: political parties are one; masonic lodges are another. We could say that religions could be another. But there is another that exists, even if we don't want to say it. It's the communitarian network. Whether we like it or not, this network exists. So there are communities for which you can talk about "community," and there are others that, when you speak of "community," you are charged with communitarianism [*communitarisme*].

[*He smiles. Some laughter from the audience.*]

Clearly, you understand, there is immense intellectual dishonesty in all of this. So, CM98, we propose a choice: we say that we clearly should come to a decision about certain things. First it is necessary for us to say that we are Antilleans. We should not define ourselves as *domien*—as "overseas people" [*ultramarins*], as "blacks of France," and so on. We are Antilleans, [and] an Antillean, according to the *great* majority in France, is a descendant of slaves. . . . [W]e can be descendants of slaves and French citizens. This is an identity choice [and] a political choice. It permits us to set into place a certain number of tools [*outils*] so that this identity can be affirmed [*s'affirmer*]; this political choice can prosper and we find that Antilleans [are] capable of carrying out a group project, in positions of responsibility, whether at the municipal, general council, regional, or national level.

In Romana's intervention, we are once again confronted with the problem of group mobilization in the context of French white supremacy's anticommunitarian values. He argues that some groups are able to defend their groups without being accused of being divisive, while Antilleans face the heightened risk of being labeled *communitauriste*. His central thesis is that Antilleans' numerous ethnoracial identity options pose a *problem of visibility* ("He could define himself as *ultramarin*, as *domien*, as Guadeloupean, as Creole, as Black. . . . When you have a multifaceted identity, no one sees you"). Antilleans' complicated and inconsistent identity discourse, in Romana's view, undermines their ability to act cohesively as a group. His justification for arguing that Antilleans need to "make a choice" about their collective identity is the observation that social networks are highly important for the distribution of resources and opportunities in French society. The idea, then, is that if Antilleans are unable to agree on how to define their identity (and distinguish themselves from black movements, led by French people from sub-Saharan

Africa), they will be unable to construct cooperative networks and act on behalf of their group's interests in the future. Moreover, Romana felt that leaders of CRAN at the time, such as Patrick Lozès and Pap Ndiaye (of Beninese and Senegalese origin, respectively) were speaking out of turn by discussing Antilleans' historical experience of slavery and migration.[10]

It should be noted that Romana is fully aware that black identity can be (and is) affirmed by many Antilleans. Yet this is an identity choice he believed should be rejected. From this perspective, black (racial) identity and a regional overseas identity (*ultramarins*) are both framed as insufficiently specific of the particular ethnic heritage of Antilleans—that is, their temporal condition as descendants of slaves. Finally, he links the need for Antilleans to embrace both their French citizenship and their slave heritage to a political project ("This is an identity choice [and] a political choice". The emphasis on politics was indicative of recent transformations in CM98's activism. In recent years, the group increasingly has made explicit efforts to expand its political reach. Combining political activism with a monolithic ethnoracial identity claim is a mobilization strategy that allows CM98's leaders to portray themselves as legitimate representatives of Antillean migrants in hexagonal France. Indeed, in 2010, Viviane Romana, Serge's wife and a co-founder of CM98, was elected as a representative of Seine-Saint-Denis and a member of the Regional Council from the Socialist Party.

Conclusion

This chapter has examined a range of ethnoracial categories and temporal claims that are mobilized and constructed in French commemorations of slavery. Through participant observation, I have sought to illustrate how slavery commemorations contribute to the production of multiple discourses on the historical and contemporary meanings of racial categories, identities, and group relations. Drawing on evidence from a variety of commemorative settings, I have shown that many event organizers and panelists, as well as those audience members who decide to speak, subvert French Republic norms of color-blindness by directly addressing both historical and contemporary processes of racialization.

Several observations stand out from the foregoing examination of the data. First, commemorative venues were not only sites where participants expressed their feelings of group belonging in terms of ethnicity or race; they were also venues where people explicitly discussed the social construction of ethnoracial categories and their normative views on whether and how such distinctions should be made. Ethnoracial cascading within commemorative discussions allowed audience members and event panelists to legitimately discuss race (thus violating French norms of color-blindness) as speakers responded to each other's use of racial and ethnic categories.

Second, while representations of blackness and various diasporic identities were especially salient in visual representations and discursive exchanges, some commemorative forums were also venues where whites were labeled, characterized, and made visible as a presently existing social group in France today. Through discussion and debate, historians, activists, and members of the public resisted the historical erasure of the French Republic by unpacking how the chattel enslavement and colonialism eventually produced modern concepts of race. Moreover, their collective temporal labor forged connections between these histories and present-day racial attitudes, inequalities, and group relations. In contrast to the near complete erasure of whiteness in the commemorative speech of French politicians, some of the events profiled in this chapter allowed participants to critically discuss (and debate) the historical construction of white racialization, the ideology of white supremacy, and whites' continued sociopolitical dominance.

Finally, in unpacking the meanings associated with blackness in commemorative events, I observed that Africa and Africans are often relegated to historical roles in representations of slavery—most speakers talked about Africans as enslaved and deported people in the distant past rather than as contemporary members of the French nation and actors with a stake in the memory of slavery. In her work on racialization in Ghana, the anthropologist Jemima Pierre (2013) critiques the temporal erasure of Africans from the present. In the case of French commemorations of slavery, these dynamics risk masking and marginalizing the vast majority of French blacks of sub-Saharan African origin. The temporal claims I heard at CM98 events in particular emphasized the past and present existence and interests of Antilleans (French descendants of slaves) while minimizing racial discourse and identity in the contemporary moment. Although this finding is somewhat unsurprising, given that my methodology focused on French Caribbean events, it is also problematic. Outside of events organized by French people of African immigrant origin, the idea of Africa as the source of enslaved populations and the cultural glue tying together members of the "diaspora" remained largely in the background as historical and symbolic context. Present-day French Afro-descendants are implicitly included when commemorative organizers and audience members talk about "blacks," but they are rarely directly addressed in the way that contemporary Antilleans are routinely discussed in commemorative forums. I seldom encountered commemorative forums that explicitly privileged "Africanness" as a basis for collective identity (such as those organized by COFFAD) during my fieldwork. Despite prevalent references to the African "diaspora" and the presence of historical representations of Africa and Africans, French people of sub-Saharan African origin were *not* the focus of the commemorations I observed, regardless of their numerical majority among the black population in metropolitan France. This finding held true even at some commemorative events organized by groups whose leaders were immigrants from Africa, such as Alain Bidjeck of the Orig'in Association and Émile Batamack of Passerelle Noire.

Given the privileged status of French Caribbeans in popular discourse about French slavery, I sought to better understand the perspective of French descendants of slaves outside the commemorative movement. Do they share the race-avoidant discourse of groups such as CM98? How do they imagine the impact of the slavery past on the present? The next chapters complement the analyses thus far with perspectives from members of the French Caribbean public.

5

"We Have a History"

SLAVERY AND FRENCH
CARIBBEAN IDENTITIES

Despite the fact that French descendants of slaves come from a variety of different places—including Mayotte and Réunion Island in the Indian Ocean, Guiana in South America—French Caribbeans are often framed (either explicitly or implicitly) as the primary "public" to which commemorative events about slavery are targeted and the main social group that commemorative activists claim to represent. Do French Caribbeans outside of the commemorative movement think about race and slavery in ways that resemble the activists who claim to speak for them? To answer this question, I now turn to the perspectives of first- and second-generation Antillean migrants to assess the extent to which their feelings of attachment converge with or diverge from the representations of commemorators. This chapter unpacks the identities and temporal constructions of individuals who could potentially identify as descendants of slaves to determine the criteria they view as salient, the meaning they assign to ethnic and racial categories, and the representations of ancestry that inform their collective identities. By examining their perspectives, I aim to shed light on the degree to which commemorators and non-activists produce similar or divergent representations of race, ethnicity, and belonging.[1]

The analysis for this chapter is drawn from in-depth interviews with two samples of Antilleans living in the Paris metropolitan region, including (1) first-generation migrants from Martinique or Guadeloupe ($N = 32$) and (2) second-generation migrants who spent the majority of their childhood in mainland France ($N = 27$). I describe these respondents as *non-activists* (in contrast to commemorators) because they were not leaders in commemorative organizations when the interviews were conducted. All respondents had at least one parent of French Antillean origin. Most of the respondents were middle class and worked in white-collar or semi-skilled occupations, although it should be noted that the second-generation sample was younger and included a higher proportion of working-class individuals than the first-generation sample. Although the sample should not be interpreted as representative of French Caribbeans in Hexagonal France, it nonetheless provides rich insight into the perspectives of Antillean migrants by showing the range and salience of ethnic and racial identities in the respondents' self-concept.

The chapter first explores how French Caribbeans describe their ancestry. Next, I unpack respondents' definitions of their collective identities, highlighting the dimensions of their ancestry that they view as salient for their group membership. Then I explore the implications of Antilleans' racial classification and identification by assessing how they define what it means to be "black" in France. The conclusion situates the chapter in the argument of the book.

Ancestry Selection

Overall, my interviews revealed that ordinary French Caribbeans generally acknowledge slave ancestry as part of their genealogical heritage, but most respondents do not *primarily* see themselves as "descendants of slaves." Indeed, only 7 percent (4 of 59) specifically spoke of slave ancestry as a meaningful part of their group membership in their response to the question about identity. Ancestry is a central dimension of collective memory for ethnic and racial groups. As Max Weber ([1922] 1978) and Eviatar Zerubavel (2003, 2012) point out, claims about ancestral ties often form the basis of ethnic (or racial) belonging. In her work on black identities, the sociologist Mary Waters (1990, 1991) highlights the impact of socialization (through family structure, practices, and formal education), as well as of immigration status, in structuring how people understand their group's history. Such factors influence the "level and amount of knowledge and interest an individual has in his or her ethnic ancestry" and "shape the amount of raw material available to the individuals to form such an identification" (Waters 1990: 57). She also points to generational differences among immigrants that facilitate or hamper the intergenerational transmission of knowledge about ancestry, arguing that members of the first and second generation may derive their knowledge about ancestry from socialization and interaction with family members, in contrast to members of the third generation and beyond, who are required to make more conscious efforts (Waters 1990: 57). From this perspective, an individual's "ancestral options" are subject to a range of limitations rooted in his or her group membership and access to knowledge about his or her genealogical past.[2]

People with ancestral ties to enslavement do not always identify as "descendants of slaves." For example, the sociologist Tanya Golash-Boza (2011) found that Afro-Peruvians' conceptions of blackness are not closely tied to slavery, despite Peru's sustained involvement in the transatlantic slave trade. Further, most Caribbean societies, including the French *départements* of Guadeloupe and Martinique, include a heterogeneous mix of ethnic groups and color categories. Guadeloupeans and Martinicans can lay claim to a variety of origins, including African, indigenous Caribbean, European, and Asian (particularly Indian and Chinese) groups.[3] Moreover, phenotypic distinctions in Caribbean societies foster recognition of subtle gradations between "whiteness" and "blackness." Asking my respondents to describe their memories of these distinctions (and what they represent) was often an occasion for them to describe the broad range of skin tone, hair texture, and facial features they observed among their own family members—differences that they generally explained as evidence of racial mixture from European, Asian/Indian, indigenous Caribbean, and African sources.

Respondents disagreed over the precise meaning of the various categories partly because such classifications are inherently relative and because of generational differences and migration status. Thus, first-generation migrants who had grown up in the islands expressed a much more detailed understanding of phenotypic distinctions because of their use in everyday life; second-generation migrants, by contrast, often heard phenotypic distinctions mentioned only in passing, during vacations to the Antilles. Intermediate categories such as *métis(se)* and *mulâtre(sse)* generally connoted the offspring of racially different parents (most often "white" and "black," but also "black" and "Indian," for example). Most respondents agreed that terms such as *batard indien(ne)* (Indian bastard) or *coulie* referred to features that indicated ancestry from India.[4] *Chabin(e)* was one of the most contentious categories, as some respondents (especially second-generation migrants) used it to refer to anyone who was considered "light-skinned" (*avoir la peau claire*), whereas first-generation migrants often policed the term more strictly, reserving it for a specific combination of phenotypic features (i.e., "copper"-colored hair, light-brown eyes, and light skin). Darker-skinned people were referred to not only as *noir(e)* but also as *nèg*, *nègre*, or *négresse* (often *belle négresse* for attractive dark-skinned women), as well as other terms, such as *bleu* (blue).

I assessed respondents' ancestral belonging by attending to their discourse over the entirety of the interview. Some spontaneously described themselves as having ancestors who were enslaved, but most respondents mentioned slave ancestry in response to specific questions I posed to them. In general, interviewees acknowledged their slave ancestry in response to questions about

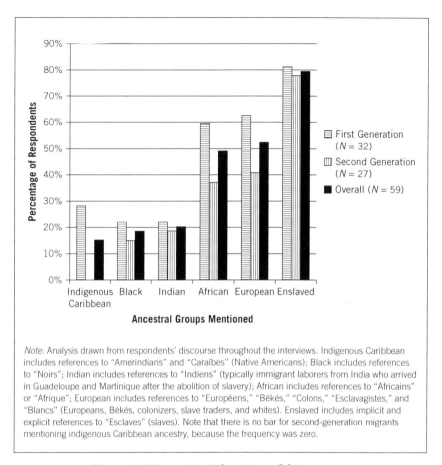

Note: Analysis drawn from respondents' discourse throughout the interviews. Indigenous Caribbean includes references to "Amerindians" and "Caraïbes" (Native Americans); Black includes references to "Noirs"; Indian includes references to "Indiens" (typically immigrant laborers from India who arrived in Guadeloupe and Martinique after the abolition of slavery); African includes references to "Africains" or "Afrique"; European includes references to "Européens," "Békés," "Colons," "Esclavagistes," and "Blancs" (Europeans, Békés, colonizers, slave traders, and whites). Enslaved includes implicit and explicit references to "Esclaves" (slaves). Note that there is no bar for second-generation migrants mentioning indigenous Caribbean ancestry, because the frequency was zero.

Figure 5.1. *Non-activists' description of their ancestry.*

their collective identifications ("How would you describe your identity?"; "What does it mean to be Antillean?"; "How would you compare Guadeloupeans and Martinicans?"), their awareness of phenotypic classifications within Antillean culture ("What were the words or terms you heard growing up for describing skin color and traits?"), or their exposure to narratives about slavery ("Did you hear about slavery in your family?"; "Did you learn about slavery at school?"). As shown in Figure 5.1, they most frequently described their ancestors as slaves (80 percent), followed by Europeans (53 percent), Africans (46 percent), Indians (20 percent), blacks (19 percent), and indigenous Caribbeans (15 percent). All of the non-activist Antilleans reported having ancestors who were enslaved, "African," or "black," but few respondents used all three terms to describe their ancestry.

Imagining Enslaved Ancestry

Respondents typically imagined their slave ancestors as having been objects of suffering and agents of contribution to the French nation. For example, Michèle, a first-generation student, used both frames when she described what her family members taught her about their enslaved ancestors:

> *Michèle:* [My] parents told us that . . . our ancestors were slaves, that they were brought over for the cultivation of sugarcane . . . and bananas, for French commerce . . . that very much contributed to France's wealth for centuries, a little detail that certain French people forget. . . .
>
> *C.F.:* Did your grandparents talk about slavery, or only your parents?
>
> *Michèle:* It was especially the parents—in fact, my mother. She gave us some anecdotes. . . . [I]n terms of childrearing, for example, [when] the children were causing a ruckus, they would be whipped during the time of slavery. . . .
>
> *C.F.:* How did you feel when your parents taught you that your ancestors were slaves? Do you remember anything?
>
> *Michèle:* Um, not really. It was . . . through books that you get [knowledge about] your slavery culture, because parents don't know a lot about it, either. In fact, it's [from] anecdotes that parents and great-grandparents gave [that] we know we're children of slaves. You're sure to have a certain hatred toward slavery, but, then, it's true that because you haven't lived through it, you can't say much about it, except that it was a bad thing and that in principle one shouldn't treat humans that way.
>
> *C.F.:* When you say "a certain hatred," what do you mean?
>
> *Michèle:* It's a hatred toward France of that time, which accepted this triangular commerce in the islands—a hatred for the fact that they whipped the slaves, that slaves were killed and women were raped. When you hear these stories, you feel a certain hatred, and you really want apologies.

Michèle's strong feelings of resentment for the unjust suffering of her ancestors were echoed by many Antilleans, especially those who recounted emotional experiences of learning about slavery and identifying with slaves in particular (rather than other ancestry groups). Matthieu, a first-generation migrant, shared this gripping account of his reaction to watching movies about slavery:

C.F.: Are there films about slavery that stick out for you?

Matthieu: The last one I saw was *Middle Passage* [*La Traversée*]. [It's] an Antillean documentary. Then there are, of course, the classics: *Roots* . . . , *La Rue Cases Nègres* [*Sugar Cane Alley*] . . . , *La Case de l'Oncle Tom* [*Uncle Tom's Cabin*].

C.F.: What did you think of *Middle Passage*?

Matthieu: [It was] hard. . . .

C.F.: What aspect?

Matthieu: The suffering. A film I really like is *Amistad*.

C.F.: Why?

Matthieu: That one is hard. I put myself in the place of my ancestors, you know? I [said to myself], "He was there, tranquilly, in Africa. He was living life normally. He was sold for [*pause*] a mouthful of bread—you know?—in such conditions." All of that for sugar-cane, for rum . . . sugar, cotton, like in the United States. When I saw the conditions that they went through, it's abominable. The first scenes in *Amistad* [show] when he was young, he was captured, and afterward in the boat—the suffering he endured. . . . [H]e vomited on himself; the person next to him died. You . . . wash yourself with seawater. All of that is hard for me. I always said that before I die, I have to go to Gorée island. Oh, yeah. I will go out of respect for my ancestors, because that's where everything started.

C.F.: And what did you think of *Roots* in relation to *Amistad*?

Matthieu: I already saw that film in the Antilles [when] I was young. I must have been twelve, thirteen years old. Afterward, I felt hatred toward whites. . . . They whip you; they call you Toby [instead of] Kunta Kinte. . . . [*Roots*] raised people's consciousness. . . . Certain people wanted to push slavery aside [*occulter esclavage*]. [Now] they saw the reality of what happened.

This respondent's emotional reaction to these films reflected, in part, his identification with the protagonists (i.e., Sengbe Pieh in *Amistad* and Kunta Kinte in *Roots*). We can see this projection at work in Matthieu's subtle shift from using the third-person pronoun "*he*" ("He was sold for . . . sugarcane") to using the second-person pronoun "you" ("You wash yourself with seawater"). Putting himself in the place of his imagined ancestors, Matthieu felt angry toward whites for the wrongs he saw depicted in the films. Similarly, Aurélie, a first-generation migrant, told me that she felt hatred for whites after watching *Roots* and Spike Lee's *Malcolm X*. When I asked her to explain, she said, "[It's] because you tell yourself, 'Our ancestors have suffered for nothing!' . . . It's like people who were deported because they were Jews. Here, [it was] because he was black."

A few Antilleans talked about their enslaved ancestors primarily as a source of pride. Jacky, an actor and second-generation migrant, emphasized the contribution frame when he spoke of his slave ancestry:

> The whole world looks to Versailles. I'm proud to say, as the great-great-grandson of slaves, that my great-great-grandfather gave his blood so that Versailles could be built, that Louis XIV . . . had all the wealth that the Negro trade brought to France. When I see Versailles, I have this pride in me that says, "Yeah! The ancestors were strong people!" The ancestors were heroes, human beings who accomplished something that a lot of sociologists, a lot of specialists of the question haven't even scratched the surface of. . . . [They were] human beings who survived the horror in which they were plunged. Each time I think about it, I have tears in my eyes.

Similarly, Christian, a project manager and first-generation migrant, was proud to be a descendant of slaves because of the group's perseverance and historical trajectory:

> The history of slavery, for me, is a source of pride. . . . Given what we've been through, given what our ancestors went through to get to where they were, and do you realize? [Now] we are here, having a discussion. We are in a café. . . . Once, we didn't have the right to come in here. At that time, we were seen as animals; writings still existed that said the black is an imbecile, a docile child. No, I'm proud when I see the path, what we've been through [*ce qu'on a parcouru*], where we came from, what we've done, and where we are.

Like Matthieu, who projected himself onto the protagonists of *Roots* and *Amistad*, Christian conveyed his identification with slavery by using the first-person plural pronoun "we" and the objective pronoun "us." In Matthieu's narratives, slavery is not simply a phenomenon that affected other people. Rather, it is represented as a history *about him* because it involved (some of) his ancestors.

Not all Antilleans expressed strong identification with their enslaved ancestors. Several respondents acknowledged their slave ancestry only indirectly, and some told me that although they knew (or believed) that some of their ancestors were enslaved, they did not feel completely identified with that historical experience. This was especially true for second-generation migrants and respondents who saw themselves as mixed (*métis*). For example, I asked Marilyne, a student and second-generation migrant of Moroccan and Guadeloupean origin, whether she felt like a descendant of slaves. After a long pause, she laughed softly:

> *Marilyne:* Um, in fact, the history of slavery really touches me. If someone talks to me about another form of slavery—I don't know, slavery in the Pacific—it doesn't touch me. I know it's horrible. It's the same thing: slavery. But it's this slavery in particular that touches me, because from time to time I think about my last name [*nom de famille*]. Does this last name come from a former slave master [*un ancient maître*]? I ask myself questions, and I wonder. Did my ancestors live through this? . . . But to say that I'm a descendant of slaves? Well, concretely, yes—I am, when you look at the facts. But I don't feel like my dad, [who] says, "I have the soul of a slave." I couldn't say that. I don't think so. But it really touches me. I feel that it's a part of me. But I have a little bit of difficulty with things related to family heritage. I don't know which part is, what part is transmitted from one generation to the next, unconsciously. Because people often tell me—I have an aunt, in fact, who lives in Guadeloupe and who is very spiritual. She explained to me that, um, from generation to generation there are things that get passed on, even unconsciously. For example, she has a theory that says that if blacks don't smoke a lot, it's because cigarettes are a form of enslavement, and since blacks have been enslaved, they don't want to get caught up in this new form of slavery. But it's supposedly an unconscious thing. There you go.
>
> *C.F.:* Do you believe it?
>
> *Marilyne:* Not really. I'm black and I smoke. [*Laughter.*] . . . This aunt, my mother's sister . . . , is Moroccan and went to live in Guadeloupe with my father's family. In fact, she didn't know Guadeloupe—she's Moroccan—but she knows me. When she left for Guadeloupe, one or two years, she came back, and when she came back, she told me, "Seeing Guadeloupeans, I thought about you, and I realized that there were things about you that I didn't see before but now show me that you're Guadeloupean." I told her that I didn't understand what she was talking about. She told me, "The attitude, the things I didn't see before because I didn't know Guadeloupe, now that I've lived in Guadeloupe, even if you haven't lived in Guadeloupe, it's obvious that you're

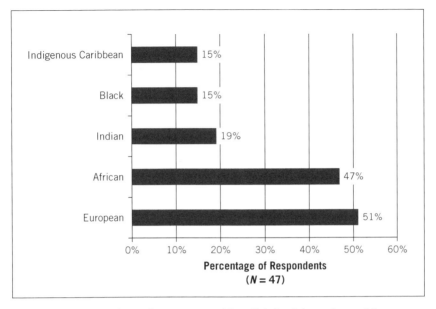

Figure 5.2. *Additional ancestries cited by self-defined descendants of slaves.*

Guadeloupean." I don't know what she meant, but it made me happy. She was saying [that it was] in the attitudes . . . mannerisms. . . . I don't know if it's true, but it showed me that perhaps I do, in fact, have a family heritage. I don't know what it is, where it came from, but there has to be something.

Slightly more than half of all respondents who acknowledged slave ancestry also used other terms to refer to ancestral groups. Figure 5.2 shows that 51 percent of self-defined descendants of slaves mentioned having European or white ancestry, 47 percent also referred to their ancestors as African or of African origin, 19 percent used the term "Indian," and 15 percent each described their ancestors as black and indigenous Caribbean. What these numbers suggest is that about half of those who saw themselves as descendants of slaves viewed their ancestry in monolithic terms, and half recognized additional ancestral ties.

Imagining European Ancestry

Waters (1991) found that African Americans tend to ignore or to be unaware of their white ancestors. Many Antilleans in this study, by contrast, acknowledged having European forebears. Respondents used a variety of terms, including "European," "colonizer," "white," and "*béké*" to describe their ancestors from Europe. Typically, respondents mentioned their European ancestors in the context of discussing three themes: (1) their knowledge of phenotypical categories in the Antilles, (2) their identity, and (3) their genealogy. About a quarter of the respondents mentioned white European ancestors in the context of describing phenotypical distinctions in the Antilles. Sophie, a first-generation migrant from Guadeloupe, used examples drawn from her family to explain the range of phenotypical differences and ancestral origins:

> *Sophie:* My father's . . . grandfather was white, and on his mother's side, there were blacks but also some mixture—so, white and mixed. My father came from what we call a mulatto [*mulâtre*]—someone with kind of straight hair and light-skinned [*clair de peau*]. . . . [O]n my mom's side, her mother, her great-grandmother, [they] were all *black black* [*noirs noirs*]. By contrast, on my father's mother's side, they are people with a little bit of Syrian [or] Lebanese origin. One of them had married a Negro woman [*négresse*]. . . .
>
> *C.F.:* Have you done your genealogy?
>
> *Sophie:* I started, but it's not finished. I'm doing it now.
>
> *C.F.:* So the words [you heard] were "mulatto"—
>
> *Sophie:* "Black" [*noir*], *chabin*—
>
> *C.F.:* What's the difference between *chabin* and *mulâtre*?
>
> *Sophie:* My husband, for example—they say that he's a *chabin* because he has Negro traits [*des traits négroïdes*], but he's light-skinned. . . . Me, I'm a *négresse*.[5] That's what I am.
>
> *C.F.:* You're not considered light-skinned?
>
> *Sophie:* Yes. I am not a black, black *négresse*, but I think that in relation to my sister I was a *négresse*. To me, I was a *négresse*.
>
> *C.F.:* It's relative.
>
> *Sophie:* And, in fact, *négresse* is a beautiful word for me. I put it as "beautiful *négresse*"; [that's my] rebellious side, the hard-headed side, [with] strength of character. For me, it's very positive [*valorisant*] because until I was nine, it was not something that was positive, because I was there, the little *négresse* . . . , on the lowest end of the social scale.

In contrast to the many interviewees who claimed to be proud of their enslaved or black ancestors, no Antilleans explicitly said they were proud of their white ancestry. However, many respondents did feel that racial mixture was a positive thing, even if they did not express particularly positive feelings about their white ancestors. For example, Sandrine, an architectural assistant and first-generation migrant, identified strongly with her African origins and her enslaved ancestors but also said that she was proud of her mixed heritage:

> On my father's side, my grandfather is a white. My grandmother is a lady . . . with strong African features. On my mother's side, my grandmother is a Caribbean [*caraïbe*], and my grandfather is a fat black, really big [guy]. . . . [W]hen he walked, he'd shake the whole house. . . . So all of that made me.

A few respondents, such as Philippe, a first-generation migrant, mentioned white ancestry as an argument against racial separatism and racism. As he put it, "The Antillean population is multiform; thus, [we're] a multiform people. All Antilleans have white and Indian blood in their veins, OK? I have Caribbean [*caraïbe*], Indian, and African blood."

Some interviewees told painful stories about being rejected by white family members or having mixed-race relatives who were the illegitimate offspring of whites who refused to recognize them. Several also mentioned knowing that their ancestors were white because they had raped their enslaved or slave-descended foremothers. Pierre, a first-generation migrant, poignantly explained how he felt about the historical legacy of racial mixture and rape in his genealogy:

> *Pierre:* I know that my great-grandmother was raped.
> *C.F.:* By whom?
> *Pierre:* A guy, a white guy, a [slave] master [*Un mec, un blanc, un maître*]. But it was just toward the end of slavery, you see? . . . [D]espite the end of slavery, it didn't stop right away. It's something that's remained. She was raped . . . and she went crazy afterward. . . . [T]he dude wanted to apologize by adopting the child. [He wanted] to take the child home, give him a good education. She refused. . . .
> *C.F.:* What does having a slave master in your genealogy represent for you?
> *Pierre:* [*Laughs.*]
> *C.F.:* Nothing?
> *Pierre:* All right. We're going to talk about mixture. [*Laughs.*]
> *C.F.:* Do you feel like a descendant of slave masters or not?
> *Pierre:* I'm going to ask you a simple question, and for once, you're going to respond even if you don't want to—just this time. If you knew that your father was a rapist and that he was Chinese [*laughs*] . . . would you feel Chinese?

C.F.: Even if I felt Chinese, I would more so feel traumatized.

Pierre: Traumatized, yes, but would you feel Chinese? Traumatized is obvious.

C.F.: I don't know.

Pierre: [*Laughs.*]

C.F.: It's true. I don't know. I imagine I wouldn't.

Pierre: Me, if my mom told me that she had been raped by a Chinese [*laughs*], I wouldn't feel Chinese, because it's my mother who raised me, with her culture. You see? There's something interesting about mixture [*la mixité*]. . . . [T]he notion of race is relative. . . . Cheikh Anta Diop believed in race.[6] Aimé Césaire believe[d] in race. . . . But their belief in race wasn't a blind belief. They had already put relativity in race—that is, they believed it was cultural. What makes race isn't one's color; it's one's culture.

Pierre's tragic recounting of his grandmother's experience of sexual violence by a white rapist underscores why some Antilleans did not speak fondly of their European ancestors. Knowing that one of your ancestral groups has victimized, harmed, or otherwise oppressed another set of your forebears understandably generates boundaries against the perpetrators rather than feelings of solidarity and identification.[7] Finally, although Pierre did not mention this factor explicitly, the segregation of Antillean society (especially that of Martinique), where whites and descendants of colonists (*békés*) routinely practice endogamy and socially exclude Afro-descended Antilleans means that many French Caribbeans with whites in their family tree lack intimate relationships with those same family members. Sandrine, the architectural assistant who acknowledged her white ancestry and expressed pride in her mixed background, had few interactions with whites growing up in Guadeloupe. When I asked her whether she had contact with whites on the island, she replied:

> They don't mix with people—even the kids. They put the kids in private schools. . . . [T]he *békés* don't mix with us, but I had some friends there. . . . I don't have anything against the whites. I have some really good buddies back in Guadeloupe. . . . I have a childhood friend. . . . [H]is mother was a *béké*, but she's a *béké* who married a black, so she's a fallen *béké* [*une béké déchue*].

Waters acknowledged the historical legacy of violent racial mixture during slavery as a plausible reason why African Americans emphasize their black ancestry and rarely mention white or other ancestral groups. She found that African American descendants of U.S. slaves generally identify as black but "do not mention or know about other ancestries in their backgrounds", pointing out that "much of the intermixing of blacks and whites that occurred during slavery was a result of rape and coercion of black slaves by white slaveholders. As a result, families might very well be reluctant to pass along specific lineage information about the white slave-owner father responsible for the violence against the mother" (Waters 1991: 60). Thus, feelings of resentment and rejection, stemming from stories of ancestral rape and other forms of violence, may also play a role in diminishing the social significance of European ancestry for descendants of slaves in France.

Imagining African Ancestry

Most Antilleans I spoke with described their African ancestry in vague terms because they were largely unable to trace their genealogy to specific African nations or ethnic groups. Corinne, a first-generation migrant, discussed not knowing where her African ancestors came from.

> *Corinne:* I don't know an Antillean who knows his African roots. . . . I can't say where I come from. I can't say which country. . . .
> *C.F.:* Would you like to know?
> *Corinne:* Of course! But I would like to know just as much where I come from in Africa as where I come from in India, where I come from in England, you see? . . . [T]he difference between descendants of slaves in the United States and descendants of slaves in the Antilles [is that] we don't seek out our African roots. . . . [T]hat's my impression. . . . There isn't anybody who has told me, "I come from this or that tribe in Africa," you know?

Alain, a first-generation migrant, spoke of Africa as an ancestral source but also as a mythical place:

> *C.F.:* What's your perspective on Africa?
> *Alain:* It's kind of seen as a source . . . as an origin—the origin of something, like the base of a lot of nests, the base of a lot of history. It's also a bit of an imaginary place [*un endroit un peu fantastique*], a little mythical [*mythique*], it is part of [our] roots, also, and unfortunately, there are people [there] who have a tendency to be a little aggressive with one another, so you're afraid to go there. . . . [I]t isn't violent everywhere, but imagining this violence, you tell yourself, "I don't know about that!" [*Laughs.*] I want to go there, but what could happen to me? But otherwise, [I see it] very positively.

I want to go there to know it, to see it. The landscapes look magnificent. I would really like . . . to meet the people who live there.

Most Antilleans who acknowledged African ancestry emphasized that they, themselves, were not African. Their refusal of African identity partly reflects contemporary group boundaries between French of sub-Saharan African and Antillean origin. Sophie, a teacher and second-generation migrant, illustrated this distinction:

> My conception of Africa is that it's also in some way the country of my ancestors. So how can one not love their ancestors? When you do not love your ancestors or when you reject your ancestors, what does that make you? That means that you have a serious issue [*un gros souci*]. [But] I'm not going to say that I'm African. . . . I never told you that I'm African. I said that I'm black, I was born in the Antilles, and I've experienced this Antillean [and] Caribbean culture, but I'm not going to say, to be politically correct . . . , that I'm African. . . . I'm [also] not going to tell you that I don't love Africa or Africans. So in some ways . . . I live my Antilleanness and my *négritude*.

Jacky, a first-generation migrant, was one of the few respondents who associated his African ancestry with an African identity:

> *Jacky:* I'm an African. What can I say? I'm an African. I'm a Negro and I'm African. Naturally, I'm different. Naturally, I don't speak Wolof, Bambara, Lingala. . . .
> *C.F.:* When you say that you're African, what do you mean?
> *Jacky:* I am black. Blacks come from Africa, so I'm African.

Only two interviewees—both members of the second generation—reported knowing the origin of their African ancestors. Both respondents were able to trace back their ancestry to Benin. Olivier, whose parents came to mainland France from Martinique, says he learned the origins of his African ancestors because his mother had met the former president of Benin:

> She was lucky. . . . [H]e told her where we come from and said that . . . our [last name] is a village in Benin. I've noticed that physically, when I meet Beninese [people], there is a physical type that is close to us. Especially my father and my grandfather, I saw that they were really close to the Beninese [type]. I learned afterward, recently, that 46 percent of Africans who went to Martinique were Beninese—almost half were Beninese.

Defining Collective Identity

When I asked non-activists to define their identity, they usually provided a range of answers rather than just one label, demonstrating the multidimensional nature of their collective identification. As shown in Table 5.1, almost all of the non-activists (93 percent) mentioned ethnoracial identities. Several patterns stand out with regard to their responses. First, a slightly lower proportion of second-generation migrants mentioned ethnoracial groups as part of their self-conception (89 percent, compared with 97 percent of first-generation migrants). National identity was the second most salient category, with 37 percent of respondents indicating that they felt "French."

Here, too, a difference in terms of migration status is apparent: second-generation migrants reported French identification at a higher rate than first-generation migrants (44 percent compared with 31 percent). Personal identity (e.g., defining oneself as a "simple person," "easygoing," or "intellectual") was mentioned by 19 percent of the respondents. Only women mentioned gender as a salient identity. While most of the respondents were Catholic or had been raised Catholic, religious identity was salient for only 5 percent of the non-activist sample. Conspicuously absent from the list is political identification. Although some respondents did describe themselves as involved in their community or currently engaged in (non-commemorative) activism, none explicitly defined their identity in terms of political beliefs or belonging to a political party.

TABLE 5.1. NON-ACTIVISTS' IDENTITY FRAMES			
Categories	Percentage of first generation (*N* = 32)	Percentage of second generation (*N* = 27)	Percentage of Non-activists (*N* = 59)
Ethnoracial	97%	89%	93%
National	31%	44%	37%
Personality	22%	15%	19%
Gender	9%	11%	10%
Other*	6%	7%	7%
Religious	6%	4%	5%
Age	0%	7%	3%
Don't know	3%	4%	3%

Note: Figures exceed 100% because responses were not mutually exclusive.

*The "Other" category includes identifying in terms of one's profession, family, sexuality, being "Parisian," and so on.

National Identity

As mentioned above, migration status (and place of birth) played a role in mitigating feelings of French belonging. Antilleans' complicated attachments to France were demonstrated by the fact that most respondents—even those who identified as "French"—reserved the word "France" for the mainland and discussed the overseas departments as separate, quasi-national entities. Some second-generation migrants felt they were "French" because (mainland) France was their place of birth and the place where they were raised. Gladys, the owner of a beauty shop and a second-generation migrant, felt strongly that having been born in mainland France made her French, but she also described Frenchness as an inalienable part of her identity:

> *C.F.:* When you think about your identity, do you feel French?
> *Gladys:* I'm 100 percent French. I was born in France, [so] there's no problem. However, I'm of Guadeloupean origin. . . . I feel French because I am French. I'm not going to feel American or something else. . . . [Some] Antilleans tell me that their nationality is Guadeloupean. Wait a second, [I say]: on your identity card, the nationality is marked "French." It's not marked "Guadeloupean."

Carole, a student and second-generation migrant, was raised by her Martinican mother in an affluent suburb outside Paris and. Her father is from Ivory Coast, in West Africa, but did not play a significant role in her life. Carole used the word "black" in a descriptive way to refer to herself and other people of African or Caribbean origin, but she described her identity mainly in terms of being French:

> I feel at home only in France. . . . I was born in France. I grew up here, and I am French, completely. But I continually feel obligated to specify that I'm of Antillean origin [because] of other people. Otherwise, as far as I'm concerned, I'm French.

When I asked her whether she also identified with the African side of her family, she replied:

> I would say that . . . the Antillean side takes precedence. I don't know why, but I don't really put it out there. Maybe it's the fact that I don't live with [my father], but I don't really put it out there that I'm also half Ivorian. So when people ask me, "Where are you from?" I say "France." "What origin?" is usually the question that follows, so I say, "Antilles."

That helps people understand, because they know that the Antilles are in fact France. . . . So it's easier for me to say that I'm French of [Antillean] origin—that my mom came from Martinique—than [to say] I'm half Ivorian. Also, I've always lived here, so for me it's my country. . . . I was raised here, in the French way, with the same basic principles, the same values . . . , the same education.

Carole's family situation (being raised by her mother) made her feel closer to her Antillean heritage and distant from her African side. But emphasizing her Antilleanness was also a way to assert her French belonging to people in mainland France who sometimes perceived her as an immigrant.

Some respondents felt French because of the influence of French culture (e.g., education and values) in their lives. This definition of Frenchness was accessible to (and expressed by) both first-generation and second-generation migrants. For example, Jean-Luc, a forty-four-year-old information technology (IT) manager, was born in Paris but moved back and forth between metropolitan and overseas France during his childhood. He describes his identity as "French of Martinican origin." When I asked him what that meant, he said:

It means that I am French. I was educated according to the French model, so perhaps even my way of thinking is very French. But maybe there are aspects of the Antilles that are part of my personality. . . . I can't define myself as a Martinican for the simple and good reason that I wasn't born there. There are things that I don't have. So because of that, I'm of Martinican origin. . . . I know about things from there, but I see things like a French [person].

Others described themselves as French but saw the French component as less influential than other aspects of their collective identity. Marc, a first-generation migrant, saw himself as French but did not feel that the "French" dimension was particularly meaningful:

I used to play around and say that I was Antillean-American-French because . . . you can mix up being Antillean and American. We could use the word "Caribbean," because Antillean culture is inevitably influenced by other islands. You can't deny [what] the mix of English, French, and Spanish has given to the Caribbean. So there is, first of all, an Antillean identity that comes from this, so we're Caribbean or Antillean. This concept is purely French. It's . . . the English equivalent of "West Indian." But . . . when we went to Miami or New York [and said] we came from

Martinique, [they replied], "Martinique? Where's Martinique?" . . . [But if we said], "Near Cuba, Jamaica," then it was OK— right away they understood the part of the world that we were talking about. That's why I prefer to say, "Caribbean" rather than "Antillean." In France, Antillean really only means Guadeloupe [and] Martinique.

Similarly, Michèle, a first-generation migrant, made it clear that being French was a minor part of her identity:

[I'm] Martinican before anything else. . . . I'm a Martinican woman, so I have more of the Antillean mentality. I really like observing and understanding Antillean culture. More than anything, I'm Antillean, and then I define myself as French.

Later, I asked her to tell me what being French meant to her:

More than anything, it means belonging to a multicultural country. . . . [I]n France, you have several identities, several cultures. It's not just one culture. And "French"—actually, I don't use [that word]. I call myself "French" only on paper [*sur les papiers*]. [T]ake the example of French music: I listen to it, but I don't really like it. It isn't me, you know? However, I like to call myself French in terms of France's rich history, . . . because it's a magnificent country in terms of its monuments, its historical past—Versailles, the Eiffel Tower, the Haussmanian buildings. It's part of living in . . . Paris. . . . Also the French Revolution—you can feel French because of that.

The ambivalence in Michèle's feelings about being French was typical of the French Caribbeans I interviewed. While she said she called herself "French" only on paper (i.e., legal citizenship) and did not have a great deal of affinity for what she viewed as "French" culture (i.e., music), she felt some pride for aspects of French history (e.g., the Revolution).

Only a few respondents expressed deep attachment to their French identity. Pascal, a sixty-year-old first-generation migrant, was adamant and a bit chauvinistic in describing his admiration for France, despite slavery:

I admit it's not good, but I'm . . . extremely nationalistic. I'm very French, and I've always defended France. . . . I'm very happy to be French, very proud of being French . . . , but I have Martinican origins. . . . It isn't contradictory for me [because] in Martinique, I have ancestors who came from France . . . four hundred years ago. So I can't spit on [France]. But

I also have some [ancestors] who came from Africa, and I don't spit on them, either. That's normal. . . . But the ones who came from Africa were taken by force. They didn't choose to come here.

I asked Pascal to explain why he felt "extremely nationalistic":

French society makes choices, or made choices, that correspond to my aspirations. . . . [I]f [President Nicolas] Sarkozy gets on my nerves in some ways, it's because I see that he's breaking French rules, and I think it's very important to me for France to stand for something. There's a way of thinking—I'm sorry to say this to an American woman—but when France took certain positions against . . . American hegemony, well, [we] were right. That's our position . . . , and when that imbecile [George Bush] tells us that we're the only ones to do or not to do something, I say, "But when in 1789 we had the Revolution . . . we were the only ones in Europe. There were kingdoms everywhere. Everyone was against us, but we still did it, and we imposed this idea of revolution on the entire world." So I don't see why today we shouldn't have originality in various domains. We have originalities and I'm proud of it.

Overall Patterns in Ethnoracial Identification

Table 5.2 specifies the ethnoracial frames that respondents mentioned when defining their identities. Most often, respondents said that they identified as "black" (39 percent) or that they saw themselves as "Guadeloupean" or "Martinican" (39 percent). Antillean identity was salient for 36 percent of respondents. In such cases, interviewees either meant that they felt attached to the community of Antilleans (people from the French overseas Caribbean islands [the DOM]) living in Hexagonal France or they felt Antillean because they were born in the Antilles. Caribbean identity was mentioned by 12 percent of respondents and suggests broad solidarity with Caribbean populations (outside the French DOM). African identity (usually an allusion to slavery) was mentioned by 12 percent of the non-activists, and 10 percent said that being mixed was an important part of their identity. Significantly, while the vast majority of respondents acknowledged their enslaved ancestors, only 7 percent (4 of 59) specifically spoke of slave ancestry as a meaningful part of their group membership in their response to the question about identity. This may suggest that activists have quite a challenge on their hands in generating interest in slavery among the French Caribbean masses. A final important finding is the social irrelevance of European ancestors for non-activists: 3 percent mentioned slave-owner ancestry as an important part of their iden-

TABLE 5.2. ETHNIC AND RACIAL COMPONENTS OF NON-ACTIVISTS' IDENTITIES		
Identity frame	Frequency (*N* = 59)	Percentage of non-activists
Black	23	39%
Specific island	23	39%
Antillean	21	36%
Caribbean	7	12%
African	7	12%
Mixed	6	10%
Slave ancestry	4	7%
Indigenous Caribbean	3	5%
Creole	3	5%
Indian	3	5%
Slave-owner ancestry	2	3%
European	2	3%
White	1	2%
Asian	1	2%
Moroccan	1	2%
Note. Figures exceed 100% because responses were not mutually exclusive.		

tity, 3 percent saw European heritage as meaningful, and 2 percent saw having white ancestors as a component of their self-conception. Below, I briefly examine the two most salient ethnic and racial identities.

Black Identification

An interesting paradox emerged as I reviewed instances in which respondents referred to themselves as black: although the vast majority (92 percent) of non-activists self-categorized as black, only 39 percent actually mentioned being black as a salient dimension of their collective identity. Indeed, even Antilleans who downplayed blackness, identified as racially mixed (*métis*), or rejected a black identity altogether nonetheless used the term "black" as a description for themselves or their group membership, particularly when recounting their encounters with various ethnoracial groups (including whites) or their experiences with discrimination. What this finding suggests is that most Antilleans saw themselves as belonging to the *group category* black partly because they are aware of how whites and other groups in mainland France perceive them. Yet, blackness is a meaningful identification—a real *social group*—for only a subset of the sample. Thus, Virginie, a second-generation migrant, identified primarily as black partly because she felt that the majority population saw her that way:

> *Virginie:* It's horrible to say this, but I would define myself by my color. I know that I'm black in France. . . . I know that I'm Antillean. I would say that I'm Antillean to someone from the metropole. But if I say to someone from the Antilles that I'm Antillean, they wouldn't see me as Antillean.
> *C.F.:* What would they see you as?
> *Virginie:* Metro [French].
> *C.F.:* And why is it horrible to say that?
> *Virginie:* Because I should say that I see myself as an Antillean, but I can't because over there they wouldn't recognize me as Antillean. It's difficult to say this, because it's my roots. I'm out of place there. I don't know—for example, in the United States, there are African Americans. I would be an African European, without really trying to find another attachment to an island, even if I feel Antillean. I can't say it, because they wouldn't see me that way—except here, in the metropole.

On the one hand, Virginie feels that people in mainland France primarily see her as black, and she deploys Antillean and blackness as synonymous identities in the Hexagon. On the other hand, people in the islands tend to remind her that she isn't a "real" Antillean because she was born and raised on the mainland. What is evident in her account is a heightened awareness of being externally categorized by both non-blacks in France and Antilleans in the DOM. Understanding the distinction between black categorization and black identity is a complex affair that I return to at the end of the chapter.

Island-Specific Identification

Not surprisingly, identification in terms of particular islands was mitigated by generational status. Thus, 47 percent of first-generation migrants described their identity in terms of attachment to Guadeloupe or Martinique, compared with 30 percent of second-generation respondents. Of the respondents who mentioned Guadeloupe or Martinique as the *most* important part of their collective identity, all but one were first-generation migrants. Clara, a first-generation migrant from Guadeloupe who moved to Paris for college, described the shifting salience of her island identity:

C.F.: How do you define your identity?

Clara: It depends. Here in France, I'm, above all else, Guadeloupe-an. However, in Guadeloupe, obviously, [and] for the rest of the world, I'm a Frenchwoman from Paris [*une française de Paris*] because it's simpler for me. . . . When I meet someone abroad, I say, "I'm French. I live in Paris" [*said in English*]. It's a hell of a lot simpler. Here you can kind of get into a discussion, explain, "You know, in fact, I grew up . . . in the French West Indies" [*said in English*]. [If I try to] explain that it's a French *département* and all that, it gets a little bit complicated. So let's say that when I'm abroad, I'm French, from Paris, to simplify things.

C.F.: And what does being Guadeloupean mean to you?

Clara: It's as if I belong to a completely different country [*un pays à part entière*]. Me, in my head, I don't even talk about my "island." I talk about my "country," because for me it's almost a completely different nation. . . . I have two cultures—or I have one culture derived from a mixture [*pour moi j'ai deux cultures, ou alors j'en ai une issue d'un mélange*], but I believe I have two, and I adapt myself according to where I am.

Although Clara grew up in Guadeloupe, she felt that she was now perceived as French (or Parisian) because she had left the island and moved to the metropole. The sharp distinction in her mind between "France" and the islands is evident in her own awareness of the nationalism she feels as a Guadeloupean.

Respondents who described their identities in terms of their specific attachment to Guadeloupe or Martinique often made light of differences between the populations of the two islands. Most respondents talked about stereotypes of Guadeloupeans and Martinicans as attitudes held by other people. Rarely did interviewees admit to having low opinions of the other group. Robert, a second-generation migrant, identified as Martinican (his parents' place of birth). While he said that relations between Guadeloupeans and Martinicans in mainland France were good, he jokingly took jabs at Guadeloupeans out of a sense of shared cultural intimacy:

Robert: When I see a Guadeloupean, the first thing I do is tease him.

C.F.: About what, for example? [*Laughs.*]

Robert: Jokes. . . . [L]ike, for example, the slaves arriving in Martinique [were] the most intelligent, the most beautiful. . . . [T]he ugliest ones and the morons were sent to Guadeloupe. The Guadeloupean [would] answer, "Yes, when the slaves arrived, the most docile and malleable were kept in Martinique and the most rebellious went to Guadeloupe." So, it's . . . jokes like that; it's little battles.

Raphael, a second-generation migrant with Martinican heritage, also mentioned lighthearted teasing between the groups:

> *Raphael:* It's true that from time to time you get little jokes, little comments . . . like the French who make fun of Belgians, the Swiss.
> *C.F.:* What kind of jokes are made about Martinicans?
> *Raphael:* Oh, . . . Guadeloupeans . . . tend to compare us [Martinicans] with the poor little servants of the whites . . . , and Martinicans tend to compare Guadeloupeans to people who are . . . stupid, simpletons.

The oblique reference to slavery in Raphael's response is striking. The joke here is based on the idea that Martinicans tend to be stigmatized as "servants" to white people.

The Multiple Meanings of Black Classification and Black Identification

What do Guadeloupean and Martinican migrants mean when they use the word "black"? Do they adopt thin or thick understandings of blackness? The considerable gap between the percentage of non-activist Antilleans who self-classify as black (92 percent) and those who count blackness among their primary collective identities (39 percent) suggests that some respondents self-categorize as black in a descriptive way or as a kind of shorthand to make themselves understood. About midway through my fieldwork, I decided to further investigate the multiple meanings of black categorization and identification for my respondents, given recent black movements, the prevalence of black representations in commemorative discourse about slavery, and the frequency with which Antilleans spontaneously used the word to describe themselves. To that end, I asked a subsample of the respondents ($N = 37$) the following question: "What does being black mean to you?"

Antilleans' understandings of blackness were quite heterogeneous. Indeed, as Table 5.3 shows, I identified nine connotations for the word "black," including (1) phenotype, (2) culture, (3) historical heritage, (4) imposed categorization, (5) pride/happiness, (6) racism/disadvantage, (7) personal attribute, (8) struggle/suffering, and (9) oppositional categorization. Several of

TABLE 5.3. NON-ACTIVISTS' UNDERSTANDINGS OF BLACKNESS			
Meaning of blackness	First generation (*N* = 17)	Second generation (*N* = 20)	Non-activists (*N* = 37)
Phenotype*	41%	25%	32%
Culture**	41%	20%	30%
Historical heritage**	18%	35%	27%
Imposed categorization*	29%	25%	27%
Pride/happiness**	41%	15%	27%
Racism/disadvantage*	24%	10%	16%
Personal attribute**	0%	20%	11%
Struggle/suffering**	6%	10%	8%
Oppositional categorization*	6%	5%	5%
Other	12%	0%	5%

Notes: (1) The "Other" category includes responses such as "hard work" and intersectionality (e.g., combining black identity with gender). (2) Responses do not add up to 100% because answers were not mutually exclusive.
* Denotes category that corresponds to "thin" blackness.
** Denotes category that corresponds to "thick" blackness.

these categories (phenotype, imposed categorization, racism/disadvantage, and oppositional categorization) can be understood broadly as indicative of thin blackness: recognition of one's external categorization as black and the disadvantage and stigma that may result from such labeling. Thick blackness is represented by discourse that depicted blackness as dimensions of identity (e.g., culture, history, emotion [pride/happiness], personal attributes, and suffering). What the data clearly illustrate is that respondents do not have a monolithic understanding of what blackness means. But not only do Antilleans lack consensus on a single definition; as individuals, they often drew on both thin and thick conceptions. In other words, respondents did *not* generally treat these representations of blackness as mutually exclusive.

Thin Conceptions of Blackness: Phenotype, Racism, and Categorization

Caribbeans mobilized thin descriptions when they defined "black" in terms of phenotypical features and exposure to racism and discrimination. Thin conceptions of blackness were also evident when respondents mentioned imposed categorization (being labeled black by others) and definitions of blackness that were based on an opposition to whiteness. Overall, phenotype was the modal definition of blackness for the sample, with 32 percent of respondents using criteria such as skin tone, hair texture, and facial features. François, a sixty-seven-year-old first-generation migrant from Guadeloupe, rejected a black identity and felt that being categorized as black meant having a certain skin tone: "It's a color. . . . I don't identify as black and certainly not as a Negro." When I asked him what "Negro" meant, he said, "It means 'a beast of blood,' the slave. . . . [N]o one's going to make me a slave. . . . I don't want to be called a slave. I'm a citizen. I'm a sir [*monsieur*]." Adrien, a first-generation migrant who was also from Guadeloupe, identified as black and thought of the term as a combination of different features:

> *C.F.:* What does being black mean to you? Do you identify yourself as black, or is it just a skin color [to you]?
> *Adrien:* I identify myself as black, yes. They've talked a lot about it in the media recently. There's an article that was saying [that] there are a lot of ways to see skin color in Guadeloupe; there are a dozen different names: *coulie, batârd indien, béké, blanc matignon,* and *peau chapée.* . . .
> *C.F.:* And what would you be in Guadeloupe? Which category?
> *Adrien:* I would be black because my hair is clearly frizzy [*crépus*]. Right now it's short, but normally it's frizzy.[8]
> *C.F.:* And what would I be?
> *Adrien:* You would be mixed [*métisse*], I think.
> *C.F.:* Why?
> *Adrien:* Because I can clearly see that in your family, you have—one of your two parents is white, or your grandparents. [*Silence.*] No?
> *C.F.:* No, [but] my grandparents on both sides are mixed.
> *Adrien:* Ah, OK.

Adrien was not the only respondent who did not categorize my phenotype as black. While many of the respondents thought I could pass as a typical Antillean in Martinique or Guadeloupe, there was little consensus about the category into which I would fit. Although some respondents simply saw me as black (particularly those who saw themselves as light-skinned), they used a broad range of labels to describe my phenotype, including *métisse, mulâtresse, négresse pas très foncée* (not too dark Negro woman), *sapotille* (the color of the Caribbean sapodilla fruit), *chappée coulie* (almost Indian), *chabine* or *claire de peau* (light-skinned), *presque chabine* (almost light-skinned), and *entre chabine et noir* (between light-skinned and black). During fieldwork, I noticed that wearing my hair in twists (a style French Antilleans refer to as *vanilles*) often prompted respondents to perceive my hair texture as smoother and less frizzy (or "nappy") than when I wore my hair in an afro. In such cases, respondents seemed to perceive me as "less black" and more mixed. The diversity of descriptions applied to my appearance also demonstrates the relational and contextual nature of black phenotype and intermediate categories.

It is also important to note that Antilleans' understanding of blackness as phenotype is shaped not only by their familiarity with intermediate classifications but also by the historical stigmatization of black features within which these categories derive their meaning (Lirus 1979).[9] Thus, on some occasions I felt that male respondents told me I was light-skinned because they thought it was flattering to do so. Indeed, calling a woman *chabine* in the French Antilles is often a pickup line in and of itself. Many of the respondents I spoke with were very conscious of the stigma attached to black phenotype and often expressed criticism and disdain for other Antilleans' anti-black prejudice. (Respondents almost never admitted to harboring such feelings themselves.)

Youri, who had second-generation migrant family ties to both Martinique and Guadeloupe, described his experience learning about the negative meanings attached to blackness within his family:

> *Youri:* One of my mother's sisters had . . . European features. She was, truthfully, quite privileged by one of their aunts, who I think was white or mixed. And it's true that all of this is to say that in Antillean culture there are a lot of traces of the slavery period. . . . [T]he thing African Americans and Antilleans have in common is that we experienced deportation from Africa to the Americas . . . and the idea that whiteness [*la blancheur*] . . . is beautiful. . . . [T]he white was the most beautiful; the white was the model, and this discourse was absorbed over centuries of slavery by Antillean populations—that you had to be light-skinned, you had to have smooth hair [*les cheveux lisses*]. . . . There's a saying in the Antilles: instead of saying that person is "too dark," it is said that you were born badly [*tu es mal né*]. It means that you're a failure [*tu es raté*], you know? You have very dark skin. Whereas light skin and European physical attributes [*les attributs européens physiques*], among Antilleans, is valued. I think that it's a difficult thing.
>
> *C.F.:* Did you suffer from that?
>
> *Youri:* I don't think I did directly, but, then, I have memories of when I was going to the Antilles. I feel like there were mocking remarks [*moqueries*] or people used certain words because I had the darkest skin, my nose wasn't thin enough, my lips were too thick,

> [and] I didn't have straight hair. That's something that you feel
> in the Antilles. . . . I have an African American friend who lives
> in Atlanta. . . . African Americans have [a desire to] search for
> Africa [*cette recherche de l'Afrique*]. . . . Antilleans have a hard time
> accepting their African side, in my opinion. For example, if you
> say to an Antillean, "Are you from Africa?" or "You are African,"
> he's going to take it the wrong way, because for him Antillean
> culture doesn't have anything to do with Africa. There are traces
> of Africa—that's true. But it's such a different culture; it's a way
> of living that is so different. . . . [A]side from my skin color and
> my ancestors, nothing is left to connect me to Africa.

This eloquent portrait illustrates how some Antilleans view the historical
legacies of slavery and the impact of the trade on racial attitudes among their
own group members. What is also clear from Youri's reflections is that my
presence, as an African American, prompted him to highlight the traits that
he thinks all descendants of slaves have in common—deportation from Africa and the valorization of whiteness—as well as particularities (i.e., his
impression that African Americans seek out their "African" side whereas
Antilleans seek to suppress or negate it).

In addition to defining blackness as phenotype, 27 percent of interviewees felt that being black was about being externally categorized as such.[10]
These respondents were hyper-aware of their visibility. Mélissa, a second-
generation migrant, said that being black meant being "visible. . . . [Y]ou
have to accept it and live with it. That's all." Cédric, a first-generation migrant, explained that despite his own universalism, others viewed him as
particular and "black":

> I'm black because people send me back to what I am [*on me renvoie à ce
> que je suis*], but fundamentally, I don't see color. . . . I'm a human being.
> I'm universal; I don't see my color. I'm a person like all people. It's like
> when you see someone who has a handicap and you remind him of his
> handicap. But that's not a [good] comparison. It's not the same thing. . . .
> I mean that it's how people are going to consider [me]. . . . It's the other
> person's gaze [*le regard de l'autre*].

Olivier, a second-generation migrant, also emphasized the gaze (*le regard*) of
others in his understanding of what it means to be black:

> You don't want to define yourself as black at first because it's other peo-
> ple's gaze that defines you. . . . When you're in the streets, you're not

going around telling yourself, "I'm black." It's other people's gaze and other people's insults that make you understand that you're black. It's when you cross the street and a car passes by [with someone saying], "Dirty nigger!"

The racism and discrimination that result from denigrating black categorization (e.g., being called a "dirty nigger") were also a theme in Antilleans' thin accounts of blackness. Thus, one respondent said that being black meant "having a lot of trouble finding a job," and another referred to blackness as a "disadvantage."

In the wake of recent black movements and policy debates over the possibility of introducing ethnic statistics or affirmative action, significant media attention has been directed to the term *noir* in France. The euphemistic use of the English word "black" instead of *noir* has emerged as a trend in popular culture, as well as in everyday life, prompting some of my respondents to comment on the desirability of being categorized as black or *noir*. Several respondents were critical of Nathalie, a student and second-generation migrant, who said that hearing the English word "black" got on her nerves:

> Why do they say "black"? It's considered violent to say *noir*, but saying "black" is cool and [means] that they have open minds. But, no! A *noir* is a *noir*, and it's not a big deal [*Un noir c'est un noir et c'est pas grave, quoi*]! . . . Why is there even hesitation [about what] to call us? What is the problem?

Stéphane, a first-generation migrant from Martinique, used the word *noir* as a descriptor for himself and other African Antilleans. He was critical of people in France who prefer using the English word "black" to using the French *noir*:

> I can't tolerate hearing "black," like they say today. . . . I think this word "black" is very hypocritical, because basically . . . they're looking for a word so that they don't [have to] say *noir*. . . . I saw a comedy routine by someone . . . who was saying that his language changed [when he came to France]. At first, when he got here, he thought he was black, and then he heard people saying, "No, I'm a person of color" [*homme de couleur*]. [So] he also said, "I'm a person of color." When [he] needed a black crayon [at school], he said to the kid next to him, "Excuse me, can you pass me the crayon of color?" [*Laughs.*] Today [people] say "black" because it's international; people speak English. It's a way to name yourself without saying *noir*.

Although he disliked using the English word "black" (which he saw as a way to avoid using the French term *noir*), he expressed considerable ambivalence about using *noir* to talk about himself, even though he had used it throughout the interview. When I asked him directly about whether he felt black, he hesitated:

C.F.: Do you think the word "Negro" is pejorative?

Stéphane: It's a word that I find difficult to use, because I'm used to hearing that the Negro is—that the Negro race is inevitably the one that, as the French writers said, it's impossible that a soul could exist in a black body. Who said that?

C.F.: I don't know.

Stéphane: Was it Rousseau or Voltaire? Or both? . . . Personally, ["Negro" is a word] that I have a hard time using.

C.F.: Do you prefer *noir*?

Stéphane: No. [But] anyway, I don't tolerate people saying "black." [*Laughter.*] . . . I feel like saying we're black because we belong to the Negro race or that we're black because we're Antillean. I don't know how to answer this question because we're a little bit mixed. . . . I'm going to say something a little hard about my mom. [*Laughs.*] . . . She kind of looks in blind awe at what the white race represents. . . . I remember one day when she was with me in Paris. She traveled a lot. She's tired now, but she used to come a lot, and every time she came here it was with [such] happiness. . . . [S]he thought everything was beautiful. That's the way she was. . . . I would say, "But no, Mama, there are also beautiful things in Martinique. What you're saying isn't true." . . . She was conditioned [that way]. . . . One day, I remember . . . we saw an African who was sitting on a bench, and I saw my mom. Her eyes were stuck on this man. I asked, "What's wrong, Mom?" She said, "It's impossible that this man is so black." That's when I became aware of the path that separates blacks in Africa from blacks in the Antilles. So can you still say that we're black—black? My mama was very—she is even lighter-skinned than I am. But can you still say that you're black when you think that way? I don't know.

C.F.: Do you consider yourself black?

Stéphane: I think that I am of the Negro race [*race négroïde*]—that is to say, I come from a mixture. I'm not white. That's clear in my head . . . because it's clear in everyone's head. Does that mean that I consider myself black? I don't know how to respond to the question. I'm not part of the white race. That's clear. But, on the other hand, does the black race have several stages of colors or social categories? I don't know.

Thick Conceptions of Blackness: History, Culture, Emotions, and Struggle

As we saw earlier, about a third of the sample also felt that blackness was a meaningful part of their identity. In general, their thick conceptions of blackness fell into four categories: (1) narratives of historical heritage (related to slavery, colonization, and African origin), (2) references to distinctively black culture, values, and perspectives, (3) emotions (principally pride and happiness), and (4) narratives about struggle (i.e., having "problems" or facing complications in one's everyday life).

In terms of history, one respondent told me that being black meant being part of a lineage that included slavery and stretched back to ancient Egypt:

> It's that I come from this land. For me, it's that being Negro is all of history, the history of the Pharaohs . . . , Isis, all of the men from Africa. Africa is history, you know? The history of slavery. For me, it's a source of pride.

Several respondents were vague when they mentioned blackness as a historical heritage. For example, they would say that being black meant "having a history" and would mention slavery only when I prompted them for more details.

Cultural understandings of blackness ranged from references to African or diasporic traditions, practices, and language (e.g., speaking Creole) to descriptions of distinctively black attitudes and styles. One first-generation respondent vividly described what made blacks culturally different from other groups:

> Well, first, it's skin color, and we're black [because of] cultural belonging [*appartenance culturelle*] . . . the style. We're black because it shows. [If] you look at [our] feet when we walk, you can tell if someone is black or not. We're black because of what we wear. We're black because we don't like dog shit on the sidewalks. . . . I think being black is a state of mind. It's definitely not just skin color.

Michel, a second-generation migrant, felt that being black was a personal attribute, a quality that made him distinctive. "It's part of my identity," he said. "I use the word 'black' often to mark this difference . . . , so it's part of my identity because I'm different."

Fred, a first-generation migrant from Guadeloupe who owned a gourmet food company, felt that blackness was more meaningful than simply skin tone or phenotype and emphasized positive emotions (i.e., feeling pleased with being black):

C.F.: What does being black mean?

Fred: Well, it's funny. . . . [W]hen I was in Guadeloupe, I wondered whether I was black, you know? I'm more [black] here. [*Laughs.*] But being black for me, it's a way to be different from others, so I'm really happy.

C.F.: Really happy? Why?

Fred: Because I don't like being like other people. . . . I think that being black today is very good, because there are things to show. I think black cultures have something to teach the world. . . . [W]ith the worldwide [economic] crisis today, maybe there are things linked to African culture . . . that can be used for rethinking the models that were being used, because I think we've really already shown the positive aspects of Europeans and Asians, but maybe we haven't sufficiently used what African culture could contribute to humanity. And the black comes from Africa. As much as I define myself as Creole, I don't deny an African affiliation. In traditional music, gwoka, we know where it comes from. Even in the Creole structure, we know that there's an African part in us, and I think that it's a good thing for humanity. I'm happy to be part of the population that may have something to contribute to others, because it doesn't have the same history. Also because this history—how do you say it? We have a history—not of a people, but of a population that was unjustly picked on and so has resources to contribute to others, and maybe now is the time to bring these resources to others.

In the social context of Guadeloupe (with its wide range of phenotypic distinctions), Fred questions whether he is really "black." Significantly, he feels less ambiguity about his categorization (i.e., thin blackness) in predominantly white Hexagonal France. Yet beyond this distinction (and his own awareness of being "different"), Fred believes that there are distinctively black traditions and values, rooted in Africa, that not only are a source of personal pride but also can potentially offer resources and tools to the world. Importantly, when he says, "We have a history," he is not only expressing black pride. He is also constructing a temporal understanding of racial belonging.

Blacks are not just people who existed in the past. They are also a group that he perceives as extant today, a group that shares a heritage.

Conclusion: French Descendants of Slaves

This chapter has considered the complex ways in which ordinary individuals from the French Caribbean islands imagine their belonging. Unpacking these dimensions of identification and classification helps elucidate possible areas of divergence and convergence among the self-understandings of ordinary people and the group boundaries produced by commemorators. French Caribbean migrants generally acknowledge slave ancestry as part of their genealogical heritage, but the majority of respondents did not *primarily* see themselves through that historical lens. Further, although the vast majority of interviewees self-categorized as black, most did not *primarily* frame blackness as the basis of their collective identity. Ordinary Antilleans do not easily fit into the ethnic or racial boxes that commemorators and politicians would impose on them. In part, this complexity reflects the historical legacies of color hierarchies and intermediate classifications in the Antilles. But Antilleans' ambiguity over their identities and the meaning of their ancestral ties is also fostered by the relative absence of institutionalized sources of knowledge about colonial history and culture in the French educational system (Fleming 2011), and the status of slavery as a *non-lieu de mémoire*—an absence rather than a presence—in French collective memory.[11] As a result, despite the existence of blackness and slave ancestry as elements of their self-concept, many French Caribbeans are ill equipped to make explicit connections between racism in the past and the exclusion they face in the present. In other words, they are unable to do the requisite time work. While they may indeed feel as though they belong to a group with a common history, they do not generally discuss that history in terms of race.

6

Legacies

It began with the closing of nearly all of Guadeloupe's 115 gas stations on January 21, 2009. By the next week, the entire island was paralyzed as a broad coalition of activists, labor unions, and members of civil society banded together to impose a general strike. They called themselves the Liyannaj kont Pwofitasyon (LKP), Creole for Collective against Exploitation.[1] The group soon formulated a popular, and controversial, rallying cry—"La Gwadloup sé tan nou, la Gwadloup a pa ta yo" (Guadeloupe belongs to us, Guadeloupe does not belong to you)—drawing a line in the sand between the predominantly black population and the white minority (the *békés*), who exercise disproportionate control over the economic and political structures in Guadeloupean society. Although the *békés* are less of a presence in Guadeloupe than in Martinique, the LKP *grévistes* blamed the persistence of colonial relations (and the continued domination by the mostly white elite) for a whole array of contemporary problems facing the majority population.

The forty-four-day strike was the longest and most entrenched social movement to hit Guadeloupe in the postcolonial era. Officially, the affair ended—with mixed results—when an agreement was signed by the LKP's leaders, the French government, and local officials on March 4, 2009. While Guadeloupe was the uncontested epicenter for the overseas uprisings that year, strikes and protests also emerged in Martinique, French Guiana, and Réunion Island over the same time period, as activists and ordinary people took to the streets to decry *la vie chère* (skyrocketing prices for first-necessity goods), high unemployment, and the pervasive sentiment that French politicians in Paris had failed to ensure the welfare and equal opportunity of its citizens in the French overseas departments (DOM). Élie Domota, the leader of the movement, emerged as a visible and charismatic figure in the French public sphere, speaking frequently in both standard French and Antillean Creole to the press and the crowds who came to hear him. His trenchant critique of modern-day colonialism and capitalism run amok in the islands earned him admiration from many Antilleans and censure from some whites, who were concerned that his claims smacked of "reverse racism."[2] Among other things, Domota came to be known for defiantly proclaiming that the movement would not allow "a band of *békés* to reestablish slavery" (*une bande de békés rétablir l'esclavage*), a statement that his opponents used to accuse him of instigating racial hatred. In his own defense, Domota explained that "saying Guadeloupe is and remains constructed on relations of class and race is shocking, although it is the truth."[3] To rectify lingering inequalities, the LKP issued an extensive list of more than one hundred demands that was remarkable as much for its breadth as for its attention to detail.[4]

In mainland France, people tuned into the overseas uprising through media reports, as well as a number of related television and radio programs. Canal+, a well-known cable channel, aired the documentary *Les derniers maîtres de la Martinique* (The Last Masters of Martinique) in mainland France on January 30, 2009, billing it as an exposé of the *békés* and their relation to the majority population. Controversy erupted when footage from the film showed Alain Huygues-Despointes, an eighty-two-year-old *béké*, expressing disappointment that historians did not explore "the good side of slavery" and affirming his desire that he and fellow whites "preserve their race." The show also called attention to the small size of the *béké* community (presented as 1 percent of the Martinican population) and its considerable grip on agricultural land and ownership of distribution monopolies and related businesses in the Antilles. Numerous talk shows and debates were held in mainland France to discuss the underlying causes of the DOM uprisings. On such occasions, most panelists portrayed contemporary dysfunctions in the islands as colonial legacies. For the first time in the postcolonial era, the economic structures of the DOM were placed at center stage for metropolitan audiences, garnering headlines in major newspapers and embroiling officials within Elysée Palace and the Overseas Ministry in almost daily—and very public—conflict with LKP leaders and their supporters in mainland France.

The 2009 strikes were an important historical moment. Activists in Guadeloupe and Martinique infused their mobilization with explicit references to the colonial past, including the history and legacies of enslavement. Back in the Paris region, I attended protests at which black and Caribbean people marched in solidarity with the LKP movement. Activists held signs linking colonialism and slavery to contemporary discrimination, such as one placard

Figure 6.1. *Protesters marching in Paris on February 21, 2009, at the height of the uprisings of 2009 in the French overseas departments. The banner reads, "Long Live the Struggle of Antillean Workers."*

Figure 6.2. *White protesters from the General Confederation of Labor joining blacks and people of color in Paris, February 21, 2009. The banner, which combines French and French Antillean Creole, reads, "Solidarity: Together, Together, to Win! Demands! Negotiations!"*

Figure 6.3. *A protester marching in solidarity with Antillean workers on February 21, 2009, holding a sign displaying broken chains.*

that read, "1492–2009: Profitasyon."[5] To what extent did this discourse reflect the temporal constructions of French Caribbeans on the mainland? To address this question, I examine how non-activist Antilleans describe the legacies of slavery. Discourse about the legacies of enslavement are an important arena in which racial temporality is being constructed in representations of slavery. However, the issues at stake are whether and the extent to which these legacies are actually understood in terms of race. Whereas commemorators depict slavery's reach into the present as wide-ranging (significant not only to Antilleans but also to national and transnational concerns), non-activists tend to describe slavery as more directly relevant to the islands where it took place and, less frequently, to African nations that have fared poorly in the postcolonial period. This suggests that ordinary Caribbean migrants do not perceive many clear causal links between their everyday experiences in metropolitan France and the history of French colonialism.

The Oxford English Dictionary defines the word "legacy" as "anything handed down by an ancestor or predecessor." When ordinary people and commemorators refer to the "legacies of slavery," they typically mean to call attention to the ways in which the slavery past continues to haunt the present. Legacy narratives are not always only about the causal effects of slavery; they also convey how actors frame the *contemporary relevance* of slavery (e.g., arguing that lingering discrimination against blacks justifies the commemoration of slavery, whether or not slavery was itself a direct cause of anti-black prejudice). The success or failure of commemorators' collective action depends, in large part, on their ability to legitimately argue that the slavery past and the silence that engulfed it both contribute to a host of contemporary problems. Legacy narratives about the present-day consequences of slavery are a common feature of commemorators' historical narratives, despite differences in the particular legacies groups frame as salient. Contemporary legacies are almost always described in negative terms and include everything from cultural attitudes, social behavior, and psychological disorders to power relations and economic conditions. Commemorators portray their own activities as *addressing* (though not necessarily solving) the problems they claim slavery has wrought.

Reconstructing the causal chain of events from the slavery past to present-day problems is crucial to the moral entrepreneurship of reparations advocates. Causal stories about the impact of the slavery past on the present are forms of "diagnostic framing" that activists use to characterize "a problem and the attribution of blame or causality" (Snow and Benford 1988: 198). Drawing on the social movements literature, Rhoda Howard-Hassmann (2004) argues that contemporary supporters of reparations for slavery have been largely unsuccessful, in part because of difficulties they face in framing their causal narratives.[6] For example, she argues that African Americans have not obtained compensation for slavery (unlike Japanese Americans interred during World War II) because the "victims of direct harms are dead, perpetrators are diffuse, some of the actual harms were legal at the time they were committed, and the causal chain of harm is long and complex" (Howard-Hassmann 2004: 823).

Interpreting the Legacies of Slavery

How do Caribbean migrants conceptualize the legacies of slavery? To what extent do they see racial processes and patterns as the consequences of slavery? I focus here on responses to the question "Do you think that there are still consequences or traces of the history of slavery?" though in some cases, respondents spontaneously provided discourse on this theme in earlier parts of the interview. This question was asked toward the end of the interview questions, after respondents had already been probed about their migration experiences, identities, experiences with racism, perceptions of group boundaries, and exposure to historical narratives about the slavery past.[7] The vast majority of non-activist respondents (53 of 59) described present-day consequences of the transatlantic slavery past.

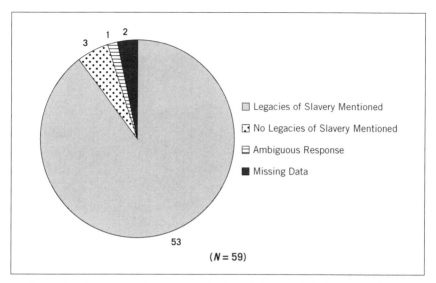

Figure 6.4. *Frequency of non-activists' acknowledgment of the legacies of slavery.*

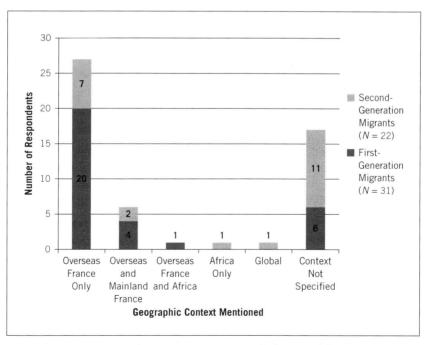

Figure 6.5. *Where non-activists situate the legacies of slavery.*

Legacy claims	First-generation migrants (*N* = 32)	Second-generation migrants (*N* = 27)	Total overall migrants (*N* = 59)
TABLE 6.1. TYPES OF LEGACY CLAIMS			
Economic and political dynamics	37.50%	37.04%	37.29%
Inter-group boundaries	46.88%	40.74%	44.07%
Intra-group dynamics	34.38%	37.04%	35.59%

Only three respondents, all of whom were second-generation migrants, felt that there were no lingering consequences of slavery. One of the first matters I attended to when analyzing the data was determining the geographic boundedness of respondents' discourse about the aftereffects of slavery. Did respondents think that the history of slavery played a role in their everyday lives in mainland France, or did they see these legacies as mostly restricted to the overseas departments and territories? Unpacking this important distinction is crucial for understanding how Antillean migrants might assess the relevance of commemorative activism and mnemonic entpreneurship for group members on both sides of the Atlantic. Among the first-generation migrants, 81 percent (25 of 31) provided a geographic context for their legacy discourse, compared with 50 percent (11 of 22) of the second generation. Of those who indicated a geographic context, the modal response for both generations was overseas France.[8]

What is remarkable about Antilleans' legacy discourse is not only the long list of consequences produced by the respondents but also the *scope* of their theories for how the slavery past affects the present. That is, respondents not only saw slavery as consequential in numerous ways; they also imagined slavery as historically relevant for a wide variety of domains. Indeed, as this chapter illustrates, at least one Antillean migrant in the sample described almost every area of social life, public and private, as linked to the legacies of slavery. After reading and inductively coding the responses, I identified three broad categories to capture the range of non-activists' claims about the consequences of slavery: (1) economic and political legacies, (2) inter-group legacies, and (3) intra-group legacies. Overall, respondents' legacy claims were about evenly distributed across these three categories. Support for each type of legacy was also fairly uniformly distributed in terms of generation status (see Table 6.1). It should be noted that these categories are ideal types. In reality, many of their dimensions are intertwined and necessarily interconnected.

Economic and Political Dynamics

Non-activists pointed to many contemporary aspects of economic and political relationships, particularly in the Antilles, as evidence of slavery's reach into the present. In terms of economic factors, non-activist migrants mentioned a range of examples, including the economic dominance of the white minority (*békés*), the use of the term "metropolitan" to describe mainland France, the prolongation of colonial hierarchies and relationships, and the production of wealth for whites (as a group) in the DOM and the French state more broadly. Political legacies were involved when respondents expressed the opinion that the Antilles (as a geographic region and as political entities) are not treated as fully part of the French nation—and Antilleans in particular are regarded as second-class citizens (*citoyens de seconde zone*). While most of these legacies were imagined in relation to the Antillean departments, two respondents did mention the impoverishment or colonization of Africa as economic and political legacies of slavery.

Pascal, a first-generation migrant from Martinique, observed:

> The traces [of slavery] are . . . the extension of the *békés*, who still possess most of the land. . . . Nobody—no government from the left or the right—has thought of rectifying this. But since they make a lot more money with importation and distribution [of goods] than crops, they do very little cultivation of the land, [and] as more and more of us go back there for retirement and all that, they sell the [land] for a fortune.

Similarly, Agnès, a second-generation migrant from Guadeloupe, pointed to the economic prominence of the white minority and the racialization of power dynamics in the Antilles:

> It's a society that is colonial, so it is based on the . . . [c]lass relationship but, at the same time, it is based on the relationship of race [*rapport de race*], even if we don't want to racialize the problem. When people speak of the *békés* in the Antilles, it's because there are blacks who are bosses [*patrons*] in the Antilles, but not really the same way the *békés* are. The [black] guy is the boss of his business, surely, but not of the land. So there is the weight of this relationship.

Guillaume, a first-generation migrant from Martinique, thought that social relationships and hierarchies of the slavery period persisted after abolition until the present day:

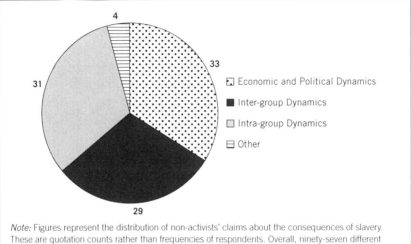

Note: Figures represent the distribution of non-activists' claims about the consequences of slavery. These are quotation counts rather than frequencies of respondents. Overall, ninety-seven different legacy claims were made by respondents. The three major categories (Economic and Political Dynamics, Inter-group Dynamics, and Intra-group Dynamics) were inductively developed from coding the claims. The figure shows that when all of the respondents' perceptions of legacies are taken into account, there is a fairly even distribution of claims among the three major categories, suggesting that Antilleans believe the slavery past is more or less equally explanatory for these three realms of social life. Further analysis would be necessary to determine whether this distribution would change once normalizing for respondents with multiple intra-category claims.

Figure 6.6. *Non-activists' legacy claims.*

When there was the abolition of slavery, um, the slaves became free. And for whom were they supposed to work? For the colonizers! The colonizers . . . hired them, so to speak, on their properties for them to work. So the slave-master relationship persisted anyway. That is, the colonizers still behaved like masters . . . [I]t stayed the same from 1848 until 1946, so, uh, it's rather, it's basically a century that we had the same representations . . . and it hasn't been broken. In 1946, it was the department and departmentalization. There, it was really necessary to try and change the system, but it persisted. . . . There is still this master-slave relationship. . . . I'm weighing my words [*je pèse mes mots*], but there is still a small part of the population that gobbles up all the wealth, and they're the descendants of the colonizers.

Another first-generation migrant from Martinique, Antoine, pointed to the terminology used to distinguish mainland from overseas France as evidence of colonial legacies: "This was already talked about it during the strikes in the Antilles—the fact that people use the term 'metropole.' 'Metropole' goes back to [the] dependencies, territories. It's necessary to say 'continental' France." His comments underscore how the 2009 strikes in the French Caribbean produced temporal narratives about the legacies of colonialism and slavery, allowing some people to mentally link past and present oppression.

Labor Relations

A connected, though distinct, theme in respondents' discourse about economic legacies is their description of contemporary labor relations in the Antilles. First-generation migrants cited attitudes toward work as consequences of slavery more than second-generation migrants did, most likely because members of the first generation had greater exposure to labor disputes and work routines in the islands. For example, Alexandre, a first-generation migrant from Martinique, was typical of many respondents who suggested that Antilleans continue to experience a form of slavery due partly to their economic domination:

> Today we're still undergoing slavery in a certain way [*aujourd'hui encore on subit l'esclavage d'une certaine façon*] . . . economically, because in Martinique we still have the *békés* who possess everything [*detiennent tout*].

He went on to give a specific example of why he thought contemporary labor relationships were structured by the colonial past:

Alexandre: When you analyze the . . . functioning of the country . . . , privileges are transmitted from generation to generation. . . . The relations to work are rather peculiar—employer to employee. It's rather peculiar.

C.F.: What, for example?

Alexandre: For example, in the sense that it's like what I see in a number of people living in the country. When he employs you, the employer, doesn't assess you in terms of . . . your competence. He makes you understand that the job is a privilege that he's giving you. So if he offers you a salary considerably beneath your profile, your competence, you should thank him rather than negotiate with him.

C.F.: It's a kind of paternalism?

Alexandre: It's a privilege that comes from this period, because, you know, there was slavery, so we were forced to work in the fields. Afterward, there was the colonial period between. You have abolition of slavery and departmentalization. How did that happen? In any case, there was no choice: it was still the sugarcane fields . . . and the employer, what he was doing—the people came to offer their work, and he was saying, "I want you, I want you, [and] I don't want you."

C.F.: It was a privilege to work.

Alexandre: There you go. Completely. And it still happens a little bit like that today. I'm going to tell you—I hope I'm not going to shock you, but, unfortunately, it still happens like this. . . . Certain employers, with regard to women, [say], "When I employ you, I'm making you the privilege of having a job, so really, if I ask you for a little service—"

C.F.: She should feel obliged.

Alexandre: There you go. That's why really absurd things sometimes happen in the country, because it's a privilege that the other gives to the woman. . . . All of the employers hate people who make demands [*qui revendiquent*], who talk too much.

Robert was the only second-generation migrant who described legacies in terms of attitudes toward work. When I asked him whether he thought there were still traces of slavery today, he replied:

> Yes, because there are still people who will say, "I'm not going to work for that white." And then, it depends on the [type of] white. . . . If it's your friend with whom you've worked, your longtime friend, you'd never say that. But if it's an old racist guy [*un vieux mec raciste*], yes, it's sure that you are not going to work for him.

He then went on to clarify that he doesn't share this attitude because he grew up in mainland France, underscoring differences between members of the first and second generations:

> From my point of view . . . I don't have this closed aspect to my culture [*j'ai pas ce coté ferme sur ma culture*]. . . . [H]aving been immersed like this in multiculturalism since I was little [*d'être baigné comme ça dans le multiculturel depuis tout petit*], you have a hard time closing yourself off in a single clan.

Social Unrest

Given that many of my interviews with non-activists were conducted in the spring of 2009, during the LKP strikes, the topic of colonial continuities and social unrest in the DOM was in the headlines. Seven respondents (four first-generation migrants and three second-generation migrants) mentioned the strikes explicitly when they described the legacies of slavery. In this context, Melissa, a first-generation migrant from Martinique, mentioned the "conflict in the Antilles" as an indicator of the presence of the colonial past. She went on to describe ongoing economic inequalities:

> Normally, there was the abolition of slavery, but in a certain way they continue . . . to have slaves. This continues in a different manner because these are people who have all the big companies, big things, so there's a certain form of exploitation.

While race may be implicit here, it is not the dominant framing in her description of the impact of slavery on the islands. Instead, she focuses on economic domination.

Inter-group Dynamics

Many respondents, particularly members of the first generation, also described the consequences of slavery in terms of inter-group boundaries. Interviewees mentioned the existence of racial distinctions (i.e., beliefs in racial differences between groups) and feelings of resentment, hatred, and distrust on the part of blacks and whites that create boundaries and division in both overseas and mainland France. It is likely that such claims were more salient among first-generation migrants due to their socialization in the Antilles and their exposure to racial grievances stemming from slavery in the DOM. One first-generation migrant from Guadeloupe stated that the slavery past affected blacks by shaping their mentalities and creating resentment against (white) French. "Frankly, I think that the Antilleans can [be] very anti-French," the respondent said. "In my family . . . there are a lot of people who prefer to despise them."

Alain, a first-generation migrant from Martinique, thought that the persistence of racial distinctions and anti-black racism, passed by whites from generation to generation, was linked to the slavery past:

> *Alain:* I imagine that there are still places where there are individuals who think that there is a profound difference between a white individual and a black individual. Yes, there are places where a real difference is made. . . . It could be linked to treatment, bad treatment. Maybe. Yes, discrimination exists.
>
> *C.F.:* Do you think that it's linked to slavery?
>
> *Alain:* Yes, because [slavery] positioned a group of individuals in their way of thinking. If, as a little one, you are taught to think

that you are strong [*fort*] and that others are different, then obviously—well, since [you were] little, you were told that blacks are less strong, less intelligent, that they're lazy. So the first black you meet, you will already . . . see him that way.

Clara, a first-generation migrant from Guadeloupe, saw inter-group boundaries in overseas and mainland France as tied to slavery:

> Black-white racism is present in the Antilles, but it's also present here. For me, it's really the direct consequence of slavery. It's that, in some way, maybe unconsciously, the whites will . . . really consider that we are a form of underclass [*nous somme une forme de sous-classe*], a lower category of people. We were once at their service. The black, he will . . . be against the white because, he will think, "This is what we've been through." I think that, yes, the direct consequence of slavery is a form of racism and contempt [*racisme et mepris*].

Some second-generation migrants also believed that slavery was responsible for contemporary racial tensions. For example, Anne, who was raised in metropolitan France, thought that blacks' resentment toward whites and whites' anti-blackness were both rooted in slavery:

> There are a lot of Antilleans who are vindictive toward whites because, to them, whites have never treated us the way they should. There is really this mentality. . . . There are a lot of associations where they talk about the memory of slavery, of not falling back into slavery, all of these things. I tell myself that if there were no more traces [of slavery], then there would not be these kinds of associations, this way of speaking that there is between people who are very vindictive. . . . I sometimes wonder whether there are people who don't feel that black women of a certain age make really good housekeepers [*femmes de ménage*], that it's in their genes, that they know how to take care of a house. Is it because their mothers and grandmothers and their grandmothers took care of the houses [of whites]? I don't know. Sometimes I ask myself about the assets and attributes of black women— having a lot of kids, knowing how to take care of a house, knowing how to cook. I wonder whether people would not expect white women of the same age to have these characteristics. So is it something that comes from the fact of keeping people on a certain level?

Antilleans' recognition of racism as a historical continuity in the experiences of their group and elaborate discourses about the continuing legacies of colonialism and slavery contrast with historical imagination of Surinamese women studied by Philomena Essed (1991: 92), who generally understood their encounters with racism as ahistorical and who lacked an extensive cultural repertoire for understanding connections between present discrimination and the colonial past. Making these kinds of temporal connections is not easy. It requires both time and effort to stitch together mental links between the racial past and the present.

Intra-group Dynamics: Colorism and Lack of Solidarity

Pierre, a first-generation migrant from Guadeloupe, included, among numerous legacy claims, the notion that "[color] hierarchy among blacks [*hiérarchisation chez les noirs*]" had produced a wound (*une blessure*) among members of his group today. In explaining the wound, he said:

> The heritage of the wound is that they told us all the time that we were shit, we were savages, we were from Africa. . . . The only value we could have was in serving the master, and the masters are the whites. It's purity; it's this; it's that. . . . A black man wasn't going to heaven unless he respected his master. . . . That's where this hierarchy among blacks comes from with regard to skin color. And so, this importance of having white blood—do you see what I'm saying? It's the importance of having white blood and all that. That's a mark of slavery. It's a wound.

Corinne, from Guadeloupe, felt that the legacies of slavery included anti-black attitudes among Antilleans. She provided this example:

> The son of one of my mother's colleagues just became the manager of Crédit Agricole in Point-à-Pitres [Guadeloupe]. There were people who [said], "I'm not going to work for a nigger!" . . . They were black! You see? It's all these little expressions that we have, on a daily basis. When there is some bullshit—when someone sees a person throw a piece of paper out the window of his car, [the person says], "Hey—there's another nigger. Look at what that nigger did." We're in a perpetual—how do you say it? Um, we're destroying ourselves [*On s'autodétruit*]![9]

Thomas, a second-generation migrant of Martinican heritage, commented:

> They talk to you about mixed people [*métis*], mulattos [*mulâtres*], *chabins*. . . . [It's] divide and conquer, choosing [from] all the blacks—for example, making the one who is the most light-skinned the boss over the oth-

ers. That gives him a certain importance, so he is happy, . . . [but it is also] creating . . . divisions among blacks. This is what I call the dysfunctions of slavery [*la tare de l'esclavage*]. . . . It's the heritage in negative terms— the trauma [*le traumatisme*], the aftermath [*les séquelles*]—and it is still present.

Thomas imagined blacks as a group ridden with self-defeating division linked to color hierarchies that whites intentionally imposed during the colonial period. This is a familiar refrain throughout the French Caribbean, and it can be found in Frantz Fanon's unsparing critique of white supremacy, "negro-phobia," and colorism in the Antilles:

> In Europe the black man has a function: to represent shameful feeling, base instincts and the dark side of the soul. . . . It is normal for the Antil-lean to be a negrophobe. Through his collective conscience, the Antillean has assimilated all the archetypes of the European. . . . [W]e read white books and gradually assimilate the prejudices, the myths and the folklore that come from Europe. . . . [T]he Antillean is a slave to this cultural imposition. After being a slave of the white man, he enslaves himself. (Fanon 1967: 167–168)

Many of the commemorative organizers and ordinary people I interviewed echoed Fanon's analysis of internalized oppression. In a similar vein, Alexan-dre, the first-generation migrant from Martinique who earlier described eco-nomic legacies, also felt that the "psychological and mental" aftermath of slavery produced color hierarchies and prevented Antilleans from being able to cooperate with one another. He provided a detailed historical narrative about color categories during slavery to back up his claims:

> My mother, my father . . . I thank them. They always talked to us about that period. They transmitted certain values to us. They always demon-strated to us that um, in fact, we are human beings. . . . [T]hey talked to us about slavery. . . . I had the opportunity to go with them to a sugarcane field, where they explained things to us so we could understand. In fact, it's visible [*ca se voit*]. There are still traces between the sugarcane fields and the master's house. . . . I had the opportunity to see the overseers [*les commandeurs*] in the sugarcane fields. The commanders were the ones who were in the fields supervising the cutting . . . other blacks . . . very light-skinned [*le teint tres clair*]. You see? It was light skin that elevated you in society. That is, perhaps one out of a thousand overseers was black. But someone who was light-skinned could not be sent into the fields; he

was, at minimum, an overseer. As a child, when you see the way people talk to one another, inevitably you ask your parents questions. My parents explained to us why things were done in this way, why certain people behaved in this or that way. Finally, it's by transmission. You see? . . . We are still in our heads. We are imprisoned, stuck in our heads. And . . . we continue to say [things like] "saved skin" [*la peau échappée*] or "nigger plot" [*complot nègre*], a dog's plot. . . . It means that any association of blacks is . . . a failure in a certain way, you see? We can't do anything together. . . . All of this shows the division there is among us, and all of this is due to our slavery past, because they always tried to divide the blacks, as everyone knows. . . . [I]n our subconscious [*l'inconscient*] . . . [there is] the idea that black is not good. . . . It's something that is still present in our heads, in our minds.

This account of slavery's psychological consequences is similar to arguments advanced in E. Franklin Frazier's *The Negro Family in the United States* (1966), as well as in the classic *The Wretched of the Earth* (1968), in which Frantz Fanon forcefully argues that colonial oppression engendered economic, social, and psychological dysfunctions on both the colonizer and the colonized. The notion that the wages of colonial domination were both material and mental was a point of agreement for Fanon and Jean-Paul Sartre, who wrote the preface for Fanon's book (Jules-Rosette 2007).[10]

Group Members' Beliefs, Behavior, and Identity

In addition to depicting the slavery past as producing intra-group conflict, many non-activist Antilleans felt that slavery was partially responsible for producing particular orientations and negative behavior that have shaped group members' ways of thinking. The most frequent type of group belief identified by non-activists was that, as a result of slavery and colonization, Antilleans had come to regard themselves in the same negative and pejorative way that whites and other outgroups had defined them. In other words, they thought that slavery had produced what Pierre Bourdieu described as *symbolic violence*—the process by which members of dominated groups come to internalize the external categorizations produced by dominant groups. Using the case of gender relations in Kabyle society, Bourdieu describes symbolic violence this way:

The dominated apply categories constructed from the point of view of the dominant to the relations of domination, thus making them appear as natural. This can lead to a kind of systematic self-deprecation, even self-denigration, visible in particular, as has been seen, in the representation that Kabyle women have of their genitals as something deficient, ugly, even repulsive . . . and, more generally, in their adherence to a demeaning image of woman. Symbolic violence is instituted through the adherence that the dominated cannot fail to grant to the dominant (and therefore to the domination) when, to shape her thought of him, and herself, or rather, her thought of her relation with him, she has only cognitive instruments that she shares with him and which, being no more than the embodied form of the relation of domination, cause that relation to appear as natural; or, in other words, when the schemes she applies in order to perceive and appreciate herself, or to perceive and appreciate the dominant (high/low, male/female, white/black, etc.), are the product of the embodiment of the—thereby naturalized—classifications of which her social being is the product. (Bourdieu 2001: 35)

It is important to note that Bourdieu conceived of symbolic violence as a form of domination that unwittingly bedevils victims—that is, dominated individuals come to appropriate demeaning images of themselves produced by the dominant group *without realizing that this process is taking place.* In a similar way, non-activist Antilleans typically described fellow group members as having bought into negative representations of themselves (or having acquired self-defeating behavior) in an unconscious manner, through the intergenerational transmission of social relations produced during the period of slavery. Such accounts are a form of "folk psychology," which Paul Churchland (1984: 56) defines as "our common-sense terms for mental states." Respondents draw on lay understandings of mental functioning and behavior to explain how the legacies of slavery affected other group members. Importantly, respondents never described themselves as current "victims" of such symbolic violence. Although they sometimes acknowledged that they, too, had internalized negative beliefs about their group, the respondents almost never indicated that they currently held such attitudes. Instead, they portrayed themselves as "awakened" (DeGloma 2010), routinely pointing to other group members as misguided people who were unknowingly contributing to their own demise by stigmatizing blacks or Antilleans. This inculcation of white racist attitudes by blacks was expressed earlier by Pierre, who observed, whites "told us all the time that we were shit, we were savages, we were from Africa," thus producing a "wound" among members of his group.

In describing the legacies of slavery, Thomas, a second-generation migrant from Martinique, illustrated how he believed some blacks had come to believe in black inferiority and white superiority:

I believe enormously in everything that is subliminal . . . , that conditions the behavior of each person. Let us take a very simple thing: . . . [y]ou watch a commercial, for example. . . . The presence of blacks in commercials represents the [group's] buying power [*pouvoir d'achat*]. So it really sends a message. . . . [T]he moment you're represented, it's to sell bananas or Banania. I'm persuaded that this constructs a man, because one constructs oneself with all that comes from the exterior. It's part of our upbringing [*notre éducation*]. From the moment I send this message, you begin to give yourself the idea of who is dominant and who is dominated. That's why this dysfunction of slavery, if they explain to you by telling you that—really, the white is stronger than the black. They explain to you that things change, . . . but if you look closely [at] the political landscape . . . , there are only white leaders, politicians.

Sébastien, a first-generation migrant from Martinique, felt that there were "immense" mental and behavioral consequences of slavery:

It's the slave's thinking [*la pensée d'esclave*], not being able to project oneself as a free man [*un homme libre*]. . . . Reflecting as a slave, behaving as a slave, not realizing that the chain is broken prevents a lot of Antilleans from going toward other populations, from going [even] to themselves and constructing something unique. It blocks them. The Antillean remains in this idea that the white is all-powerful, the *békés* are all-powerful, the Antillean doesn't have a chance. He hates the Antillean. There's still too much of that.

Finally, several respondents mentioned that group members' efforts to memorialize slavery and define their identity also represented the present-day "marks" of the colonial past.

Family Structure and Gender Relations

Somewhat surprisingly, non-activists rarely mentioned contemporary gender relations or family structure as aftereffects of slavery, even though such narratives are at the heart of highly visible commemorative groups such as CM98. Alexandre was one of only two first-generation migrants who mentioned problems between Antillean men and women as derived from slavery. "Today, we're going through the consequences, because the relationship between women and men—it doesn't work [*ca ne tient pas*]," he said. Stéphane, a first-generation migrant from Martinique, mentioned the popular perception among Antilleans that skirt-chasing men are not faithful because of slavery:

> *Stéphane:* In Martinique . . . , I often hear people say, "It's a consequence of our slavery past." . . . People are able to explain a lot of things with the past, even things that have no relation to the past.
> *C.F.:* Can you remember a few examples?
> *Stéphane:* Of course! A cheating man [*un homme volage*] in Martinique is a cheater, of course, because of slavery. The man was there to procreate. Then they took away his woman, because she was not *his* woman—it was his master who had chosen her. . . . So it's normal that the man in Martinique is a cheater.
> *C.F.:* Do you think that's correct?
> *Stéphane:* Of course! [*Laughs.*]
> *C.F.:* You think it's true that [slavery and unfaithfulness are] linked?
> *Stéphane:* I don't know. I'm not enough of a sociologist to know, but—I don't know. But, in any case, things are explained that way. I hear things like that.

Only one second-generation migrant (Virginie) linked contemporary family or gender dynamics to slavery. In particular, she felt that Antillean families were often composed of passive men and very independent women, a pattern she noted among her grandparents and parents, and in her own experience. Her argument for the historical link was that enslaved men were forced to be "producers" and were prevented from being husbands and fathers. As a result, they were unable to affirm themselves in their role as men because they could not protect their women and families.

Perceiving Slavery as Inconsequential

Having demonstrated the broad range of legacy claims made by non-activist Antilleans, I now consider the perspectives of the few respondents who said they did not think slavery had any present-day consequences. Three interviewees expressed this view. Significantly, they were all second-generation migrants. Maryse, a second-generation migrant of Martinican heritage, explained her reasoning:

> Perhaps certain people could have consequences, but for my part, I don't have any. In fact, the problem is that, from the moment they stop holding you back from advancing, you cannot blame [them]. . . . I think that if France had not allowed [us] . . . to have an education like everyone else,

had not helped us financially on the basis of [our] resources, not our color or origin, there would have been traces [of slavery]. But finally we were treated like the French, so, well, that's my opinion. Another person would not say that.

From her perspective, members of her group were treated like everyone else in France. As a result, they had no historical grievances or contemporary problems that were rooted in slavery. Her opinion contrasted sharply with those of the vast majority of non-activist respondents, who felt that racism and discrimination operated in mainland and overseas France.

Conclusion: Constructing Continuities

On February 21, 2009, I attended a protest in Paris organized by Continuité Liyannaj kont Pwofitasyon (CLKP), the group that represented the LKP movement in mainland France. As is always the case in France, estimates of the size of the crowd varied widely. Activists claimed there were thirty thousand participants, while the police acknowledged ten thousand. The truth appeared to be somewhere in between. In the crowd I met up with Alain Bidjeck, president of Orig'in Association, who had come to show his support for the strikes in the DOM. The CGT, which frequently critiques capitalism in its activism for workers' rights, was visibly present as unionists held up banners calling for solidarity with the LKP movement. The slavery past was explicitly present in the minds of many people in the street. One man held up a large white sign that read "1492–2009: Profitasyon" and showed three black figures huddled together, as if in the bottom of a slave ship, while two other men held a banner on which they had written in squiggly black letters, "Guiana with the Antilles: Same combat. Today the chains are in our heads, no longer on our feet." The presence of these two temporal claims—one underlining the legacy of slavery as contemporary exploitation and the other pointing to present-day "mental" or "psychological" chains—demonstrates the range and salience of legacy claims in the worldviews of people from overseas France.

Antilleans' awareness of the legacies of slavery in the French Caribbean constitutes an important source of knowledge that has been largely suppressed in the metropole. The findings here point to a running theme in this book: the labor (and uncertainty) involved in constructing claims about the impact of the slavery past on the present. Most non-activists I interviewed thought that transatlantic slavery had an impact on their present social interactions and the behavior of their group members, particularly those still living in the islands where slavery took place. However, it is troubling for the student of antiracism that respondents did not often describe these continuities in terms of race or racism. These findings must be read in the context of France's history of minimizing or misrepresenting slavery and colonization in the educational curriculum. Elsewhere, I have shown that two-thirds of the French Caribbeans interviewed in this study reported learning very little about the transatlantic slave trade at school (Fleming 2011). These dynamics of racial and temporal disconnection are not restricted to the French Caribbean case. The sociologist France Winddance Twine found Afro-Brazilians to be relatively silent on the links between slavery and anti-black racism. Twine argues that this silence reflects a contradictory tension between Afro-Brazilians' partial acknowledgment of their slave ancestry and their choice "not to retain memories of African slave ancestors" (Twine 1998: 119). Although my data do not allow me to determine whether French Caribbeans deliberately forget the racial legacies of slavery, these interviews suggest a reluctance—or inability—to make connections among slavery, colonialism, and present-day racism in mainland France. Without this explicit racial and temporal framing, it is difficult to imagine how French Caribbeans and other Afro-descended people can recognize and respond to systemic racism in mainland France.

7

Reparations

If—as commemorative activists and ordinary Antilleans agree—slavery has produced socioeconomic dysfunctions that stretch into the present, then the question of reparations is concerned with determining what, if anything, can be done about this damage. Examining the reparations discourse of activists and ordinary people reveals how they imagine possible lines of action for addressing the consequences of the slavery past. Within the context of French white supremacy, however, certain lines of reparative action are framed by politicians as more plausible than others. This was made clear yet again when, in 2015, French president François Hollande suggested that France owes a "moral"—not economic—debt to Haiti.

This chapter proceeds as follows. I begin with a theoretical overview of research on reparations. Next, I show how commemorative organizers broadly support symbolic interventions for repairing the past but express mixed support for economic restitution. Then I show how non-activists justify their support for (or criticism of) slavery reparations. Support for symbolic repair (i.e., through pedagogical outreach, public apologies, and ceremonies) was shared by both commemorators and non-activists, and interviewees almost universally rejected the desirability and feasibility of individual payments to present-day Afro-Caribbeans. On this point, commemorators seem to reflect the views of non-activists.

Theorizing Reparations

According to Nicolas Dodier and Janine Barbot (2009: 105–106), reparations can include, among other forms, "the sanctioning of responsible parties (legal sanction, moral condemnation, vengeance, retaliation, etc.), compensation (financial or otherwise), facing what was lost or the origin of the suffering (under the form of commemoration, evocation, for example)." I use the term "symbolic repair" to refer to instances in which actors advocated for recognition through educational outreach, affirmation of national inclusion, apologies and expressions of regret, acknowledgment by responsible parties, signaling of respect, and memorialization. Eric Posner and Adrian Vermeule (2003: 691–692) distinguish "reparations schemes" from other types of remediation on the basis of three criteria. First, while ordinary legal interventions involve transfers from "an identified individual wrongdoer to an identified individual victim of the wrong," reparations schemes may involve transfers between collective or unidentifiable wrongdoers and victims.[1] Second, reparations schemes involve "remediation of or compensation for past injustice" and are therefore, motivated by "backward-looking" justifications rather than "forward-looking" aspirations (i.e., measures primarily designed to expand the opportunity structure or bring about redistributive justice).

A historical irony of French Atlantic slavery is that reparations were, in fact, obtained following abolition. As explained in previous chapters, compensation was directed to the former slave owners rather than to former slaves. In his massive volume *Des colonies françaises: Abolition immédiate de l'esclavage*, Victor Schoelcher defended compensating the colonists for their losses on the grounds that "if the fact of possessing slaves is illegitimate, it is no less legal." Schoelcher also portrayed colonists' desire for compensation as rational, given their pecuniary interests and the dismantling of their economic power: "It is difficult to make a man understand the philosophical necessity of his ruin . . . for the elevation of a race that he is accustomed to despising" (Schoelcher 1842: 260). He apparently believed that compensation would serve to pacify the former slave owners and maintain order in the colonies[2] and blamed the metropole, rather than slave owners, for the sins of slavery.[3] When the provisional government approved the abolitionary decree on April 27, 1848, it also rejected three proposals by Schoelcher that were designed to compensate the freed slaves: (1) granting compensation to freed slaves, (2) providing freed slaves with a plot of land, and (3) redistributing land that had been formerly claimed by colonists (Schmidt 2003: 310). The French Republic did, however, implement its plan to transfer funds to colonists to offset the costs of abolition. Compensation for colonists in Guadeloupe, Martinique, French Guiana, and Réunion totaled 126 million francs (Régent 2007: 288).[4] Before abolition, a precedent for compensating the practitioners of slavery had already been established when France demanded and obtained an enormous sum of money following their defeat in the wake of the Haitian Revolution. In this case, France initially required Haiti to pay

150 million gold francs over the course of five years (30 million each year).[5] Some estimate that the sum Haiti was forced to pay France for its independence would total nearly $20 billion today.[6]

Historically, there are several precedents for groups obtaining economic forms of restitution for historical wrongdoing (Posner and Vermeule 2003: 696–697). The first successful reparations case in the United States occurred in 1946, when Native American tribes received almost $1 billion in compensation for loss of land during colonial expansion. Japanese Americans who had been interred in prison camps during World War II were awarded a total of $1.6 billion in 1988, and victims of the Tuskegee syphilis experiments (1932–1972) received $9 million in reparations in 1997. Internationally, the best-known cases of financial reparations revolve around the Holocaust, with Germany paying an estimated 100 billion deutsche marks to the State of Israel between 1947 and 1992. The movement to obtain economic reparations for transatlantic slavery is most often associated with the United States. Indeed, unlike in France, where public debate over reparations remains very marginal and not widely diffused, efforts to obtain reparations for slavery have occupied a central position in black political thought in the United States even before abolition (Verdun 1993).[7] Indeed, as Michael Dawson and Rovana Popoff (2004: 48) point out, "From Frederick Douglass to Martin Luther King, international organizations ranging from Marcus Garvey's UNIA [Universal Negro Improvement Association] to Pan African Congresses held in the 1990s, ideologies from those of W.E.B. Du Bois to Malcolm X, the idea of the reparations in real material terms, not only symbolically, has been a constant within Black discourse." More recent manifestations of the U.S. reparations movement include the founding of the National Coalition of Blacks for Reparations in America (N'COBRA) in 1987, whose singular objective consists of "obtaining reparations for African descendants in the U.S."[8] Reparations emerged as a hot issue in the American public sphere in the late 1990s, and in 2001 the National Association for the Advancement of Colored People named reparations one of its top priorities (Michelson 2002). While such efforts have been soundly rejected by the U.S. courts, they nonetheless have broad support among African Americans.[9] Using survey data, Dawson and Popoff (2004) show that 67 percent of African Americans support the idea of monetary compensation, compared with only 4 percent of European Americans. Dawson and Popoff's important study is one of the very few to assess the views of descendants of slaves regarding economic and symbolic reparations for slavery. While a plethora of scholarly work examines moral and legal arguments for and against reparations (Berg 2009; Conley 2003; Verdun 1993), empirical research on contemporary attitudes toward reparations for slavery is very limited. We can, however, derive insight about public attitudes from a study commissioned in 1997 by the television network ABC and a survey conducted in 2004 by communications scholars (Campo, Mastin, and Frazer 2004).[10] Because these studies rely on survey data, we know very little about the historical narratives and moral arguments that lie behind blacks' support for (or opposition to) reparations. Outside the United States, even less is known about how ordinary people evaluate the enduring legacies of slavery and the possibilities for restitution, as many studies on the memory of slavery throughout the Black Atlantic focus almost exclusively on the claims and representations of mnemonic entrepreneurs and participants in commemorative activity (Bruner 1996; Clarke 2006; Fanelli 2005; Holsey 2004; Vergès 2004).

The activists and officials I interviewed generally argued that the aftermath of slavery can be repaired to some extent. Yet they also maintained that reparations can never be fulfilled or exhausted because the moral damage that was done is permanent and the suffering of the dead is irreversible. It is for this reason that commemorative organizations often portray their work as ongoing and necessarily unfinished. In this respect, commemorators can be understood as "moral entrepreneurs" (Becker 1991)—actors who seek to impose and institutionalize their version of the appropriate moral order. As they gain recognition for their claims, commemorators remain committed to an ongoing effort to impose their moral order, like the "rule enforcers" Howard Becker (1991: 157) describes:

> In justifying the existence of his position, the rule enforcer faces a double problem. On the one hand, he must demonstrate to others that the problem still exists: the rules he is supposed to enforce have some point, because infractions occur. On the other hand, he must show that his attempts at enforcement are effective and worthwhile, that the evil he is supposed to deal with is in fact being dealt with adequately. Therefore, enforcement organizations, particularly when they are seeking funds, typically oscillate between two kinds of claims. First, they say that by reason of their efforts the problem they deal with is approaching solution. But, in the same breath, they say the problem is perhaps worse than ever (though through no fault of their own) and requires renewed and increased effort to keep it under control. Enforcement officials can be more vehement than anyone else in their insistence that the problem they are supposed to deal with is still with us, the fact is more with us than ever before.

Becker's account suggests that rule enforcers legitimate their existence to pursue their rational interests. Yet there are other explanations for why slavery commemorators often frame their quest for justice as perpetually unfinished business. The first has to do with the historical trajectory of African-descended populations in the postcolonial period. To the extent that descendants of slaves in particular, and blacks more generally, continue to find themselves on the bottom of the socioeconomic status hierarchy and disproportionately disadvantaged throughout the West (Patterson 2005), slavery commemorators view Afro-Caribbean marginalization as an ongoing problem that is unlikely to be resolved easily or quickly. The second has to do with the extent to which individuals view slavery and its aftermath as damage that can be treated as commensurate with *or* ameliorated by particular interventions (i.e., material compensation or symbolic repair). Doubt over the reparability of the horrors of slavery were expressed even before abolition, as Stephen Best and Saidiya Hartman (2005) point out. Those involved in the abolitionist movement (including enslaved people themselves) argued for justice even as they acknowledged that no measures could ever absolve practitioners of slavery for the wrongs that had been committed.

Commemorators' Reparations Claims

Of the semi-directed interviews I held with commemorators, forty-three respondents described the positions of their group with regard to reparations for slavery.[11] Reparations discourse was gleaned from not only interview data but also published materials produced by commemorative organizations. Overall, commemorators expressed broad support for symbolic repair and mixed attitudes toward economic restitution. Some commemorators felt that the Taubira Law was a step forward but was not sufficient—thus, the need for their organizations to continue their memory work. Moreover, seven of forty-three commemorators explicitly criticized the Taubira legislation for its failure to address the question of reparations. In fact, an early draft of the law did include a provision that would have established a committee to explore the possibility of reparations. As Doris Garraway (2008: 382) points out:

> Taubira's initial draft lacked much of the ambiguity and disavowal of the final version, notably in its definition of "European powers" as the perpetrators of the crime in question, and the provision in Article 5 for an exploratory committee to examine the question of reparations: "un comité de personnalités qualifiés chargées d'évaluer le préjudice subi et d'examiner les conditions de réparation morale et matérielle due au titre de ce crime." Two days before the commencement of public debate, however, the Commission des lois revised this article so as to provide instead for a committee charged with determining strategies for memorializing the "crime."

The abrogation of Article 5 reduced the symbolic impact (and reparative capacity) of the law in the eyes of several of the mnemonic entrepreneurs, as seen in this exchange with an activist:

> *C.F.:* I was told that the first draft of the Taubira Law spoke of a committee to discuss reparations, and that it was later removed.
>
> *Respondent:* Absolutely. They don't often speak about that. You are well informed, because they often say that the Taubira Law was unanimously adopted, but they forget to say that the most important article was unanimously removed . . . , and Madame Taubira found herself in a very difficult position because she had two strategies once the law was passed: she could either say, "The Taubira Law is great. I'm the one who drafted it, and it unanimously passed. It's a great law" or "The Taubira Law is an absolutely ridiculous thing. They unanimously removed the most important part." Obviously, she chose the first option because she needed to construct her [political] career, and it wouldn't be good for her to say that the Taubira Law was worthless. I understand why she did that. I can't hold it against her. But it is nonetheless necessary to remember this article—it was unanimously removed.

Taubira, who was appointed minister of justice in 2012, has indeed managed to build her political career. Yet while the topic of reparations was dropped from the law drafted in her name, she has continued to advocate for restorative justice to address the aftermath of slavery. At times, her public position on this issue has been directly at odds with those of white political leaders in France. This was clearly the case in 2013, for example, when Taubira expressed support for redistribution of land in the overseas departments to aid descendants of slaves only two days after President François Hollande insisted that reparations for slavery would be "impossible."[12]

Commemorators on Symbolic Repair

With regard to symbolic claims, commemorators most frequently suggested pedagogical outreach as a tool for repairing the past. About a third (14 of 43) of the mnemonic entrepreneurs talked about reparations in terms of bringing more attention to the history of slavery through the national educational curriculum or diffusing knowledge about slavery through commemorative activities and the building of museums. Commemorators often expressed the need to rehabilitate transatlantic history from obscurity, and they understood knowledge diffusion as a strategy for gaining recognition. In the wake of increased commemorative activity concerning colonial slavery in the late 1990s, the Ministry of Education enacted a series of significant, if not fully applied, changes to the teaching of the unique history and culture of overseas France. As late as 1995, the national curriculum for history courses made no mention of slavery in elementary school,[13] yet by 2002, the "black trade" was included under the heading "From the Beginning of Modern Times to the End of the Napoleonic Epoch (1492–1815)," and the abolition of slavery is acknowledged in a section on nineteenth-century history (Vergès, Condé, and Comité pour la Mémoire de l'Esclavage 2005). Similarly, curricular guidelines for middle school largely overlooked transatlantic history until the early 2000s, with few exceptions. In 1997, middle school history teachers were instructed to cover the definitive abolition of slavery in 1848 but not the first (and failed) abolition of 1794. Even at the high school level, transatlantic history has traditionally occupied a marginal place in the educational curriculum.

The Taubira Law called for the integration of colonial slavery into the French educational curriculum, but efforts in this area continue to lag. In its 2005 report, the Committee for the Memory of Slavery (Vergès, Condé, and Comité pour la Mémoire de l'Esclavage 2005) noted that colonial slavery was uniformly reduced to a two-page dossier in high school history classes. Since 2000, the overseas departments of Guadeloupe, Martinique, Réunion, and Guiana have had access to tailored curriculums designed to allow students to learn elements of their local history and geography, including greater attention to colonization and slavery. These "adaptations," however, are not included in the educational curriculum for students in mainland France. Notwithstanding the importance of these recent changes and the impact of the Taubira Law in improving the teaching of Atlantic history (Durpaire 2002), most of my Antillean respondents described the classroom as a space in which the history of their enslaved ancestors was largely ignored and silenced. Respondents frequently reported that they were taught "nothing" or "very little" about the transatlantic slave trade and that what they did remember learning was condensed to "a page" or even "a paragraph."

Daniel Voguet, the president of the Association des Descendants d'Esclaves Noirs (Association of Black Descendants of Slaves [ADEN]), a man who self-identifies as white, drove home this point:

> The first reparations are historical reparations—that is, those who are descendants of slaves should be able to know what the history of their ancestors was . . . to know that the Negro trade existed, why it existed, and what the consequences were of this ignominy.

Figure 7.1. *Françoise Vergès speaking alongside Yves Jego, former overseas minister of France, and members of the Comité pour la Memoire et l'Histoire de l'Esclavage at an awards ceremony for French academic theses written on the history of slavery, January 14, 2009. For the text of the speech, see* Potomitan, *available at http://www.potomitan .info/lafwans/verges.php.*

Later in the interview, Voguet argued for the broader import of teaching colonial history, arguing that "the whole national community should know what happened." Émile Batamack of Passerelle Noire put it this way: "It is necessary, first of all, to construct spaces that allow people to learn, to understand, to be together," while an Antillean official with the Municipal DOM-TOM Welcome and Information Center said that reparations could be pursued by "putting chapters in the history books." Several commemorators also felt that expanding access to historical archives could be useful not only for diffusing the history of slavery but also for allowing descendants of slaves to retrace their genealogical trees.

Commemorators on Material Repair

Commemorators' support for material, or economic, repair was more uneven. Very few activists approved of individual economic payments. One activist ardently believed that reparations should be made yet did not feel comfortable saying this on the record. The activist explained, "Saying that [I am] in favor of reparations. . . . [As a leader] of [my group], I cannot take this position. . . . If someone interviewed me, I would say the question is not yet developed in France. That's what I would say." Another activist was transparent about personal evolving views:

> *Respondent:* My position is that I support the cause of reparations. By the way, I wasn't always in favor of reparations. I should say that it wasn't really a question for me before 2001–2002 . . . but coming here [to Paris], and notably after the Taubira Law was enacted, I heard people who had arguments against reparations that were so odious that I became radically in favor of them.
>
> *C.F.:* What were the arguments against it?
>
> *Respondent:* There were a lot, and they were all execrable [*tous étaient exécrables*]. For example, a lot of people were saying, "It's been such a long time; it's necessary to forget about all that." I say, yes, it is convenient for you to forget certain things. That doesn't seem like a very good argument to me. I say that it's up to me to forget what I want, but you cannot pronounce amnesty for yourself. . . . Another argument is "Yes, of course we are guilty [*coupables*], but one cannot repair [slavery] because it's been too long." . . . I say, first, it is necessary to remember that reparations were made in the Antilles, but not for the slaves. They were for the masters . . . to compensate them, the poor things, for the misfortune that the abolition of slavery caused them. So there were reparations, but for the executioners [*les bourreaux*], not for the victims. . . . In the United States, they thought about the famous "a mule and an acre" formula. Even if it wasn't put into place, the principle was at least evoked. There were some who received a little money, a little land like that, but [for us] it was, in fact, the opposite. [The Martinican writer Patrick] Chamoiseau puts it very well: the slaves who asked for reparations were told "no" right away and that reparations were for the masters. So I say, you see it is quite possible to have reparations; it's simply that they weren't given to the right people. For example, Japanese who were put into concentration campus in the United States obtained reparations. When Jews who survived the Shoah asked for reparations from Germany, they obtained them. We could think of numerous other historical cases. There was a great quarrel between France and Germany, and since Germany did not pay [reparations], France occupied the Ruhr [region], saying, "You don't want to pay [reparations, so] we're going to occupy the Ruhr and use it for ourselves."[14]

> . . . [W]hen the clergy's goods were nationalized after the French
> Revolution, this was done using the logic of reparations—that is,
> for centuries, the peasants paid . . . a tenth of their salary to the
> church, so all of the money from the church came from them,
> so they should receive reparations. . . . The history of France was
> always made with reparations. . . . There are those who say, "You
> can't repair, it's impossible. . . . [Slavery was] such a huge crime."
> To that I say, but we repair all the time.

This activist drew on historical examples to show not only that commensura-
tion for historical grievances was possible but that such efforts have already
been made in various contexts. The activist went on to say, however, that
power relations were primary determinants for whether groups were successful in obtaining reparations:

> Clearly, Africa could not obtain reparations because it was still domi-
> nated even after decolonization. But when one is in a position of power,
> for example, one can obtain reparations from Germany: in 1918, because
> Germany had lost the war; in 1923, because Germany was in a position
> of weakness; and in 1945, because, again, Germany lost the war. From a
> moral and judicial point of view, [reparations are] completely possible.
> From a point of view of power relations, sometimes it is not possible.
> That's the only difference. And to the question of [the passage] of time, I
> say . . . that, for example, Haiti demanded reparations. . . . It is necessary
> to know that, under the French restoration, France returned to indepen-
> dent Haiti, threatening to recolonize it. Since Haiti was in a very weak
> position, it preferred to pay . . . a considerable sum—millions of gold
> francs at the time . . .—to keep its independence. But as soon as they paid
> it, they never stopped asking for reimbursement [from France] for the
> damages of slavery, as well as for those who had to pay to keep their lib-
> erty. France always said "no." But when France says today that it's too
> late, that reparations are not possible—you cannot say that during 100
> years and [then] say in the 101st year that it's too late. By the way, with
> regard to slavery in the Antilles, [the Taubira Law] says that slavery is a
> crime against humanity. By definition, crimes against humanity are im-
> prescriptible. . . . So even if 300 years have passed, . . . there is no statute
> of limitations. It's an eternal crime.

Taking this position publicly, however, was not possible for this activist in the
current political climate. Yannick Meyo, who worked with Orig'in Association in producing the *Africaphonie* events, went on the record saying that the

subject was still taboo in France, particularly when blacks face difficulty merely getting recognition for the racism they confront in everyday life:

> The question of reparations is very difficult in this country. I think that perhaps my grandchildren or my great-grandchildren will talk [about reparations]. . . . [W]e are so far [from it] that asking for it like that, people wouldn't understand. You see? They would not understand. Today we're [working on] accepting one another, . . . because there are some who have not yet accepted that they could be led by a black. [There are] people who have not yet accepted [seeing] a black behind the wheel of a luxury Mercedes when he's not the chauffeur—it's his car. . . . We don't even have to go back further than last week. I was standing next to a taxi with the trunk open and the luggage was being brought down. There was a guy who came to see me and said, "Where are you going?" I said, "No, he's the [driver]." . . . In fact, the [driver] was a white [man] of a certain age, and he was carrying my bags. In the minds of some people, however, I must be the cabbie. This [idea] has a source.

That source, Yannick implied, was the history of slavery and the stigmatization of blacks that solidified during the colonial era.

Several French Caribbean commemorators portrayed Africans as primarily responsible for pushing the reparations agenda. This probably reflects media coverage given to African nations' reparations claims during the United Nations World Conference against Racism in 2001 in South Africa, but the charge may also stem from some respondents' boundaries against Africans. Consider the views of this CM98 member, who sharply differentiated her ingroup from Africans throughout our interview:

> *Respondent:* When you speak with an African, the African tells you, "Our slaves, our slaves." . . . I say, no! It's not you! . . . You were not slaves! You are not descendants of slaves! Maybe your family has someone [who was enslaved], but that's different [*une autre fabrication*]. . . . [T]hey want financial reparation. . . . So in that case, how much should we ask for? . . . Personally, I find it ridiculous!
>
> *C.F.:* Why is it ridiculous?
>
> *Respondent:* Because [for us] it's symbolic. We are not going to ask after how many—three hundred or four hundred—years to be given [money]. How would they pay us? In gold? To whom? How? Be serious! . . . No, we ask that things be done in memory [of slavery]. . . . I personally would like the United Nations . . . to say

that, in terms of slavery, the Europeans, the Africans, and so on owe us recognition. . . . [I]t's something international, that slavery has been recognized as a crime against humanity. But for now, not all people, not all Europeans, recognize this.

Similarly, Patrick Karam, the former Inter-ministerial Delegate for Equal Opportunities for Overseas French, thought the suffering of the slaves was not commensurable with economic repair. Moreover, he described demands for financial compensation as both immoral and characteristic of "Africans" in France:

> *Karam:* Can one evaluate the cost? Can one financially evaluate the deaths? Can one put a monetary value on the lives of people? . . . It's horrible that this question of reparations is represented under the form of financial reparation. Reparation can only be moral. But having financial reparations [would be] insulting [to] the slaves and [to] the descendants of slaves. I notice that the immense majority of descendants of slaves don't ask for reparations. Second, those who ask for reparations a lot are of African origin—not the African intelligentsia over there; they are respectful. It's the ones who are here and who are trying to ride a wave. They should begin by asking themselves about Africa's responsibility [for slavery], because there is also some responsibility there.
>
> *C.F.:* What is the responsibility of Africa?
>
> *Karam:* [It's] like the responsibility of Europe. The descendants cannot respond to the responsibility of their ancestors . . . , but at the time, there was no colonization. . . . Who went to find the slaves and take them to [the Europeans]? Who? So, there is [African] responsibility. In his work, . . . [the scholar] Frédéric Régent, [shows] that when France abolished slavery, a delegation came from Benin to protest the action. No one is responsible for the past and for his or her ancestors—no one. I'm simply saying that if [people] look for responsibility, where do they stop? Are there also responsibilities in Africa? A question I ask is "Who are we going to ask to pay?" Whom will we compensate? You see? I don't get into this debate. I think that it's necessary to bring people together. For example, I know that in Benin there is a great ceremony [to commemorate slavery]. It's the only African country that has recognized its responsibility in slavery, the only one to admit that slavery was a crime against humanity, the only one that has dared to look at its past.

Of the commemorative groups examined in this study, only two explicitly advocated economic compensation for slavery in their official discourse. Both groups—Agir pour les Réparations Maintenant pour les Africains et Descendants d'Africains (Acting for Reparations Now for Africans and Descendants of Africans [ARMADA]) and Collectif des Filles et Fils d'Africains Déportés (Collective of Daughters and Sons of Deported Africans [COFFAD])—were Africa-centered.[15] Yet behind the scenes, collective forms of economic repair found support among some commemorators of Caribbean, African, and European heritage. However, some activists with direct ties to Africa were openly skeptical about the desirability of compensation. Patrick Lozès described the position of his organization, the Conseil Representatif des Associations Noires (Representative Council of Black Associations [CRAN]), this way:

> We ask for reparations, but not individual reparations. Individual reparations are very complex. However, we do ask that there be collective reparations, that there are museums, spaces where one can know this history—research centers, spaces for knowledge. But individual compensation seems complex because it is necessary to trace one's lineage. Say you are a descendant; you will get a quarter [reparation], but . . . once someone pays, he can tell you, "Stop bothering me with this history." . . . [I]t's not because they compensate that they should forget. . . . [We have to be] very careful with this business about compensation.

It is important to note that CRAN's official position on reparations changed in recent years, following a shift in leadership. In fact, the group's current president, Louis-Georges Tin (2013), published a book in support of reparations (both symbolic and material) that foregrounds the legacies of slavery and colonialism.

Batamack, who is of Cameroonian origin, explained why he rejected individual payments but embraced the idea of directing money to pedagogical outreach and projects to combat inequality:

> I never thought that reparations for pocket money to go to nightclubs would be useful for anything. From my point of view, that wouldn't be the reparation of anything. It is necessary to make great museums, great monuments, great universities where we learn [about] slavery, whether it's in Africa, France, the Antilles, or elsewhere, and construct institutions . . . on the ground to help with the concrete realization of things, by voting for budgets to do things, so we can reduce the rate of illiteracy. . . . People need to go to school . . . so they can be autonomous in life. . . . If we want effective reparations, this is what we need to do.

Taken together, these comments show that economic repair is far from a common goal among commemorators. Indeed, only eight out of the forty-three mnemonic entrepreneurs suggested even collective economic reform or development as a means of repairing the past, underscoring the marginality of monetary evaluations in the reparative logic of commemorators.

Perspectives on Reparations among Ordinary Caribbeans

To tap into the views of non-activist Antillean migrants, I asked the question "What do you think of the idea of reparations?"[16] The majority of interviewees (74.6 percent) expressed support for some form of repair for the past, while about a quarter (23.7 percent) did not express support for reparations. Support for reparations was notably stronger among first-generation migrants (84.4 percent) than among second-generation migrants (63 percent). I intentionally asked the question in an open-ended manner to discover how respondents imagined the meaning of reparations, without privileging one form or another. Despite the resurgence of public discourse about the economic legacies of colonialism sparked by the Liyannaj kont Pwofitasyon (Collective against Exploitation [LKP]) strikes (as well as the emphatic demand for 200 euro payments for the black populations in the French overseas departments [DOM]), I did not expect Antilleans to express broad support for economic reparations for two main reasons. First, given that market-based evaluations are more salient in the cultural repertoire of Americans than in that of the French (Lamont 1992), I hypothesized that French Antilleans overall would express moral condemnation of framing the wrongs of slavery as commensurate with monetary repair. Second, the issue of reparations has been largely obscured in debates over the memory of slavery, and few Afro-Caribbean groups, aside from COFFAD, have publicly called for individual payments. Groups that support collective economic repair (such as increased funding for infrastructure or the sponsoring of scholarships and educational opportunities in the DOM) also are rarely articulated in public debates. For these reasons, I went into the field expecting that French respondents would generally construct reparations claims in terms of cultural entrepreneurship (i.e., commemoration, museums, and pedagogical outreach).

Overall, the respondents confirmed these expectations, and the distribution of their preferred form of reparations was the same for both samples. Thus, the modal response for both groups was "support for symbolic reparations only" (53.1 percent, first-generation migrants; 37 percent, second-generation migrants), followed by "support for economic reparations only" (15.6 percent, first-generation migrants; 14.8 percent, second-generation migrants),

TABLE 7.1. NON-ACTIVISTS' SUPPORT FOR REPARATIONS			
	First-generation migrants (*N* = 32)	Second-generation migrants (*N* = 27)	All non-activists (*N* = 59)
Form of reparation supported			
Support for economic reparations only	15.6%	14.8%	15.3%
Support for symbolic reparations only	**53.1%**	**37.0%**	**45.8%**
Support for economic and symbolic reparations	9.4%	7.4%	8.5%
Support for unspecified form of reparations	6.3%	3.7%	5.1%
Subtotal	84.4%	63.0%	74.6%
No support for reparations	15.6%	33.3%	23.7%
Missing data	0.0%	3.7%	1.7%
Total	100.0%	100.0%	100.0%

"support for economic and symbolic reparations" (9.4 percent, first-generation migrants; 7.4 percent, second-generation migrants), and "support for unspecified form of reparations" (6.3 percent, first-generation migrants; 3.7 percent, second-generation migrants); see Table 7.1. The discussion that follows closely examines how respondents envision "symbolic" and "economic" repair and considers the explanations for why so many Antilleans express the need for symbolic reparations but generally oppose economic interventions.

Difficulty Conceptualizing Reparations

One of the most vivid patterns in non-activists' response to my query about reparations was a tendency for some respondents to confront me with many questions of their own. Consider these reactions from interviewees, including some who eventually expressed support for reparations:

> "Reparations for whom? . . . Who should be compensated? Of what? . . . I don't know."
> "How are you going to repair? That's the question I ask myself sincerely: how are you going to repair?"
> "Reparations for slavery? Um, repair what? Why now? [*Long pause.*]"
> "[Reparations] for whom? Why? Who would repair? Who would give? I do not know what good that would do now."
> "I don't know what to say. . . . Reimburse for slavery? Reimburse whom?"

"What would we do? Whom would the money go to? What would
they do with it? Whom would they give it to? They should give
it to all of us! Where should the money be used?"

Overall, twelve non-activists (five first-generation migrants and seven second-
generation migrants) asked these kinds of questions. Antilleans' questions
about the feasibility and purpose of reparations reflect the extent to which
reparations discourse remains a relatively abstract and ill-defined notion,
despite recent commemorative movements. This is demonstrated by patterns in
media coverage. Searching for the terms "slavery" and "reparations" in French
media sources in the 1990s produced only 107 results on Lexis-Nexis, compared
with 1,813 results in U.S. sources over the same time period. Beyond this observation, the higher proportion of counter-queries from second-generation interviewees is an indicator of generational differences in the sample. While
first-generation interviewees typically had a broader repertoire for understanding the impact of the slavery past on the present and a stronger belief in the
desirability of reparations, second-generation respondents tended to view fewer
consequences and, therefore, less need for repair.

Support for Symbolic Repair

Again and again, respondents used the word "recognition" (*reconnaissance*)
when describing their vision of what reparations should look like. Sylvie, a
second-generation migrant of Martinican origin, eloquently explained Antilleans' need for recognition:

> *Sylvie:* I think that it's always the same problem: as long as the recog-
> nition [*reconnaissance*] of slavery has not taken place, [and] there
> has not been an asking of forgiveness by the slaveholding people,
> as long as there has not been a real gesture, there will be a need
> for recognition that slavery happened, that they say, "Forgive us.
> France was a slaveholding country." Everything happens through
> recognition [*tout passe par la reconnaissance*]. They, in fact, apolo-
> gized for the Holocaust. I think that slavery made more damages
> [*dégâts*].
> *C.F.:* What were the damages?
> *Sylvie:* It's an entire people who were put into submission and that
> tried to rebel and were completely picked on [*brimée*]. So there
> was an enormous amount of death, rape . . . violence, and there
> was a lot of pressure on the Antillean people. I think that it's all

this that hurts Antilleans now. It's that they don't recognize their
former slave condition [*leur condition d'ancien esclave*].

C.F.: It hurts because they do not recognize . . . ?

Sylvie: Yeah, it's true that when you aren't recognized as something,
it's as if you're nothing. And it's hard to be nothing.

Cédric, a first-generation migrant from Martinique, wanted an apology from
the French state:

> For me, the first reparations are through recognition [*reconnaissance*], that
> they say, "Yes." That they really put this debate on the table and speak
> without taboo or holding back . . . and that they stop beating around the
> bush, because as long as we beat around the bush, we'll never get ahead.
> There will always be this issue of racism, [being] a visible minority. I think
> that . . . this problem deserves to be posed and to be said and that France
> should say, "Yes! We committed a crime. Yes, we did it with the law," and
> that they don't . . . say, "Yes, there were African chiefs [who participated];
> there was this, [and] there was that." [France should say], "We wanted to
> develop Europe. . . . Well, we did it. We knew what we were doing. . . .
> We ask forgiveness for what we did. We ask forgiveness in the name of the
> French Republic." I think that would already be a big step.

Christelle, another first-generation migrant from Martinique, concurred:

> To move forward [*avancer*] . . . , we need an apology. They never asked
> for . . . forgiveness for what they did, what our ancestors went through. I
> think that it's important that one day the president of the French Repub-
> lic say, "We apologize for having made your ancestors [and] black Afri-
> cans go through atrocities."

Robert, a second-generation Martinican, thought that gaining recognition
was sufficient to repair the past and avoid repeating it:

> It's necessary to be aware of what happened in the past; it's necessary to
> be aware of the errors committed so that they don't begin again. . . .
> That's it. For me, it's recognition—recognize the errors of the past so that
> they are no longer committed.

For these respondents, naming slavery a "crime against humanity" was not
enough to signal regret on the part of the French state. Further, the sym-

bolic recognition some respondents desire involves elements of racialization. Christelle, for example, wanted France to apologize specifically to blacks, something the state cannot and will not do if it refuses to recognize race.

Education

Several respondents, all of Martinican origin, mentioned educational outreach and pedagogy as a means of spreading awareness about the history of slavery and rectifying the past. Carole, a second-generation migrant with Martinican roots, put it this way:

> I think that, to begin with, they should inscribe it in textbooks to teach the youngest [children] and inscribe it in the history of the world, in the textbooks . . . of countries implicated [in slavery]. That would be a good form of reparation.

Mathieu, a first-generation migrant, also framed reparations in terms of education. He said that he had studied colonization at school because he grew up in Martinique but that such opportunities were lacking in mainland France:

> It's simple: textbooks. It's unacceptable that today in France, there is no material on abolition, on slavery, on colonization in the textbooks. . . . [I]n high school, I studied Aimé Césaire—notably, his book *Discours sur le colonialisme*—but not in France. Sorry. When I came to France, they talked to me about Victor Hugo and company. Sure, [that literature] is good, but it didn't speak to me. . . . What is reparation? It's a kid of Antillean origin who is born in France . . . [who can] open his textbook and talk to his teachers [about] how this happened in France—about how France is a nation of colonizers and it did this.

Raphael, a second-generation migrant, also emphasized the importance of using talk (and education) about slavery to help Antilleans feel respected:

> *Raphael:* I believe that the best [reparation] is to explain what they did. It's to talk, at least.
> *C.F.:* Education?
> *Raphael:* Education is very important. At least, I believe that children here, from the Antilles, could at least have a feeling of respect. Because I do not see why they continue to perpetuate—it's perpetually like this. As soon as someone insults a Jew, it's the end of the world. Right away, they go back to World War II. . . . There

seems to be a double standard [*deux poids, deux mesures*], you know? They don't do anything about something that lasted four hundred years, but for something that lasted five years—yes, it produced millions of deaths, but how many deaths did slavery produce?

Raphael felt that slavery and the Holocaust were commensurate in the sense that each historical tragedy merits recognition and objected to the two events being weighed using different metrics (i.e., *deux poids, deux mesures*) in the public sphere.

Support for Economic Repair

Non-activists generally conceived of economic reparations in terms of development (principally in the Antilles, but a few respondents also mentioned Africa), the dismantling of white minority dominance in the Antilles through the eradication of monopolies and the redistribution of land, and support for group members' educational attainment. Very few respondents expressed support for reparations in the form of payments to individuals. Michelle, a first-generation migrant from Martinique, was one of the very few interviewees who expressed strong, spontaneous support for some form of financial repair. Her justification was the fact that former slaveholders in the DOM had received compensation for their losses following the abolition of slavery:

> The *békés* were in fact given 60 million francs back then for having lost the slaves, so they were compensated for the loss of the slaves. France compensated them. That's messed up [*c'est abbérant*] not only from a financial point of view, but also from the point of view of respect.

Pierre, a first-generation migrant from Guadeloupe, said that he agreed with French Representative Christiane Taubira's stance on reparations and thought that individual payments were "useless":

> *Pierre:* I'm on Taubira's side. . . . [For the] reparations she asks for . . . [France] could say, "We will help you finance [initiatives], not give money to each person. We will finance structures that will allow you to develop . . . hospitals, schools, an agricultural system." You see? Investments in an agricultural system. Things like that. . . .
> *C.F.:* Why not give money to descendants of slaves?
> *Pierre:* Why? To go get a drink? [*Laughs.*]

C.F.: Why not?

Pierre: So that each individual is free to do what he or she wants? No, . . . I am against that, because it's a trap. . . . In what way will that reconstruct us? . . . If I buy a house, how does that help reconstruct us? A population was affected, not only an individual. It's a population; it's a continent; it's Africa that was affected. We're often told that . . . Africa before 1500 consisted of kingdoms. . . . Less than three hundred years later, in 1700, there weren't any left.

C.F.: Do you think Western nations should do something for Africa?

Pierre: Not for Africa. But Africans themselves do not want reparations in general. . . . [O]ften, what is said to descendants in the Americas [is] "You don't know if you are a descendant of an African enslaver [*africain esclavagiste*]. . . . You do not know." There were wars between slaveholding countries. . . . [T]here wasn't any unity [among] Africans. . . . [Yet] I've never heard anyone say that the Europeans were savages because they killed one another [in the world wars]. Those were the normal situations of the time. . . . So it's normal that each kingdom tries to fight to survive; some fight against the slaveholding system and others fight for its expansion. . . . To return to the subject of reparations, it's not an individual, even, for example, for Africa, for the destroyed kingdoms. Well, even if you belong to those kingdoms . . . it's the kingdom that needs to be reconstructed. You understand?

C.F.: OK. But how? How to do [reparations]?

Pierre: . . . Taubira [is asking] for compensation for the infrastructure that will allow the islands to become nations or, at least, autonomous departments . . . that are capable of providing an education to their children, health care, [and] an agricultural system that allows for nourishing the entire population.

Pierre's description of African involvement in the slave trade underscores the fact that African societies are not a monolith. If some Africans enslaved others, he suggests that this must have been because various African nations were at war with each other. Rejecting anti-African stigmatization, Pierre points out that Europeans are not generally portrayed as "savages" for slaughtering each other. While he rejects the desirability of individual payments, his vision of reparations is tied to nationalistic aspirations—an imagined future in which collective reparations empower Guadeloupe and Martinique to support their populations' well-being.

Opposition to Economic Reparations

By and large, non-activists either dismissed the idea of economic repair outright or expressed serious reservations about financial compensation, which was consistent with my expectations. Figure 7.2 summarizes respondents' criticisms of an economic approach to reparations for slavery. Overall, they expressed concerns that attempts at economic repair are not feasible, are not useful or necessary, and would create a backlash against group members.

In general, most non-activists' skepticism about economic reparations had to do with the practical challenge of determining who should receive compensation, who should pay, and how the damages themselves should (or could) be calculated. Many respondents thought reparations were impractical because they had difficulty imagining slavery as commensurable with monetary value. Thierry, a second-generation migrant, thought economic reparations were unfeasible due to group members' ethnoracial mixture and the lack of clear criteria on which to base Antilleans' claims:

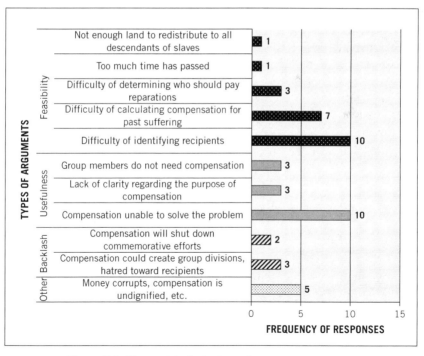

Figure 7.2. *Non-activists' criticisms of economic reparations.*

How should they be evaluated? . . . Who owes what to whom? There have been mixtures—notably, in the Antilles. Should one [have] half a reparation for the black side of the person, for the two-thirds of one-quarter of whatever he had? Or if he's mixed with [Indian heritage], does that cancel out everything? . . . The problem is that this business of reparations is often based off of what happened with the Jews [in World War II], but with the Jews, . . . there is proof of their [losses]—for example, fortunes [in terms of] paintings that were taken. But slavery: how do you evaluate it? Who reimburses whom? . . . How? It would be a crazy thing. How would you do it?

Guillaume, a first-generation migrant from Martinique, explained why economic interventions would be difficult to put into place:

> *Guillaume:* Reparations? Um . . . [r]epair what happened and compensate—how? . . . If they compensate with money, they'll ask for land. From money, it goes back to this—the land. Whose land? From the land that they gave to the colonizers. . . . It's not their land; it's land that they were given. Um, what I'm going to say is mean, but Africans weren't here before, so perhaps they do not have the legitimacy to have the land, either. But I said that on purpose, to shock you. But, um, if it was necessary to do something to compensate [for slavery]—wow! It [would be] huge.
> *C.F.:* Is it too much to do?
> *Guillaume:* Yeah, because we're four hundred thousand people in Martinique! Compensating four hundred thousand people—you can't even give four hundred thousand people a plot of land to do anything [with]. Then it would be necessary to break certain habits . . . [in] the organization of the society. You have the *békés* who are descendants of the colonizers who will always keep a part of [the compensation]—it's true! . . . Reparation, I believe, would come from . . . better recognition for blacks of the Antilles.

While Guillaume thought that something should be done in reparation for the past, he did not see how the wrongs of slavery could easily be treated as commensurate with payments to present-day individuals, particularly given ambiguity over how the proper recipients would be determined.

The most frequent argument against economic reparations was simply the idea that money would be unable to solve the problems engendered by the slavery past. Often, respondents took this stance because they believed that slavery had caused moral, psychological, or spiritual damage that could not be repaired by financial means. A frequent line of argument for Antilleans was that "money cannot heal the wounds" of slavery. Thus, Fred, a migrant from Guadeloupe, supported symbolic reparations but rejected the idea of financial repair because

> it's not a solution for the real problems, which are more so in the heart than a question of money, you know? So it's not very politically correct, but they speak of giving compensation to descendants of Jews who were exterminated during World War II. I think they're getting off-track. . . . I don't think it's the right path; it's not the right way to try to repair things.

Hélène, a first-generation migrant from Martinique, expressed immediate opposition to reparations. When I asked her if she was thinking of financial reparations, she admitted that this was the case. As she continued talking, however, Hélène expressed strong support for symbolic repair while pointing out the inability of money to address the real problems facing her group members:

> *Hélène:* Reparations? I don't think of reparations. I think that it's necessary to open up. You know, it's like a wound that closed up badly [*c'est comme une plaie qui s'est mal refermée*]. It's necessary to open the wound again, clean it up a little bit. Put some words—*words*—on it and explain. Let each person take his part of the responsibility.
>
> *C.F.:* But when you say that you're not for reparations, are you thinking about financial reparations? . . .
>
> *Hélène:* Yes, that's true. I must have been thinking about that. I must have thought of a thing like that, while this is situated at a different level. It's necessary that we open it up, that we really talk. But let them say who was at the origin of this and really explain to children how it happened to people who are still here: to Antilleans, to Moroccans, to [Afro-descendants] and let them say, "Here you go! . . . [T]his is how it happened, in these conditions," and let them recognize it. . . . We know how it happened, but it's necessary that the actors recognize it.
>
> *C.F.:* The actors? Who are the actors?
>
> *Hélène:* Well, the actors—that means the French [and] all those who participated in these things. There weren't only the French, because the Arabs also participated in this. The Spanish, the Dutch, the English. Let them recognize that at one time, they acted this way:

they sold [people]. And for the French, more precisely, because there are Antilleans who are still there, there are the *békés* who are a reminder of the colonizers [*qui rappellent les colons*]. So let them break this thing there, break the thing with power in Martinique.

Youri, a second-generation migrant, did not completely dismiss the concept of economic repair but was skeptical of both its practical feasibility and its ability to rectify the trauma:

Reparation is a very good question. But it's a big undertaking because if it is necessary to have reparations with money, it's millions and even billions! . . . I do not think money can repair the wounds [*les blessures*]. . . . I think what could repair the wounds is forgiveness [*le pardon*], open-mindedness [*l'ouverture d'esprit*], exchanging with different people regardless of their origin, their culture, or the color of their skin. That's what could make a reparation. Money is a superficial reparation, but because of the wounds, especially because they're anchored deep inside of us, I think that it's necessary to do spiritually . . . like love, respect, compassion, and dignity. These are the things that repair. All the gold in the world, all the money in the world could not repair such damages [*prejudices*].

Aside from these criticisms of money's ability to heal moral and spiritual wounds, several respondents thought there were additional reasons that economic repair could not help Antilleans. Sébastien, a first-generation migrant from Martinique, thought financial reparations would not help group members because money given to blacks would end up in the pockets of the *békés*, who own many of the stores and distribution chains in the Antilles:

If you give more money to blacks, you'll compensate the *békés* twice as much. . . . [O]ne must certainly not give money to the [black] populations. They're going to spend it in the stores. . . . I would have put reparations on the economy. . . . [P]recisely because we did not have a mule and an acre [*un mulet et acre*], I would have put the reparations to say that "you will learn languages if you want to become an interpreter. . . . [Y]ou set up your micro-credit, [and] we will allow you to have a deal [*"deal" said in English*] . . . for the payment." That's what I want. But I'm afraid of giving 200 euros to [black] families.

Maryse, one of the few Antilleans who thought that slavery had not left any traces on the present, thought that economic reparations were unnecessary because blacks, in her view, no longer experienced mistreatment in France:

One cannot say that since the end of slavery, blacks have been mistreated, because we have had the same lifestyle [*niveau de vie*] as the French. . . . I don't think they need a financial reparation, because they've been treated relatively well.

Given the lack of de jure segregation and the lack of recognition given to colonial history in French education and collective memory, it is perhaps remarkable that more Antillean respondents did not express Maryse's view—that is, that blacks have little to complain about in the metropole. That most respondents in this study thought that Afro-Caribbeans faced lingering challenges related to the colonial past suggests that some French blacks not only are broadly aware of their group members' disadvantages but also view their difficulties through a historical lens, despite the French state's efforts to downplay the significance of colonialism. What may be lacking, however, is a clear understanding of how exactly present-day problems in the metropole are linked to the history of slavery and colonialism.

Fear of Reprisal and Backlash

André, a second-generation respondent, thought that demanding economic reparations would produce group boundaries and possibly stimulate a backlash:

I can halfway understand it, and on the other hand, I'd say, "It would be stupid," because it happened a long time ago. . . . [It would be good] to try not to make any more distinctions, yes, precisely to [reduce] discrimination and to try to change things. . . . [Reparations] lead to hatred and tension. I think it's a bad thing, maybe. I don't know what to say. . . . Reimburse for slavery? Reimburse whom? Nations that would be expected to pay wouldn't understand. . . . I think it would lead to conflict. . . . I can understand [the feeling], "Hey, you did this for so many centuries, [so] you've got to give something in return," but, I think also that . . . with the economy today . . . in a moment of crisis, it's not really the time to [ask for reparations]—that would make things more complicated. . . . [They would say], "You're never happy."

Two respondents also felt that receiving financial reparations would result in whites' ultimate dismissal of efforts to remember and talk about the history of slavery. Michel, a second-generation migrant of Guadeloupean heritage, stated:

I don't believe financial reparations are the solution. OK, say there are some who will be compensated. Very good. Um, I don't know—but [what about] in five years? What will happen? "He was compensated . . . and we won't talk about the abolition of slavery anymore." . . . So I'm against [financial reparations].

The possible (and probable) backlash that these respondents describe constitutes what Vincene Verdun (1993: 744–745) refers to as "the problem of finality": the idea that compensation for slavery could nullify future reparations claims by descendants of slaves.

Understanding Opposition to Reparations

Nearly a quarter of the non-activist respondents (14 of 59) expressed general opposition to reparations for slavery. A higher proportion of second-generation migrants (33.3 percent) rejected reparations than did members of the first generation (15.6 percent). This finding supports the hypothesis that Antilleans born and raised in mainland France feel less of a connection to the slavery past and therefore are less likely to perceive a need for repair. Second-generation migrants were the only interviewees who emphasized that "too much time had passed" when discussing reparations. For example, Nathalie, a second-generation migrant, did not think there were any consequences of slavery. When I asked her about reparations, she responded:

> *Nathalie:* OK, but what would they repair?
> *C.F.:* For example, one could speak of financial reparations, but also of other forms of reparation for slavery.
> *Nathalie:* I think that it's a little too late. It's too late. . . . The guilty parties are no longer here. Um, I don't see why they would give me something in reparations for something that was done several centuries ago. But in all the conflicts there have been in the world, it would be necessary to give reparations. I think that at the end of the day, it's necessary . . . to recognize one's wrongs, and it's necessary at the end of the day to forget about this idea of reparation. . . . Reparations would be opening new conflicts. I think that in the end blacks wouldn't benefit.

Mylène, another second-generation migrant who did not think of slavery as relevant to the present, thought reparations were pointless because the guilty parties are no longer present and apologies would serve only to appease people's guilty consciences. Although she did not say so directly, she implied that whites would be the ones who would feel appeased by symbolic recognition.

Yet not everyone who rejected reparations did so because she or he failed to link contemporary racial problems to the colonial past. Sometimes respondents rejected the notion of reparations because they framed their policy desires in terms of "justice" rather than "repair." This was the case for two second-generation migrants. Clara, from Guadeloupe, conceptualized the legacies of slavery as racial divisions and whites' belief in the inferiority of blacks, but she thought that both economic and symbolic repair would ultimately be counterproductive:

> I believe that [reparations are] a bad idea. How would it be determined? Who would get what, for what function? . . . In fact, I don't know anything about it—how to put it into place from a purely practical, operational point of view. Then, I want to say that this . . . [could] perhaps free the descendants of the colonizers of guilt: "OK, we did you wrong, but at the same time, don't bother us anymore with your stories about commemoration and all that. . . . It's over." . . . And then, this [would] also feed feelings of conflict, hatred: "You kept me down." . . . I think that it's necessary to go to the next step afterward: more justice, more equal opportunity. Finally, in Guadeloupe, 1 percent of the population holds more than 50 percent of the . . . land. That's not normal. Let us reestablish a bit . . . of order. There is a monopoly. Normally there are laws that regulate—in fact, competition. Let us apply them; simply apply the laws.

In Clara's view, the main problem today for members of her group is the need to address contemporary inequalities. Rather than framing the solutions in terms of "reparation," she called for "justice" through the application of French laws that would dismantle the *békés'* economic domination, echoing demands that were at the heart of the LKP movement that spring. Similarly, Pascal, a migrant from Martinique, rejected the general notion of reparations but affirmed the need for a more just distribution of wealth and resources in the Antilles:

> The only thing I ask for is justice. . . . [I]t isn't normal that people continue—the people who are descendants and the inheritors of the fruit of slavery [*fruits de l'esclavage*] find themselves today perpetuating it through modern commerce, while the same ones who were put into slavery are prevented from developing normally and from having the freedom to develop themselves.

Conclusion

This chapter has examined an important arena of temporality: the ways in which people imagine addressing the damage of colonialism and slavery. Race factored into some respondents' conceptualization of reparations, as they used racial categories to describe both the white majority and minority groups that should receive redress. In Chapter 5, I showed that most respondents thought that the slavery past was still consequential and relevant to present-day concerns; however, the people I interviewed did not generally view these legacies as reparable through economic or material means. Economic or financial compensation did not resonate with the majority of people I spoke with, activists and non-activists alike. Instead, they overwhelmingly expressed support for symbolic forms of recognition, arguing that the "wounds" of the slavery past had created social and political relations that had stigmatized blacks broadly and excluded Antilleans on both sides of the Atlantic from being viewed and treated as fully French. This suggests that efforts to frame reparations in terms of money or individual payments (such as the LKP's demand that Antillean families receive 200 euros per month, to be paid by the French government, or COFFAD's demand for individual compensation for slavery) would not receive the enthusiastic support from many Caribbean migrants in mainland France—perhaps especially from those who fit the profile of this mostly middle-class, upwardly mobile sample.

The opinions and attitudes of French Caribbean migrants matter for the development of institutional and economic policies in large part because there are just as many Antilleans living in mainland France as in the DOM. Moreover, these migrants have proximity to the seat of French political power in Paris. Thus, activists who claim to represent them are regularly consulted by local and national officials in Paris through offices such as the Inter-ministerial Delegation for Equal Opportunities for Overseas French and the Overseas Ministry itself. Antilleans' strong support for symbolic repair suggests that migrants continue to feel disrespected and excluded from civic life and look toward French politicians to signal their inclusion through commemorative efforts, educational policies (e.g., giving a more central place to the history of the former colonies in the national curriculum), and official statements of regret. While France has begun to make some progress on the commemorative and educational fronts, most officials have systematically avoided making any statements that would constitute an official "apology" for slavery, in large part due to fears that international law would require reparation. Further, in recent years, the predominantly white political establishment, including the socialist François Hollande, has taken a hard line against reparations. As a result, in the eyes of many, slavery remains a crime without resolution. In the absence of clear definitions of the guilty parties, individuals and groups who were responsible for slavery and benefited from the trade have largely avoided being shamed and stigmatized. By contrast, descendants of slaves continue to bear the racialized stigma of having been oppressed, with the color of their skin representing an open wound of past discrimination and present-day exclusion.

Conclusion

RACE-ING THE PAST AND
THE PRESENT

When many Americans think of France, they imagine the Eiffel Tower, fancy cuisine, the seductive crooning of Josephine Baker or, more disturbing, the specter of ISIS-inspired terrorism. Yet, many people still do not associate France with slavery and colonial violence despite its sprawling, transoceanic empire. This study aims to recenter racialized slavery and colonialism in analyses of contemporary French society, drawing connections between present-day inequalities and past oppression. Like other European nations, the French engaged in settler colonialism as well as the profitable business of capturing, enslaving, deporting, and exploiting Africans and their racialized descendants. This heritage remains largely suppressed in the French educational system and underacknowledged in scholarly and popular discussions about France. Against this trend, *Resurrecting Slavery* aims to recenter the intertwined histories of transatlantic enslavement and colonization in the analysis of French society and power relations today.

Racial Temporalities and French White Supremacy

Beyond contributions to scholarship on collective memory, this work attempts to shift the way scholars and observers analyze race relations in France. Rather than merely acknowledging racism (or worse, highlighting anti-Maghrebi discrimination while minimizing anti-blackness), my approach draws on Fanonian critique and global critical race theory by framing France as a white-supremacist society. I make this argument by insisting that the racial legacies of colonialism and transatlantic slavery have quite obviously not been erased. As scholars, we do French minorities (and the cause of social justice) a disservice when we are vague or imprecise about the specific nature of these racial legacies. It is not enough merely to investigate "race" and "racism" in France. We must also unveil and challenge the ongoing reality of white social and political dominance in the present. As Charles Mills (1997, 2015) argues, white supremacy requires epistemic practices that deny, mask, and mystify the social realities of white dominance. Suppressing—or misrepresenting—racial and colonial history and hiding behind color-blind ideology help maintain the status quo. In order for commemorations of slavery to challenge white supremacy, they will need to shed light on structural racism in the past and the present. Framing racialization as a historical and structural reality (rather than as an interpersonal phenomenon) is incredibly important, given that French elites tend to portray racism as the mere acknowledgment of race—or as being "racially unkind."

By drawing attention to the voices and experiences of black French activists and people of color, I have emphasized the difficulties involved in crafting connections among the racial past, present, and future in a white-supremacist society that denies the social realities of race. I have emphasized three features of French white supremacy: anti-racialism, asymmetric racialization, and anticommunitarianism. All of these factors contribute to political and institutional roadblocks that stand in the way of minority mobilizations. One of the most troubling aspects of French white supremacy is the difficulty of rendering the *groupness* (Brubaker 2004) of white French people visible in debates over migration and immigration, race, and diversity. In other words, while minorities are regularly accused of being *communitariste* or divisive when they bring attention to their marginalization, few observers of the French case acknowledge that widespread racism against non white minorities is itself indicative of *white* communitarianism. Scholars and activists can help counter this erasure by helping the French understand and accept that white racism is not a new phenomenon in their country. Slavery and colonialism both played important roles in constructing modern notions of race in France. French intellectuals and politicians were highly influential in crafting the ideology of white supremacy and scientific racism. Despite these social realities, very few French politicians—even those involved in commemorating slavery—frame Napoleon as the anti-black racist and white supremacist that he was.[1]

As critical race scholars argue, ideologies of color-blindness reproduce the economic and political power of those informally recognized as "white." Ruth Frankenberg (2001: 74) suggests that white racial belonging "is in a continual state of being dressed and undressed, of marking and cloaking." Minimizing or erasing French whiteness from representations of slavery and colonialism contributes to the cloaking of white belonging and white domi-

nance in France. Being clear about the historical construction of white supremacy as an axis of oppression in French society—one that continues to
exist in the present day—is vitally important for understanding both the
promise and the limitations of slavery commemorations. French minority
activists involved in resurrecting the slavery past are playing an important
role in countering French erasure of whiteness by providing opportunities for
political consciousness-raising and fostering intellectual exchange. This is
true even for some of the more race-averse groups, such as the 1998 March
Committee (CM98), that foster dialogue about white racism (past and present), despite their criticisms of contemporary black movements.

It is likely that the dynamics of French white supremacy have been inten-
sified by recent terror attacks that not only have taken the lives of innocent
people but also have further stigmatized black and brown minorities. In 2015,
Occasion, an online journal at Stanford University, published a special issue
on the *Charlie Hebdo* attacks. One of the most insightful articles was by
Amandine Gay, a writer and filmmaker who is most recently known for her
work on an Afro-feminist documentary focusing on the lives of black French
women.[2] In a contribution titled "Deny and Punish: A French History of
Concealed Violence," Gay (2015: 1) sharply critiques the suppression of
France's history of racial slavery and colonial violence:

> My country has forged an enduring mythology about itself. The myth
> starts with our motto, Liberty, Equality, Fraternity, and ends with the
> UN's Universal Declaration of Human Rights. And yet, France has har-
> bored two of the most prominent slave-trade ports (Bordeaux and
> Nantes), it has been one of the most ferocious slave-owning transatlantic
> powers, and it has quickly evolved into an equally fierce colonial empire
> that then imported back home its technologies of torture and genocide.

Referring to the widespread influence of Robert Paxton's (1972) revelatory work
on France's collaboration with the Vichy regime, Gay (2015: 2) notes that
"France's slave-owning and colonial history has not been 'Paxtonized.' . . . [On]
the topics of slavery and colonization, the French government excels at fostering
silence about the extent of its historical record of crimes against humanity."

This minimization of French slavery and colonial violence persists, despite the flurry of memorial activities seen since 1998. While discussing this
project with my followers on Twitter in 2015, a teacher outside Paris revealed
that her middle school students were "surprised" to learn that the overseas
departments were once colonies where people were enslaved. She wrote,
"They said, 'But madame, they couldn't be slaves! They are French!'"[3] As
mentioned in Chapter 1, the historian Sue Peabody, also encountered persis-

tent disbelief and erasure surrounding French chattel slavery. In her book *There Are No Slaves in France* (1996), she wrote, "On a recent trip to Paris to do research on 'French slaves,' I was informed by the indignant owner of a boarding house that I must be mistaken because slavery had never existed in France" (Peabody 1996: 3). Resisting this widespread historical ignorance is challenging work. Further, various pressures in French society reward Antillean activists—such as CM98—for framing slavery primarily as an ethnic, rather than a racial, issue.[4] Drawing connections between race relations in different time periods is an important component of racial temporality, the mental links people make among racial processes across time. Social scientists should pay greater attention to how people manage (or fail) to understand race as a temporal phenomenon, because racial categories, hierarchies, and forms of oppression have histories that reach into and shape the present.

In underscoring the importance of racial temporality (and the dangers of its erasure), I wish to qualify and clarify my claims. I am not suggesting that transatlantic slavery should be understood only in terms of its racial legacies. Nor am I arguing that conceptualizations of blackness today should be restricted to narrow interpretations of transatlantic enslavement. I concur with Michelle Wright (2015), who points out that many black identities (especially those of black queer people and black women) are marginalized by what she terms the "Middle Passage Epistemology"—that is, the rigid association between black belonging and being a descendant of transatlantic slavery. Yet as important as it is to acknowledge the heterogeneity of identities that encompass the complicated and unstable signifier known as the "African diaspora," it is also true, as Wright herself concedes, that recognizing racism today requires looking back to the Middle Passage.

Revisiting Collective Memory

Developments around the commemoration of slavery in France have not emerged in isolation. Examples of recent commemorations include the one hundredth anniversary of the abolition of slavery in Brazil (1988), the United Nations resolution declaring the transatlantic slave trade a "crime against humanity" (2001), the two hundredth anniversary of the Haitian Revolution (2004), the United Nations' designation of an "International Year to Commemorate the Struggle against Slavery and Its Abolition" (2004), and the bicentennial of the British abolition of the slave trade (2007). Since 2007, eight U.S. states (Alabama, Connecticut, Delaware, Maryland, New Jersey, North Carolina, Tennessee, and Virginia) have apologized or expressed "regret" for slavery, and both the House of Representatives and the Senate issued similar declarations in 2008 and 2009, respectively.

In France, the memorialization of slavery continues to proliferate through the national May 10 commemoration, Antillean-focused May 23 events (spearheaded by CM98), and, most recently, the establishment of an ambitious museum in the French Caribbean. On May 10, 2015, President François Hollande inaugurated a museum dedicated to the memory of slavery in Pointe-à-Pitres, Guadeloupe. Known as Mémorial ACTe, the institution does not specifically focus on transatlantic enslavement. Instead, its permanent collection and exhibitions aim to represent and assess the worldwide histories of human bondage.[5] Why are these commemorative activities happening now, on both sides of the Atlantic, long after the official abolition of transatlantic slavery? Research on commemorating difficult pasts has identified a period of "latency" after tragic or traumatic events, which can often result in several decades of public silence before the emergence of commemorative activity (Rivera 2008; Vinitzky-Seroussi 2002; Zerubavel 2003). But in the case of transatlantic slavery, the "latency" for Western nations has stretched well over a century. In contrast, racialized minorities have long organize efforts to commemorate the enslaved—both before abolition (Brown 2008) and immediately thereafter (Brundage 2005; Nimako and Small 2010). Because transatlantic slavery incorporated racist ideologies to justify the deportation and bondage of Africans and their descendants, its commemoration in multicultural societies is a minefield of historical resentment, sources of division and grievances. As a result, various stakeholders are likely to have very different (and opposing) interpretations of both the history of slavery and its relevance (or insignificance) to the present. More generally, in commemorating difficult historical events, "competing moral entrepreneurs seek public arenas and support for their interpretations of the past" (Wagner-Pacifici and Schwartz 1991: 382). Prime examples from the literature include the Vietnam Veteran's Memorial (Wagner-Pacifici and Schwartz 1991) and the memory of apartheid in South Africa (Teeger and Vinitzky-Seroussi 2007).

Studies in this area outline three approaches to commemorating difficult pasts. First, "dissensual" (Wagner-Pacifici and Schwartz 1991) or "multivocal" (Hass 1998; Kertzer 1988; Vinitzky-Seroussi 2002) commemorations include diverse interpretations of the past and/or divergent groups within the same space or time.[6] Second, "fragmented" commemorations (Conway 2009; Vinitzky-Seroussi 2002) have been theorized as a form of mnemonic segregation in which commemorative activities are dispersed across different spaces or spaces for distinct audiences with diverse historical interpretations and attitudes. A third commemorative strategy for dealing with difficult pasts is the production of consensus (Teeger and Vinitzky-Seroussi 2007). Vered Vinitzky-Seroussi's model (2002: 32) predicts that multivocal commemorations are "more likely to emerge in a consensual political culture, when the commemorated past is no longer part of the present agenda, and when agents of memory have limited power and resources. In contrast, a fragmented type of commemoration will be engendered in a conflictual political culture, when a strong link exists between the past and present debates, and in the presence of powerful agents of memory."

This depiction of fragmentation and multivocality in commemoration has been challenged in studies by Hiro Saito (2006) and Brian Conway (2009). Both of these studies examine transformations in historical representations over time to demonstrate inadequacies of Vinitzky-Seroussi's theory. Using the case of Japanese memorialization of the Hiroshima bombing, Saito shows that the impact of chance events (a nuclear fallout incident in 1954) can bring previously divided mnemonic entrepreneurs together in consensual commemoration.[7] Similarly, Conway (2009) analyzes the case of Bloody Sunday commemorations in Northern Ireland to argue that fragmented commemorations can give way to consensus with increased temporal distance between the traumatic event and the present, shifting political culture, and efforts on the part of mnemonic entrepreneurs to use the past in service of a politics of reconciliation.

My findings on the commemoration of slavery in France and the construction of divergent racial temporalities build on Vinitzky-Seroussi's model by addressing an alternative explanation for the development of fragmented commemorations. Specifically, I argue that the *path dependency* of historical patterns of boundary construction and group formation can contribute to the production of mnemonic fragmentation.[8] This factor is largely overlooked in Vinitzky-Seroussi's approach, which explains the presence or absence of fragmented mnemonic forms mainly in terms of political culture, timing, and power relations. The French Caribbean case is especially useful for examining the impact of historical fragmentation. These path-dependent sources of fragmentation include the historical displacement of populations via slavery; the incontrovertible geographic distance between overseas France and the metropole; discontinuities solidified by the initial abolition of slavery in 1794 and its reinstatement in 1804; and the heterogeneity of the French black population, itself a consequence of historical fragmentation produced by France's colonial and postcolonial policies.

In addition to drawing attention to historical sources of fragmentation, I provide insight into how divergent interpretations of the past are related to variations in the boundary work of ordinary people and memory entrepreneurs (e.g., the criteria they view as salient for defining group membership). Taking this constructivist perspective to the study of commemoration is in marked contrast to research that treats group membership as a "black box" that does not need to be explained. The task, then, for scholars of collective memory is not simply to reveal the boundaries that characterize commemorative fields and their entrepreneurs but also to uncover how individuals and groups construct their historical imagination by assessing the relationship between boundary work and attitudes toward the past at the micro, meso, and macro levels of analysis.

One advantage of contrasting the micro-level perspectives of memory workers and ordinary people is the ability to identify areas of resonance and divergence in their historical imaginations. This is important because unpacking the historical representations and identities of ordinary people illuminates the conditions of reception (Holub 1984; Mailloux 1998) that determine how forms of collective memorialization are likely to be viewed by members of the public. At the meso level, I shed light on the orchestration of commemorations by showing how individuals negotiate group boundaries within interactive social settings (such as public debates and open discussions). Analyzing these interactive mnemonic practices, as well as the role of cultural performance and commodification in diffusing interpretations of the past, reveals that fragmented commemorative forums allow for multivocality (sometimes even when divergent voices undermine the identity claims of mnemonic entrepreneurs) when the goals of the group include stimulating dialogue in order to "raise awareness" or attracting large crowds (e.g., by providing opportunities for cultural consumption and entertainment).

Racial Legacies and Temporal Labor

It is important to emphasize that two broad types of efforts at temporal labor were evident in this study. One category of time work (promoted by the French state) involves obscuring the racial structure of the slave trade. By avoiding references to the racial identity of slave traders (or by referring to whites only as abolitionists), politicians typically represent the past in ways that both accommodate and mask the white-supremacist present. These efforts to mystify the racial structure of the French slave trade are challenged by the temporal agency of some activists, educators, and officials who are trying to draw connections between past and present racism. On the one hand, we have seen politicians engage in selective remembering and asymmetric racialization; however, commemorative activists construct representations of slavery that invoke the racial or ethnic politics of their group membership while also recognizing whiteness. This temporal labor on the ground contests politicians' "blackwashing" of slavery.

White French people are not the only group members who are glossed over in commemorative events. People from "overseas France" are broadly portrayed as the primary community of memory concerned with slavery, while French of sub-Saharan African origin are not always explicitly linked to commemorative discourse. How does this happen? In official memory produced in political speech, the term "black" is sometimes used to refer to African slaves—historical protagonists—rather than to present-day populations in France. Present-day blacks are alluded to when commemorators describe their memory work as antiracism (and a fight to end anti-black stigma), but present-day blacks in France are rarely directly categorized as such or described. Nonetheless, visual representations of Africa and Africans provide implicit cues about the ties between French blacks of African immigrant origin and the history of transatlantic slavery.

Ironically, while the Afro-French are "masked," they are also potentially empowered by the symbolic recognition that commemorators and politicians accord to the notion of blackness, despite the fact that blacks are typically represented as historical, rather than contemporary, figures. By recognizing blackness as a socially real and existing group category, politicians and commemorators legitimate its use. In this way, the political context enables contradictory claims by opposing groups. Framing French Caribbeans as the most relevant contemporary interest group for the memory of slavery and restricting black categorization to historical figures empowers groups such as CM98 and Collectif-DOM, which reject a black identity. Yet by giving symbolic recognition to the fate of blacks in French history, politicians also legitimate the category of blackness, expanding the political opportunity structure for groups, including those that represent Afro-French, to make claims in the name of contemporary blacks.

Commemorators' claims about the relevance of slavery to the present invoke an ongoing tension. On the one hand, activists call on the French government—and the wider public in mainland France—to symbolically repair slavery by conferring recognition on the colonial past. That is, they seek to frame their objectives as relevant to the nation. On the other hand, as seen in Chapter 2 (on political discourse) and Chapter 6 (on legacies), overseas France is routinely portrayed as the main sphere in which slavery left lasting marks. This localization of collective memory makes sense, given that slavery was institutionalized in these territories. But in privileging overseas France—and, to a lesser extent, the African continent—as the primary *imagined realms* in which the legacies of slavery continue to operate, commemorators and ordinary people risk undermining efforts to explain the relevance of enslavement and colonialism to the national community (and the metropolitan public in particular). Further, relegating the memory of slavery to the islands means that it is all the more difficult to unveil the impact of slavery on the mainland (e.g., in the form of economic wealth, white supremacy, and systematic racism).

To be clear, I am not dismissing the need to raise awareness about the specific legacies of slavery and colonialism in the overseas departments and territories (DOM-TOM). However, I am arguing that these social realities must be discursively mapped onto the intertwined histories of racial and colonial oppression for people of color and their white allies to challenge racial domination in France. People living in the DOM-TOM face multiple forms of oppression and socioeconomic disadvantage. The DOM are not only among the poorest regions in France; they are also among the poorest regions in the entire European Union. Guadeloupe and Martinique, sites of French colonization and slavery, are now sites of environmental devastation. In recent years, scientists and activists have brought attention to the impact of the toxic pesticide chlordecone, which has infiltrated the islands' food supplies and may be linked to elevated cancer rates and other health complications (see Valo 2013a, 2013b). While CM98 and other French Caribbean organizations have worked hard to highlight socioeconomic and environmental problems that Antilleans overseas (and in the metropole) face, their resistance to racial analysis may also make it difficult to recognize pollution and health disparities as linked to environmental racism.

One policy implication of this study is the need to combine commemoration with antiracist pedagogical outreach that fosters temporal connections between the racial past and present. These efforts must guard against asymmetric racialization (e.g., focusing on minorities while avoiding whiteness) and should specify how colonialism and slavery contributed to the Hexagon historically (e.g., through the production of wealth for mainland France). Further, commemorative and educational initiatives need to acknowledge the presence of Afro-descended people(s) in mainland France during *and* after the colonial period. Such an approach would serve the double purpose of clarifying the importance of remembering the slavery past and affirming the presence and inclusion of metropolitan blacks in the French national community.

Limitations

While I have tried to minimize distortions and errors in my analysis, this project certainly involves limitations, practical and otherwise, that should be taken into account when assessing its findings. It is important to note that French Caribbeans do not "speak for" all French blacks. It is quite probable that French people from former colonies in sub-Saharan Africa view these issues quite differently. Future research should probe not only the multitude of French black perspectives on the history and legacies of slavery and colonialism but also the views of other French minorities and white French people. Another limitation concerns the study's methodology. While snowball sampling was the ideal strategy for gaining access to gatekeepers and key actors in the field of slavery commemoration, this method undoubtedly biased the pool of respondents in the direction of more elite and well-connected groups (i.e., those with ties to legitimating groups such as the Committee for the Memory and History of Slavery and funding organizations such as the Overseas Delegation for the City of Paris). This sample also did not include interviews with the most radical organizations—Tribu Ka and Indigènes de la République— in part because they were not deeply implicated in organizing commemorations of slavery during my fieldwork. However, racial temporality and representations of colonial history are not produced only in official commemorative settings. Anticolonial activists such as Houria Bouteldja (2016) are increasingly bringing attention to the connections among French colonial history, white domination, and contemporary racialization. The non-activist sample is largely composed of middle-class and upper-middle-class respondents. The composition of the activist and non-activist samples was both an artifact of the research design (targeted snowball sampling) and the theoretical choice to focus mainly on the historical imaginations of French Caribbeans. The non-activists should be understood as "everyday" Antilleans only insofar as they are not involved in organizing commemorative events and therefore provide insight into "everyday" historical narratives and lay theories of historical causality and repair. It is likely that working-class and poor Antilleans would express different perspectives from those analyzed here.

Finally, the fields of commemorative activism and ethnoracial politics in France are in a state of continual flux. Allegiances and grievances among and within groups shift quickly, and future work in this area will need to take account of these rapid transformations. In my experience, it was difficult to keep up with the constantly shifting landscape of interpersonal conflict and political differences between and among commemorative activists. For example, some of the groups that did not publicly support slavery reparations during the course of my fieldwork now strongly advocate for economic repair. During a visit to Paris in 2015, many years after my data collection, I noticed that commemorative activists and groups that were once at odds with CM98 were now engaged in public collaborations. More work is needed to fully track and analyze these developments—particularly in light of an emerging "Black Lives Matter" movement in France.

Future Research

Despite rising attention to the reparations question during the 1990s (Michelson 2002), and recent "statements of regret" by former slaveholding nations (as well as the U.S. Congress itself in 2008 and 2009), the ordinary perspectives of people of African descent remain severely undocumented and poorly understood. This study contributes to a growing body of interdisciplinary scholarship that considers the memorialization (and silencing) of transatlantic history in post-slavery societies (Bailey 2005; Braxton and Diedrich 2005; Brown 2008; Bruner 1996; Hourcade 2014; Trouillot 1995). These studies tend to focus on the production of collective representations in art and literature (Finley 2002), history textbooks (Washburn 1997; Weiner 2014a), commemorative events and movements (Araujo 2010, 2012; Garraway 2008; Higman 1998; Nimako and Small 2010; Pierre 2013), specific apologies and controversies (Clarke and Fine 2010), and heritage tourism (Essah 2001; Holsey 2004). By contrast, the literature on public opinion toward the history and legacies of slavery is sparse, relies on survey data, and has mostly focused on the narrow issue of reparations for slavery.

Future research should systematically investigate how racialized minorities—particularly those who identify as "black"—understand the history and legacies of transatlantic slavery and colonialism. Future work on commemorations should also explore the trajectory of the racial and ethnic divisions chronicled in this book. Are previously warring factions converging? How are commemorators themselves changing and shifting in their racial and ethnic ideologies? And how are activists responding to the French state's ongoing "state of emergency" and repression of political protest in the wake of recent terrorism? Another important dynamic that is not explored here is the impact of new Afro-feminist activism in France.[9] How are Afro-feminists framing the intersectional impact of slavery, colonialism, and patriarchy on the present? What kind of racial temporalities inform the social analyses and activism of French black women? More work is also needed to explore how activists and ordinary people are resurrecting slavery, colonialism, and the social realities of race on the Internet. In the context of hegemonic racial denial in the mainstream media and political culture, the Internet offers an alternative space for minorities and white allies to contest color-blindness and historical erasure. How is racial temporality being constructed and debated on the Internet via social media, blogs, and Internet forums?

To understand and combat racism, the French must summon the courage to address the links among slavery, colonialism, and the social construction of white racial domination. Perspectives on the European slave trade in black bodies, and the consequences of that horror, vary among lay people, activists, and politicians. Those differences are not benign. Perspectives on the past are many, but only a few are compatible with a vision of the present that enables racialized minorities to recognize and respond to systematic oppression.

There is no easy way, in France, to connect commemorations of slavery with antiracism, as the state continues to deny the existence of race while stigmatizing black and brown people for acknowledging their social realities. The open question that remains is whether French minorities will be able to overcome past oppression, resist white supremacy in the present, and disrupt the racial status quo in years to come.

Appendix A

RESPONDENTS TABLE

TABLE A.1. RESPONDENTS: OCCUPATIONS AND AGES OF NON-ACTIVIST ANTILLEANS			
First-generation migrants (N = 32)		**Second-generation migrants** (N = 27)	
Occupation	Age	Occupation	Age
Administrative coordinator, publishing company	35	Accountant	27
Adviser, financial company	25	Consultant	34
Architectural assistant	36	Student	25
Broker	26	Student	22
Chief operating officer, telecommunications company	44	Social worker	27
Consultant	37	Social worker	38
Demographer	37	Owner, entertainment management company	40
Director of aeronautical maintenance	52	Ticket agent, public transportation service	37
Engineer	33	Owner, beauty shop	23
Entrepreneur	34	Student	19
Health administrator	54	IT consultant	31
IT consultant	34	Student	27
IT developer	36	Actor	36
IT manager	44	Railroad switch operator	46
Journalist	40	Ticket agent, airline company	23
Nurse	43	Chief operating officer, marketing company	32
Nurse	48	Nurse	36
Nurse	46	Subway conductor	46
Project manager, automobile company	51	Student	18
Psychiatric nurse	50	Sales clerk, grocery store	28
Retired chief flight attendant	60	Restaurateur	55
Retired civil servant, telephone company	67	Student	22
Secretary	44	Contract worker, television company	25
Singing coach	50	Student	21
Social worker	38	Store manager, grocery store	28
Student	24	Director of clientele, entertainment magazine	29
Student	25	Program evaluator, financial company	35
Teacher	53		
Teacher's aide	31		
Textile buyer, fashion company	28		
Ticket clerk, railroad company	38		
Writer	56		
Average age	41	**Average age**	31

Appendix B

INTERVIEW QUESTIONS

1. Questions Générales
   a. Qu'est-ce que vous faites dans la vie?
   b. Est-ce que vous êtes né ici ou aux Antilles?
   c. Pourriez-vous me parler un peu de votre famille? (Probe: Mariage, enfants, frères/soeurs, parents)
      i. Est-ce que vos parents ont vécu en France hexagonale?
         1. Si oui: Est-ce que vos parents ont parlé de leurs expériences ici?
      ii. Est-ce que vous êtes en contact avec votre famille aux Antilles?
   d. Parlez-moi de votre arrivée en France hexagonale. Comment-avez-vous vécu votre transition ici?
   e. Parlez-vous créole? (Probe: en famille? avec vos amis? l'importance?)
   f. Avez-vous voyagé dans le monde? (Si oui: ou? Comment est-ce que vous vous sentiez là-bas?)
      i. Connaissez vous les Etats Unis? Avez-vous voyagé là-bas? (Si oui: comment est-ce que vous vous sentiez aux States?)
   g. Quelles sont vos activités principales? (culturelles, politiques, sociales, etc.)
      i. Avez-vous adhéré à une ou plusieurs associations ou groupes? (Lesquels? Pourquoi?)
      ii. En matière religieuse, êtes-vous croyant?
2. La Société Française et les Antilles
   a. On va passer aux autres questions plus larges: comment décririez-vous la société française?
   b. Que pensez-vous de ce qui se passe aux Antilles actuellement? Quelle est votre lecture de la situation?
   c. À votre avis, qu'est-ce qu'il faut faire pour régler la situation?
   d. Qu'est-ce que vous pensez des békés?
      i. Avez-vous eu du contact avec eux?
      ii. Connaissez-vous des blancs pays? d'autres blancs aux Antilles? (Probe: quel est le rapport entre les blancs et les autres Antillais là-bas?)

    e. Quelles sont les différences entre les Antillais en France hexagonale et les Antillais vivant aux Antilles?

    f. Connaissez vous la Martinique (ou la Guadeloupe)? Comment est-ce que vous vous sentez là-bas?

    g. Quel est le rapport entre les Guadeloupéens et les Martiniquais? (Probe: en France hexagonale et aux Antilles)

    h. Est-ce que vous voyez plutôt des différences ou des similitudes entre les Guadeloupéens et les Martiniquais?

        i. S'il la personne évoqué des différences: Qu'est-ce qui explique ces différences?

    i. Quels sont les challenges et les défis concernant les Antillais?

    j. Quelles sont des solutions qu'on peut imaginer pour les problèmes que vous venez de décrire?

3. Identité

    a. Comment définissez-vous votre identité?

    b. Qu'est-ce que ça veut dire d'être X? (Antillais, Guadeloupéen, Martiniquais, Caribéen, Africain, etc.)

    c. Pour vous, existe-t-il une communauté noire en France? (Probe: qu'est-ce que ça veut dire, d'être Noir?)

    d. Est-ce que le fait de venir ici a changé votre regard sur votre identité?

        i. Si oui: comment?

4. Discrimination et Racisme

    a. On entend parfois qu'il y a des gens qui ne sont pas traités équitablement en France. Qu'en pensez-vous? Si vous êtes d'accord avec cette proposition, qui sont les gens qui ne sont pas traité équitablement?

        i. Si oui: Qui sont les personnes discriminés? Est-ce qu'il y a des gens plus discriminés que les autres?

    b. Avez-vous été traité équitablement dans votre vie?

    c. Avez-vous déjà vécu des discriminations?

        i. *Si oui:* Comment avez-vous réagi?

            1. *Dans quel contexte?*

                a. *L'école?*

                b. *Logement*

                c. *Travail?*

                d. *L'espace publique?*

                e. *D'autres?*

        ii. Vos parents vous en ils transmis des éléments pour affronter les discriminations?

    d. À votre avis, quel est la meilleure façon pour affronter les discriminations?

    e. Qu'est-ce que vous pensez de l'action positive? (Probe: qu'est-ce que cela représente pour vous?)

    f. Qu'est-ce que vous pensez des statistiques ethniques?

5. Relations Intergroupes

    a. Quel est le rapport, dans votre expérience, entre les Antillais et les Africains?

    b. Quel est le rapport entre les Antillais et les blancs ici?

    c. Etes-vous déjà allé en Afrique? Quel est votre regard sur l'Afrique?

6. Esclavage

    a. Maintenant on va passer aux questions sur la commémoration de l'esclavage

    b. En 1998 il y avait une marche silencieuse à Paris en mémoire des victimes de l'esclavage et en 2001, le gouvernement Français a adopté la loi Taubira, désignant la traite négrière comme crime contre l'humanité. Est-ce que vous étiez en courant de ces événements? Qu'avez-vous pensé de ces actions?

    i. Avez-vous assisté aux événements autour de cette histoire? (quels étaient les objectifs?)

    ii. Que faisiez-vous d'habitude en Guadeloupe (27 mai) ou en Martinique (22 mai) pour la journée de commémoration?

c. Depuis 2006, le 10 mai est reconnu comme la date nationale pour la commémoration des mémoires de la traite négrière, de l'esclavage et de leurs abolitions. Il y a également le 23 mai qui est reconnu depuis 2008 comme journée des mémoires pour les habitants de métropole issue de l'Outre-Mer. Que pensez-vous des débats et de polémiques autour de ces dates?

d. L'article 4 de loi du 23 février 2005 soulignait le rôle positif de la présence française outre-mer. Etiez-vous en courant de cet article? Quel était votre réaction?

e. Avez-vous déjà étudié l'histoire de l'esclavage et de la traite négrière?

    i. Si oui: Que savez-vous de cette histoire? Quelles sont les sources de vos connaissances?

    ii. Avez-vous entendu parlé de l'histoire de l'esclavage en famille, quand vous étiez petit?

f. À votre avis, est-ce qu'on peut déterminer qui étaient coupable de cette histoire? (Probe: Européens? Africains? Pas de responsables?)

g. Qu'est-ce que vous pensez des réparations?

h. Probe: réparations financières? autres réparations?

i. Pensez-vous qu'il existe encore des conséquences ou des traces de l'histoire de l'esclavage?

j. On entend parfois des Antillais ou bien des blancs qui préfèrent oublier cette histoire. Que pensez-vous de cette idée?

7. États-Unis

a. Que pensez-vous d'Obama? (Probe: Conséquences pour la France? Pour les Noirs?)

b. Que savez-vous sur la question raciale aux États-Unis?

c. Que représentent les Noirs Américains pour vous? (Probe: qu'est-ce que vous aimez chez les Noirs Américains? Qu'est-ce que vous reprochez aux Noirs Américains?)

d. Pensez-vous que les États-Unis représentent un modèle pour la question raciale, ou est-ce que la France représente un modèle? (ou ni l'un ni l'autre?)

Appendix C

METHODOLOGICAL REFLECTIONS

This work draws from twenty-three months of qualitative fieldwork in the Paris metropolitan region between 2007 and 2009, with additional data collection in the spring of 2010. The Paris region was an ideal field site for this study, given its status as the major locus of French Caribbean migration and commemorative activism within the mainland. I used a mixed-methods approach, combining historical analysis of political discourse with ethnographic observation and in-depth interviewing. Below, I briefly describe the research site and different types of data analyzed in the project.

POLITICAL SPEECH

To explore how public officials talked about the slavery past and constructed collective identities, I used an archival database of more than 100,000 texts compiled by the Direction de l'Information Légale et Administrative (Office of Legal and Administrative Information) to construct a data set of speeches, statements, and public interviews delivered by public figures that mention the word "slavery" (*esclavage*).[1] An initial search identified 487 texts that I reviewed to assess their relevance. After excluding references unrelated to transatlantic slavery, I subsequently identified and analyzed 225 texts written by 61 public figures between 1980 and 2010.

INTERVIEWS WITH COMMEMORATORS

Before beginning my fieldwork in 2007, I reviewed press coverage of commemorations since 1998 to produce an initial list of commemorative groups that had been active in metropolitan France. I contacted representatives of these groups and used these first exploratory interviews to identify additional organizations and contacts. In all, I conducted semi-directed interviews with fifty leaders and members representing twenty-three commemorative organizations in the Paris region. I also interviewed eighteen commemorative informants to gain greater insight into the relational dynamics between groups.[2] Interviews were usually conducted in a public place (a restaurant or café) and lasted about two hours, although some were considerably longer, including a twelve-hour interview with a key informant that began over a homemade lunch and lasted through dinner. The objectives of these interviews were (1) to determine the personal and collective identities of commemorative activists, (2) to assess the motivations and goals of groups responsible for organizing commemorative events about slavery, (3) to reconstruct the organizational history of the specific commemoration in question, and (4) to identify the relationship between commemorative activities and antiracist organizations in France. Interviews were transcribed verbatim into French by research assistants, all of whom are native French speakers. I analyzed the transcripts using Atlas.ti, a qualitative data-analysis software program, and constructed matrices in Excel to compare responses across cases.[3] Only those individuals who indicated that they wanted to be named are identified in the text. Respondents (and their respective organizations) are listed in Appendix B.

Some of the interviews were conducted during a period of unprecedented mobilization among Antilleans in Guadeloupe and Martinique. Beginning in January 2009, a group of grassroots activists representing civil society groups and labor unions joined forces under the banner "Lyannaj Kont Pwofitasyon" (Creole for Alliance against Exploitation) to protest rising unemployment, exorbitant prices of first-necessity goods, and other forms of economic exploitation in the French overseas departments. The protests immobilized Guadeloupe and Martinique over the course of forty-four days, and activists demanded, among other things, a 200 euro increase in the monthly wages of Antilleans living in the islands. More broadly, the movement focused attention on the legacies of slavery and colonization through criticism of the economic prominence of the small white community in the Antilles (the descendants of white colonists commonly referred to as the *békés*). Given the substantial media coverage of the conflict (particularly in forums catering to Antilleans such as France-O and the radio station Tropiques FM), I added a set of questions to measure respondents' interpretations of the emerging crisis in the French West Indies.

ETHNOGRAPHIC OBSERVATIONS

To complement interviews with commemorators, I attended forty events as a participant observer (including official ceremonies, as well as meetings of grassroots organizations, marches, cultural shows, and educational exhibitions) over the course of 2008, 2009, and the spring of 2010. Most of these events took place in the city of Paris, but some were also held in the northern suburb of Saint-Denis, home to many French Antilleans and other ethnic minorities. I filmed a subset of the events in addition to taking field notes and conducting informal interviews with the people who were present.

NON-ACTIVIST PERSPECTIVES

To compare elite and activist resurrections of slavery with everyday perspectives, I also conducted in-depth interviews with fifty-nine first- and second-generation French Caribbean migrants.[4] I identified respondents through snowball sampling via ethnic and cultural associations, political groups, newspaper announcements, labor unions, as well as Caribbean internet forums and personal contacts to achieve variation among respondents. About half of the participants were from Martinique and half were born in Guadeloupe. Respondents were not paid for their participation. In labeling these individuals non-activist, I do not mean that they were not involved in any sort of activism at all. Rather, I mean to specify that they were not themselves directly involved in planning or organizing events related to the commemoration of slavery.

These structured interviews were designed first to elicit respondents' spontaneous references to the past (for example, moments when participants referred to aspects of French or Antillean history when discussing their identity or race relations in France), as well as their responses when asked directly about their views on the history of slavery. I began by asking resondents to talk about their migration to Paris, travel abroad, personal and group identities, perception of inequality in France, encounters with racism and discrimination, and how members of their group get along with sub-Saharan Africans, Maghrebis, and whites in France. I also queried them about their views on diversity policies currently being debated in France, such as the collection of ethnic statistics and the implementation of affirmative action. Toward the end of the interviews, I asked questions about their general attitude toward remembering (or forgetting) slavery, examined how they described the consequences of slavery, and explored whether they thought responsibility could be (or should be) attributed for the wrongs of the past. Additionally, I inquired about their views on reparations and other forms of restitution. To determine how they learned about the history of slavery, I asked them to specify the sources of their knowledge about the topic (e.g., the school, the family, films, and literature) and their level of involvement in commemorative events both in Paris and in Guadeloupe and Martinique. In order to protect respondents' anonymity, pseudonyms are used for non-activists throughout the text.

First-generation migrants spent the majority of their childhood growing up in the overseas departments, though some did experience short periods of schooling in mainland France. Members of the second generation, by contrast, spent the majority of their childhood growing up in the metropole and mostly experienced Antillean society and culture during vacations with family members. All respondents in this sample were born with French nationality and had at least one parent of French Antillean origin (some respondents had one parent who was of European, sub-Saharan African, or North African origin). Most of the respondents were middle class and many had acquired advanced degrees, though it should be noted that the second-generation sample was younger and included a higher proportion of working-class individuals than the first generation. Differences between the groups should be read with these caveats in mind. For the Respondents Table, see Appendix A; for the full set of interview questions, see Appendix B.

The French Caribbeans I interviewed in Paris generally felt that they were categorized as black in their everyday interactions, even if they were not considered black in their home societies in Guadeloupe and Martinique. While David Beriss (2004) found that Antillean activists avoid acknowledging race, most of the Antilleans I interviewed who were involved in the commemoration of slavery self-categorized as black. This finding was equally true for ordinary Antilleans I interviewed who were not involved with the movement. One of the more surprising findings of this study is that even some individuals who referred to themselves as racially mixed (*métis*) or criticized the politics of black identity nonetheless often used the term "black" to describe themselves. Although French Caribbean societies typically recognize a range of phenotypic and racial categories between the poles of black and white, French Caribbean respondents often reported being externally categorized as black in the metropole, even if they were seen primarily as light-skinned or mixed at home.

POSITIONALITY AND REFLEXIVITY

As a qualitative researcher influenced by black feminism (Hill Collins 1990, 2013), I take seriously the relationship between my positionality and the data I construct in the field. As an African American woman, my perspective on the topics explored in this book are informed by my evolving understanding of racial oppression and of transformations in my own identity and politics. Like the Martinicans and Guadeloupeans I interviewed, I am a kind of migrant. Born in Tennessee and raised in the North, I grew up in a very different racial context from the one my parents experienced in the wake of desegregation. This migratory aspect of my African American identity also plays a role in how I think about race and white supremacy on both sides of the Atlantic. Over the course of completing this project, I began to see that France is to the United States what the North is to the South. As northern white liberals use the South to deny their own racism, France does the same with the entire United States. Yet at the same time, there are real reasons why blacks sought to live in the North—and why African Americans, from Josephine Baker to Langston Hughes, were drawn to the City of Lights, even as racism ravaged the U.S. North and white supremacy reigned in France.

It is embarrassing to admit that my racial identity was not yet grounded in a serious study of black history and political traditions when I traveled to Paris in my early twenties. While I felt very strongly about the immorality of racism and had many questions about how race and racism operate domestically and globally, I did not begin this project with strong opinions or answers. Those began to emerge only toward the end. In many ways, this work allowed me to incrementally figure out my own views on racism and the legacies of slavery through an ongoing exploration (and critique) of the racial ideologies and narratives I encountered in the field. As a scholar of race influenced by black feminist thought, I recognized that reflexive engagement with my own relationship to the data was crucial to the strengthening of my analysis and the completion of this book.

ISSUES OF TRANSLATION: LEARNING FRENCH AND FRENCH HISTORY

My approach, at the start of the project, was largely ahistorical. I often felt inadequate during the course of the work, not only because of the linguistic learning curve but also because of my own lack of historical knowledge. When I began the project nearly a decade ago, I was not yet well versed in the history of French race, racism, or colonialism. I often felt that I did not know enough about these topics to write anything of significance about them. Without the background of French or Francophone studies, I often felt like an interloper. My primary objective was to take an inductive approach, examining how French people talked about these topics themselves. Most of my cognitive energy was tied up with simply trying to understand what people were saying in the interviews and at events.

During the data-collection phase, I decided to privilege the words of everyday French blacks and people of color over the scholarship on race politics in France. In part, this was a decision born of necessity: I simply could not deal with a mountain of foreign-language qualitative interviews and a mountain of foreign-language scholarship at the same time. I was also frustrated with the fact that much of the scholarship on race in France seemed overly concerned with academic debates and less attentive to the perspectives and voices of French blacks themselves. Of course, I could not understand French minority voices without some grounding in French history and culture—or, at least, my understanding would remain superficial unless I made an effort to connect the data to relevant literature. The trouble, however, was identifying the relevant literature, given the paucity of sociological research on race in France. As a result, this research became much more interdisciplinary than I had anticipated at the outset, as I increasingly turned to historiography and interdisciplinary scholarship in Francophone, Caribbean, and black/diasporic studies.

It took me years of nibbling around the edges of French colonial history to finally begin to develop a rubric for understanding the broad outlines of French Atlantic slavery and its relation to contemporary race politics. I struggled to learn and retain the crucial details of slavery's establishment in the French Caribbean, as well as the distinctions in its unfolding among the various islands and territories. The chronology of chattel slavery (in the Atlantic and Indian Oceans), as well as French colonization of Africa, also remained vague to me until later stages of the project, when I began to obtain a clearer understanding of the temporal unfolding of French racial and colonial history.

Improving my French during the process of conducting qualitative research and learning French history was daunting. When I conducted my first interview in Nantes with representatives of Les Anneaux de la Mémoire, I felt that I understood only about 50 percent of what the respondent was saying. Later, when listening to the audio file, I realized that I had understood even less than I thought. Knowing that I would need to carefully verify my interpretations of respondents' words, I made sure to employ a methodology combining audio recordings, native speakers' transcriptions, and extensive coding with Atlas.ti. With that said, I am certain that some things were lost in translation, even after years of fieldwork, analysis, and writing. This text, therefore, should be understood as my imperfect, though systematic, grappling with the data, not an unfiltered, objective representation of race politics in France.

In earlier stages of the project, reading and analyzing transcripts from the interviews was relatively straightforward, but reading academic literature in French felt laborious. Although my interview transcripts were in French (not translated into English), they were in fact written texts of interviews I had already constructed and conducted. Thus, analysis consisted of resurrecting and reengaging words and meanings I had already heard. It was only later in the project that I began a more dedicated and sustained engagement with history, reading academic work in both English and French. I attained reading fluency in French during the write-up phase of the dissertation, only *after* my fieldwork, and eventually immersed myself in the historiography of French racism and colonialism. In the last stages of this project, I was able to read French as well (and quickly) as I could read English, even if I occasionally had to look up a word or phrase.

While living in Paris, my French writing skills were advanced enough to communicate fluidly with French respondents, city officials, and other professionals, but not fluent enough to write a full-length academic manuscript. Although speaking French felt challenging, my verbal expression and comprehension were sufficiently fluent for me to begin appearing on French radio and television, engaging in political and social analysis (as well as debates) only a few months after my arrival. During my fieldwork (which coincided with Barack Obama's first presidential campaign), I was regularly invited as a French-speaking commentator on most of the major French networks, including France 2, France 3, France-O, France24, iTele, and Canal+.

PRIVILEGE AND FIELDWORK

Being a U.S. citizen, African American, and middle class were all factors that shaped my relationship to the research project and the research subjects. At times, I felt guilty about enjoying my time in France, not only because my topics of inquiry—slavery and racism—are so grotesque but also because as a middle-class African American in Paris, I benefit from a context that venerates African American expatriates while stigmatizing French blacks. During my twenty-two months of fieldwork, I was a graduate student at Harvard University and a visiting student at the elite Institut d'Études Politiques. My status as a graduate student with affiliations at more than one elite university opened doors—professionally and personally—that made my nearly two years in Paris a uniquely privileged experience. As an

African American, I experienced ethnic privilege vis-à-vis blacks in France, benefiting from the positive regard many French have for African American expatriates. As black immigrants from African and Caribbean nations sometimes enjoy the "boost" of being viewed as better than native African American descendants of slaves, so, too, do African Americans abroad sometimes receive greater acceptance than "native" black populations in Europe.

As a middle-class woman with considerable symbolic and social capital, I also received opportunities denied to my respondents. My personal and professional connections landed me a gig as a spokesperson in Paris for Democrats Abroad and, later, Barack Obama's campaign. As a result, I was often asked to appear on French TV and radio to discuss and debate U.S. politics, international issues, and questions related to race and justice in France. Certainly, this access meant that French media reached out to me in ways that reproduced the invisibility or obscuring of French black voices. I also lived in the center of the city in a relatively posh, predominantly white neighborhood near the Luxembourg Gardens, thanks to connections I forged with the African American expatriate community. That I did not live in the *banlieues* (marginalized surburbs) or a neighborhood that was more ethnoracially mixed was a source of anxiety for me during the research. I worried that my work would be seen as inauthentic or that I would be viewed as an interloper for living in a predominantly white neighborhood in the center of Paris. Pressured by the exigencies of finding housing quickly, I decided that as a single woman living abroad, it was more important for me to find a safe and convenient place to live than it was for me to try to fulfill my imagined ideal of politically correct fieldwork.

While I worried about imposing an "American" perspective on the data in early stages of the project, the truth is that I was not particularly opinionated or informed enough to do so as a graduate student. It worried me that I did not feel opinionated about race politics in earlier stages of the project, but now I understand the value of that incubation period. I appreciate that back then, when people would ask what I thought of an issue (e.g., ethnic statistics in France), I was honest about not being sure about my stance. As a more experienced researcher, I now understand that "I'm not sure" and "I don't know" are very valid responses, although I felt embarrassed and exasperated in the past. Toward the end of the project, after considering these questions for nearly a decade, I finally gave myself permission to have and express strong opinions regarding the need to recognize and challenge white-supremacist racism in France.

CONCERNS OVER SCRUTINY AND SURVEILLANCE

At least one of the activist groups I approached viewed me as an unsafe person to talk to. The organization's president would not speak to me directly and instead sent an emissary who did not provide his full name. It was explained to me that the group's leaders viewed me with suspicion and expressed concerns over surveillance. Later, I came to understand that those suspicions were not unfounded. There is a history of black political organizations in France being subjected to scrutiny, surveillance, and sabotage by the French government. There are similarities here to COINTELPRO's dismantling of Black Power groups. Further, the more I learned about the history of the Weatherhead Center for International Affairs (WCFIA), the institution that funded the last two years of my dissertation, the more I realized that my status as a Harvard graduate student would not be reassuring for black organizations that were concerned about surveillance. It is a matter of public record that the founding director of Harvard's WCFIA was the chief national intelligence officer for the U.S. Central Intelligence Agency in the late 1970s.

I was, to my embarrassment, unaware of this history when I applied for a fellowship from the center and did not learn of the entanglement between the center and the CIA until I returned to Cambridge after completing my fieldwork. I have no evidence that Harvard or anyone else accessed or used my data, but the reality is that storing my data on university computers or simply using the university's Internet connections may have put my respondents at risk. It is possible, particularly in the light of revelations about government surveillance throughout the world, that documenting my respondents' political views, names, and contact information might have carried political consequences that would expose my respondents to undesired scrutiny and even repression under less than democratic circumstances. I am heartened, however, that the vast majority of my respondents said that they wanted their names to be used.

EMOTIONAL LABOR

Many sociological studies derived from in-depth interviews do not provide the reader with methodological accounts that explore the role of emotions and affect in shaping the construction, collection, and analysis of the data. This terrain is most often ceded to ethnographers and anthropologists or relegated to methodological handbooks on qualitative research. I believe this oversight is a mistake, as emotional reflexivity is just as crucial to interview-based work as it is to participant observation. The fieldwork for this project involved an enormous number of in-depth interviews conducted in a foreign language, ethnographic observations of events, and archival analysis. While I had grand plans to keep well-organized field notes and summaries of each interview, the empirical reality played out otherwise. Conducting and analyzing more than one hundred interviews in a foreign language was challenging enough. Adding archival data and multimedia artifacts such as photos and videos was very often overwhelming. Having conducted my own research and collaborated with my dissertation chair, I was already an experienced qualitative interviewer by the time I began my work in France. In addition, I acquired expertise in the use of software for qualitative data analysis. Building on these strengths, I made sure that all of the interviews were transcribed by native French speakers and used Atlas.ti to organize and sift through the mountains of data I collected in the field.

One morning, in the final stages of writing this book, I began to sob while reading about the hundreds of Guadeloupeans who, when faced with the prospects of being reenslaved by Napoleon, blew themselves up on the side of a volcano, shouting, "Vivre libre ou mourir" (Live free, or die). I had read and heard the history of Louis Delgrès and the 1802 resistance to Napoleon's brutal reenslavement of Guadeloupeans for years, but this was the first time I cried about it. I allowed myself to fully engage emotionally with enslavement and racial terror only after years of impotently intellectualizing it. I do not think I had the emotional energy, self-awareness, or courage to fully acknowledge the role of affect in my project during my twenties. The gift of writing this book in my thirties is that I write from the perspective of a woman who knows the value of owning her inner life. As a younger person, I could barely allow myself to accept the full range of my emotions in my personal life, much less in my scholarship. Owning your inner life is also something that cannot strictly be taught in the academy. It is a process of internal liberation, decolonization. I have found that I must actually live and be alive with the messy realities of life outside of the academy to enrich my scholarship with my own liberation.

Progressively attending to my inner life over the course of my twenties and thirties taught me the value of grappling with unacknowledged pain. The exploration of my emotions played out over time through therapy, self-help books, spiritual retreats, meditation, mindfulness workshops, private journaling, and, eventually, public writing on the blogosphere and social media. The process taught me that self-care requires the difficult work of fully coming to terms with my own thoughts and feelings—accepting and honoring my emotions, opinions, needs, and boundaries. Eventually (and unexpectedly), this "personal" work spilled over into my scholarship as I came to see the importance of accepting and affirming my inner life in the process of writing this book. I could not pretend to be neutral about racism, slavery, and inequality. I came to see that my non-engagement with the emotions involved in knowledge production constituted lies of omission.

There were feelings—of grief, love, anger, disgust, shame, frustration, fear, and horror—that undeniably shaped my relationship to the "data." During the fieldwork and initial stages of analysis, my encounter with the histories, narratives, dilemmas, and tragedies unveiled in the interviews, notes, and texts I collected remained on the margins. I was only vaguely aware of my own feelings, and mostly determined not to fully feel them. The project felt haunted by whirlpools of pain looming on the edges of every word I heard and wrote, lurking behind the images of racism and slavery that I "collected" and "analyzed." During and after interviews, I felt emotionally exhausted, overwhelmed, and very often depressed. It did not occur to me that these feelings could be generative—that engaging with them directly was an important source of knowledge. Instead, I aimed to unpack "other people's" tragedies and emotions without first fully acknowledging my own. Becoming more alive to my own pain as a child of racialized horror—a descendant of slaves and slave owners, victims and oppressors, heroes and scoundrels—allowed me to see the emotional and moral stakes of this work more clearly. It was a dialectical, iterative process. Considering the pain and anger expressed by black French interviewees provoked my own, even when I tried to bracket and suppress my emotional reactions under the pretense of gesturing to objectivity. This dialectical provocation unfolded over years, mostly unconsciously.

Over time, I also began to feel that many of the people who wrote and talked about these issues drove me crazy—including people I interviewed for the project. I actually had to stop reading my transcripts for a while because the views respondents shared about racism were so contradictory and upsetting. But again, I could not explain why I was upset or how my view differed from their contradictions. I just felt repulsed and demoralized. It is exceedingly clear to me, as a minority researcher, that allowing oneself to fully explore the logics of oppression takes a toll. Interviewing and reading African American perspectives on racism in my earlier research did not make me feel crazy—just sad. But interviewing French people of color often made me feel disoriented, exhausted, and confused. I am sure much of this had to do with the foreignness of the language and the culture, but it also had to do with respondents' political contradictions.

I had the good fortune to meet French people of color—especially black French women—who expressed enthusiasm, encouragement, and support. I did, however, encounter significant backlash and criticism on at least two occasions. Shortly after my arrival in France, I described my project at a seminar at the École des Hautes Études en Sciences Sociale. At one point, a young black woman passionately objected to my project's focus on French Antilleans. I understood her critique as pushing me to explicitly incorporate the larger diaspora—including Haiti and sub-Saharan Africa, into the conceptualization of my project. On another occasion, I encountered hostility from one of the leaders of CM98 who had been very helpful over the course of my project. When my request to videotape a particular CM98 event was denied (after I had been allowed to record some of their other gatherings), I pressed (politely, so I thought) to understand the nature of their concerns. In response, this CM98 representative scolded me (over e-mail), suggesting that I was ungrateful. Over the course of our exchange, I gathered the group was producing their own videos, publications, and research—and the leader's reaction seemed to be about protecting their own interests. While I felt embarrassed and very worried at the time about upsetting a primary gatekeeper, I later understood that these kinds of conflicts and challenges in the midst of fieldwork are par for the course.

As I began revising the dissertation and applying a critical race perspective to the data, I felt insecure about being one of the only scholars of race in France to describe the nation as white-supremacist. In the spring of 2015, I returned to France as a visiting professor to share drafts of chapters from the book. It had been many years since I'd spent significant time in France, and I was nervous about sharing my analysis of French white supremacy in front of French audiences. To my surprise (and relief), I received encouraging feedback, especially from French minorities—not only at my talks but also online, via social media (and especially Twitter). Although some French blacks and people of color also shared critiques, their response was overwhelmingly positive and helped me feel more confident and passionate about unveiling French white supremacy and the legacies of slavery. At the airport on my way back to the United States that spring, I encountered a young French black woman working at the ticket counter. We made small talk as she examined my passport and she asked why I spoke French so well for an American. I explained that I had spent time in France studying French racism and talking to Antilleans about their experiences. Immediately, the young woman smiled and beamed with a knowing look of recognition. She mentioned her own experiences with racism and told me that my work was important. Not only did she encourage me to finish the project; she also escorted to me through the VIP line for passport control and *gave me a hug* before turning to leave. As I walked to my plane, I felt incredibly grateful for this stranger's support and uplifting energy. The memory of this exchange—and of the many other supportive black women I met in France—helped carry me through difficult times.

One of my greatest regrets is that I did not keep a consistent private journal during the fieldwork. Entries are separated by months in the sparse record I kept of my emotional life during my years in France. Although I wanted to maintain detailed notes on my emotional state during and after the interviews, I found that I could not. I felt physically and mentally tired after fieldwork. I also remember experiencing my emotions as an impediment to writing, as not a basis from which to produce knowledge. Graduate school does not generally equip young people of color—any color, really—to understand that everything inside you, including your emotions, is a source of knowledge. Although the qualitative methods courses I took and later taught emphasized the importance of reflexivity, the reality is that professors rarely share much about their emotional processing during data collection and analysis. Emotional processing is also, by its very nature, difficult to "share." Affect is private and can be challenging to understand, much less convey. No one else can "feel" for us or reconstruct the unfolding of our subjectivity. Such emotional processing also, as a rule, is regarded and dismissed as "navel gazing" by researchers who are more wedded to positivism than I am.

Black feminist scholars such as Audre Lorde and Patricia Hill Collins acknowledge the importance of affect in knowledge production. Whether we deal in archives, interviews, or participant observation, we are dealing with emotional contexts, and acknowledging the tapestry of affect that is always already there enriches our understanding of ourselves and the data we construct. One of the uncomfortable truths of fieldwork is that the emotional context of knowledge production often involves affective repression. Emotions are sidelined, bracketed, and disregarded, unintentionally and intentionally. There is also the fact that admitting shameful or politically incorrect emotions is a risky business and can be used to undermine scholarship. Naming and critiquing whiteness in the public sphere (especially in France) is a subversive and emotionally challenging endeavor. I have been at events funded by organizations specifically dedicated to promoting diversity where the word "white" was never mentioned. It is my general view that in both the United States and France, the majority population is terribly afraid of explicitly naming and condemning white supremacy.

In my experience, insisting on the connection between contemporary racism and the history of white supremacy is risky. It involves opening oneself up to the racial terrorism and violence of those who reject the relevance or immorality of the racist past. For example, my public statements on social media about the continuing legacies of slavery prompted one anonymous Twitter user to respond, "Slavery has nothing to do with what is going on right now you fat racist cunt. YOU are promoting racism." On another occasion, my statement that the United States was founded on slavery and genocide was met with a self-described "redneck" accusing me of being "racist" and "a part of the problem." Receiving these messages was, on one level, unsurprising, and on another, profoundly disturbing. It was a reminder that raising awareness about the ideology of white supremacy, the need to combat white invisibility, and the connections between the racist past and present is often met with violence. When doing this work, one must be willing to be attacked as "racist," "divisive," and unpatriotic.

White and non-black antiracists are subject to forms of violence for telling the truth about racism. Such violence ranges from the merely discursive to the physical, as with the white mob's killing of the white civil rights activist Bill Moore. When William Cohen, white and Jewish, published his history of French racist thought, French white intellectuals maligned him as racist. As my critique of white supremacy became more strident, I also worried about the possibility of political and professional reprisals for sharing my analysis and views publicly, particularly as they pertain to my (and other minorities') complicated emotions around citizenship, inclusion, and patriotism. When Martha Nussbaum critiques patriotism, she possesses a certain kind of privilege as an upper-middle-class white woman to which I, as a queer woman of color of working-class and enslaved roots, simply do not have access. My respondents took risks in trying to be honest with me about difficult and painful things. The least I can do is meet their courage with my own by articulating my truth as I see it today.

Reflecting on these experiences taught me that making connections between the racist past and present in post-slavery societies is an inherently political act. Those who are pathologically racist experience as violence the insistence that contemporary racism (1) exists and (2) is connected to past racism. The cultural work of linking the racist past to the racist present is inherently an affront to white supremacy in post-slavery societies. Further, writing about whites, whiteness, and white supremacy as an untenured woman of color is stressful, particularly when what I have to say largely takes the form of critique. White supremacy's sacred credo for people of color— *"Don't talk about the white folks!"*—has been in effect since slavery. Those who choose to engage in this kind of work live with the foreboding feeling that an awful thing might befall them for naming whites and whiteness and criticizing the racial status quo. I worried, fairly frequently and not without reason, about the personal and professional risks of maintaining a strident critique of racism in the public sphere. I share these reflections, in part because people fairly frequently tell me that I appear confident and fearless in my engagement with the public sphere. As a qualitative researcher of race and racism, coming off as a "fearless woman of color" means I must consciously unveil the hidden emotional labor involved in this work. It is important for people to understand that outspoken women of color are not fearless. We experience fear and make a conscious decision to speak anyway.

When writing this book and sharing my analysis publicly during talks and in real time over social media, I sometimes experienced (and concealed) physiological symptoms of fear: adrenaline-fueled headaches, elevated heart rate, and shortness of breath. Like those of many other women of color active on the Internet, my antiracist views at times were met with white-supremacist and sexist attacks. In the end, I decided that the potential benefits of remaining in dialogue with the public about the work outweighed the certain costs of being quiet. At the same time, I was cognizant of the impact of patriarchal and white-supremacist aggression—real and imagined—on my emotional and physical health. As a result, I made an ongoing effort to embrace a holistic approach to well-being, prioritizing mindfulness meditation, self-care, and community. When I have felt annoyed with other scholars for not being reflexive about their race politics, I have challenged myself to be more transparent about mine—and gained new appreciation for the difficulties of practicing what I preach.

Appendix D

RECORDED EVENTS

Events described in Chapter 4 were videorecorded during my ethnographic observations (Table A.2). Overall, the corpus of data comprises 476 minutes of recorded video, which I summarized in 105 pages of transcripts. When transcribing, I made sure to distinguish speakers and to include ample evidence of both their verbal and nonverbal cues of agreement (e.g., head nodding, applause, smiling, and vocalizations such as "mmm-hmm"), as well as of disagreement (e.g., head shaking, booing, frowning, wagging a finger).

	Type of event	Date	Principal organizers	Length of observed exchange
	TABLE A.2. VIDEORECORDED EVENTS			
1	Film screening of *La marche des esclaves* (The Slaves' March)	April 27, 2008	Comité d'Organisation du 10 Mai, Passerelle Noire	74 minutes
2	Film screening of *Retour à Gorée* (Return to Gorée)	May 5, 2008	Radio France Internationale, Musée Dapper	28 minutes
3	Film screening of *L'Épopée guadeloupéenne*" (The Guadeloupian Epic)	May 7, 2008	Musée Dapper, Radio France Internationale,	52 minutes
4	Film screening of *Africaphonie* and debate on the representation of the memory of slavery in the media	May 9, 2008	Orig'in Association, General Overseas Delegation for the City of Paris	90 minutes
5	Conference/debate on "Citoyens Français et Descendants d'Esclaves" (French Citizens and Descendants of Slaves)	March 20, 2009	Comité Marche du 23 Mai 98, General Overseas Delegation for the City of Paris	120 minutes
6	Annual commemoration of the abolition of slavery	May 9, 2010	Conféderation Générale du Travail	112 minutes

EVENT 1: *THE SLAVES' MARCH* (APRIL 27, 2008)

This event was a film screening and debate organized as a collaboration of Diaspora Africaine (African Diaspora), an organization that publishes an eponymous magazine; Passerelle Noire, an association in Nantes that organizes an annual commemorative event featuring a reenactment of master-slave relations; and Comité Organisation du 10 Mai, a small group that organizes an annual march in memory of slavery. The film was directed by Guylène Brunet, a French woman of European origin, and is a documentary of Passerelle Noire's commemorative mobilization. Djibril Gningue, who was in attendance, is the director of Diaspora Africaine and is of Senegalese origin. Théo Lubin is the president of Comité Organisation du 10 Mai and Émile Batamack is the spokesperson for Passerelle Noire in Paris.[1] The panel included Brunet, Lubin, and Batamack. Brunet appeared to be white, while Lubin and Batamack both appeared to be (and explicitly identified themselves as) black. The videorecording captures the entire debate that took place after the film screening. The crowd was multiracial.

EVENT 2: *RETURN TO GORÉE* (MAY 5, 2008)

This event was a screening of the film *Retour à Gorée* (Return to Gorée [2007]), directed by Pierre-Yves Borgeaud. The film follows Youssou N'Dour, the famous Senegalese singer, on a musical pilgrimage that stretches from Africa to Europe and the United States. Overall, the film is a vector for the idea of an "African diaspora," with musical traditions (such as jazz) portrayed as a link to Africa and African people. The slave trade is prominently featured as a historical phenomenon that dispersed African people and African culture. The film portrays Africa as a source of "heritage" and cultural roots. It features African American cultural producers prominently, profiling a gospel choir, as well as the work of the poet Amiri Baraka of Newark, New Jersey.[2] The event was one of many screenings in an annual film festival called "Regards sur l'Esclavage: Mémoire Vive" (Perspectives on Slavery: Living Memory) that was held annually between 2006 and 2008 at the Musée Dapper in the posh Sixteenth Arrondissement in Paris and organized at the initiative of Catherine Ruelle, a well-known journalist for Radio France Internationale. The Musée Dapper is described as "a space of the arts and cultures for Africa, the Caribbean and their diasporas."[3] The videorecording of the debate includes remarks made by the film's director, as well as by Ruelle, and a portion of the question-and-answer session. Both Ruelle and Borgeaud appear to be white (Borgeaud explicitly refers to himself as white several times during the event). The crowd appeared to be multiracial.

EVENT 3: *1802: THE GUADELOUPEAN EPIC* (MAY 7, 2008)

The film *1802: L'Épopée guadeloupéenne* (1802: The Guadeloupean Epic [2004]), directed by Christian Lara, was also shown during the Radio France Internationale–Musée Dapper film festival. It was one the films regularly featured in commemorative events before and during my fieldwork, including screenings sponsored by the General Overseas Delegation for the City of Paris. The film portrays events in Guadeloupe leading up to the resistance to Napoleon's reinstatement of slavery in 1802. In particular, it focuses on the heroic roles of Joseph Ignace and Louis Delgrès, both French officers of Afro-Caribbean origin who led a mutiny and revolt against the French army. Both men sacrificed their lives but were ultimately unable to prevent the reemergence of the slavery regime. In addition to Ruelle, who organized the event, two speakers were present: Myriam Cottias, a historian and director of the International Research Center on Slavery, and Jean-Michel Martial, an actor who played the role of Ignace. Cottias appeared to be white, and Martial appeared to be black (and explicitly identified himself as such).

EVENT 4: *AFRICAPHONIE* (MAY 9, 2008)

This event included a film screening of *Africaphonie* (2008), a documentary about the commemoration of slavery in France and an eponymous festival that gathers musicians from the African diaspora. The project received official recognition from the Committee for the Memory and History of Slavery, and the film featured interviews with a number of well-known figures, including former president Jacques Chirac, Christiane Taubira (the legislative representative from French Guiana responsible for the law that bears her name and that designated the transatlantic slave trade a crime against humanity), and Afro-Antillean figures such as Thierry Henry (soccer player for the national team). The event took place in the lower-level auditorium of Paris City Hall. The first set of panelists and speakers included Jean-Claude Cadenet, the general overseas delegate for the city of Paris; Alain Bidjeck, president of the association Orig'in; Taubira, parliamentary representative from French Guiana; Michael Gosselin, the director of *Africaphonie*; and Modeste Sallah, singer and collaborator on the *Africaphonie* event.

The film screening was followed by opening remarks from Cadenet, Bidjeck, and Taubira. A few questions were then taken from the audience, after which there was a short homage to Aimé Césaire, who had died on April 17 of that year, in which Abossolo M'Bo, a Caribbean actor, read excerpts from Césaire's *Ferrements*, a collection of poems published in 1960, and the poem "Depuis Elam. Depuis Akkad. Depuis Sumer," published in 1948. After the homage, the debate began in earnest, with Pierre Varrod, director of publications for the Hachette publishing house and a professor of communications, as moderator. The official subject of the debate was "the transmission of the memory of slavery and the Negro trade in the media." The speakers included Elizabeth Arnac of Cinéma Lizland Films, which produced the television series *Tropiques Amers*,[4] and Jean-Paul Pierot, a journalist with *L'Humanité* and the editor-in-chief of a special issue on the memory of slavery published on May 5, 2008. Arnac, Pierot, and Varrod all appeared to be white. Vergès and Durpaire both appeared to have very light skin (the color of light tan) but visibly distinct from the pale white complexion of the other panelists. After an opening round of commentary from the panelists, several questions were taken from the audience. The crowd was multiracial. The videorecording captured the entirety of the public remarks and debates after the screening. A cocktail party was held after the event.

EVENT 5: "FRENCH CITIZENS AND DESCENDANTS OF SLAVES" (MARCH 20, 2009)

The event "French Citizens and Descendants of Slaves: The Future of the Antillean Community in Metropolitan France" was held in the lower-level auditorium of Paris City Hall and was a collaboration between the Overseas Delegation for the City of Paris and the 1998 March Committee (CM98). The event was purely an open discussion and did not involve a film screening or any cultural performance. Jean-Claude Cadenet, the general overseas delegate for the city of Paris, opened the event by making reference to the strikes that were taking place at that time in the Antilles. He then read an excerpt from the poem "Solde," by Léon-Gontran Damas, a writer from the Negritude movement, before turning over the event to Serge Romana, president of CM98 and the only panelist. Romana appeared to have very light skin (which he explicitly referred to during his remarks). The crowd appeared to be predominantly black, as there were many members of CM98 in attendance. The videorecording covers the full opening remarks of Romana (which lasted about an hour and twenty minutes) and much of the question-and-answer session.

EVENT 6: ANNUAL COMMEMORATION
OF THE ABOLITION OF SLAVERY (MAY 9, 2010)

This daylong event was held in the massive indoor pavilion of the labor union headquarters of the Confédération Générale du Travail (General Confederation of Labor [CGT]) the day before the national day of commemoration of slavery and abolition (May 10). The theme was "Haiti: A Mirror of Our History." Haiti was an especially salient *lieu de mémoire* for commemorations that took place in the spring of 2010 because of the devastating earthquake that struck the island on January 12 of that year. The cover of the event's invitation featured the figure of a black man and a black woman breaking out of chains and looking toward the sky. Despite the nod of recognition given to the Haitian tragedy, the atmosphere was festive, with activities such as prize giveaways, cultural performances of gwoka (traditional Guadeloupean drumming and dance), and two roundtable debates.

I focus here on the first panel, which included Paul Baron, a retired historian; Naissant Bernier, also a historian; Marie-France Astegiani, a vice-president of the Association des Descendants d'Esclaves Noirs et Leurs Amis (Association of Descendants of Black Slaves and Their Friends); Monique Vatonne, co-leader of the CGT's Collectif Revendicatif Confédéral des Originaires de l'Outre-Mer (Confederal Protest Collective of People of Overseas Origin); and Suzanne Dracius, a Martinican writer. Mitch Zéline, president of the association P2M and host of a radio show on Espace FM, moderated the roundtable. This was the fifth annual commemorative event held by the CGT in recognition of the abolition of slavery. The speakers were all assembled at a table draped with black cloth; a Haitian flag was affixed to the front of the table. Vatonne appeared to be white. Astegiani had red hair and appeared to be mixed, of medium-brown complexion. Bernier appeared to be black, of dark-brown complexion. Baron appeared to be black and possibly mixed, of medium-brown complexion. Dracius appeared to be mixed, of very light cream complexion. Zéline appeared to be black and was of medium-brown complexion. The crowd was predominantly black, and the videorecording includes the entirety of the debate.

Notes

INTRODUCTION

1. It should be noted that 1998 was also the fiftieth anniversary of the Universal Declaration of Human Rights, a point that activists and politicians often made in their statements about the commemoration of the abolition of slavery.

2. Mainland France is often described as "Hexagonal" France, a reference to the five-sided shape of the country's geographical borders in Europe.

3. To my knowledge, there were no large-scale official events planned by the French government for the one hundredth anniversary of the abolition of slavery in the French overseas territories. There were, however, colloquiums and speeches, most notably held at the Sorbonne, with figures such as Césaire and Gaston Monnerville (president of the Council of the Republic).

4. "Les manifestations nationales en metropole," Ministry of Culture, available at http://www.culture.gouv.fr/culture/actual/abolition/partner.htm (accessed March 14, 2011).

5. I use several terms to refer to the heterogeneous population of people in France with proximate African ancestry. "Black French" refers to the population with African ancestry in France due to migration or immigration ties to African nations or Caribbean territories, nations, or overseas possessions. This category includes people from any territory in the Caribbean, including French Antillean islands such as Guadeloupe and Martinique and Guiana, located on the northeastern tip of South America, as well as non-French possessions (i.e., Haiti). In the French context, "Antillean" (*antillais*) generally designates French citizens from the French islands Martinique and Guadeloupe, located in the Lesser Antilles. The term "overseas French" (*ultramarin*) includes all French citizens with ties to the overseas departments. The DOM comprise Guadeloupe, Martinique, Guiana, Réunion Island, and, as of 2011, Mayotte. Note that some of the overseas DOM (Réunion and Mayotte) are located not in the Caribbean but in the Indian Ocean. Occasionally, I use the terms "Afro-French" and "Antillean French" to distinguish between French people with proximate ties to African nations and those with proximate ties to the Antilles. This is a more restricted use of "Afro-French" than that in Constant 2009. Finally, when emphasizing the Antilleans of African origin, I sometimes refer to them as "Afro-Antilleans" (to distinguish the group from the minority of white Antilleans living in the DOM).

6. All translations throughout the text, unless noted otherwise, are mine.

7. Article obtained via Lexis-Nexis; author unattributed.

8. On the relationship between the French and Haitian revolutions, see also Cooper 1925.

9. Post-racialism—closely related to color-blind ideology—argues that racial groups and processes were elements of the past but have now been transcended. On post-racialism and anti-racialism in the United States, see Roberts 2011. Regarding attacks on the use of racial discourse and categories to address inequality in the United States, she writes, "When racial-justice advocates refer to the political meaning of race . . . it is interpreted as an expression of racism morally equivalent to forms of overt white supremacy" (Roberts 2011: 292). Similar "color-blind" critiques are used in France and elsewhere (including in the Netherlands) to silence forms of antiracism.

10. See http://content.time.com/time/world/article/0,8599,1887106,00.html.

11. Zyed Benna (seventeen) and Bouna Traoré (fifteen) were two minority youth who died on October 27, 2005, after being chased by French police. Muhittin Altun, who was seventeen at the time, was also electrocuted but survived with severe burns over 18 percent of his body. During the riots that took place after their death, French authorities declared of a state of emergency, a measure that some interpreted as linked to colonial repression associated with the Algerian war. The police officers, Sebastien Gaillemin and Stephanie Klein, went to trial in 2015 for "non-assistance to individuals in danger." They were found not guilty.

12. I concur with the sociologist Tanya Golash-Boza, who defines race as "a group of people who share physical and cultural traits as well as a common ancestry." She also emphasizes the relationship between the rise of "white or European superiority" and "the colonization of the Americas" (Golash-Boza 2015: 3).

13. For Max Weber ([1922] 1978: 389), ethnicity is grounded in a "subject belief in . . . a common descent" that can be rooted in "physical type or . . . customs or both, or because of memories of colonization and migration." Many scholars suggest that race is primarily a form of "external categorization," compared with ethnicity, which is thought to emerge from an internal sense of belonging (Jenkins 1997).

14. Stéphane Kovacs (2012) notes that since the mid-1970s, immigration from other European nations to France has been on the decline, falling from 66 percent in 1975 to 38 percent in 2008. During the same period, immigration from Africa has increased.

15. According to INED (January 2015), there are 64,204,000 people in metropolitan France. Census numbers from 2012 indicate 1,856,000 individuals living in France's overseas departments with 403,000 in Guadeloupe, 388,000 in Martinique, 239,000 in Guiana, and 833,000 in Réunion.

16. See Pew-Templeton Global Religious Futures Project, http://www.pewresearch.org/fact-tank/2016/07/19/5-facts-about-the-muslim-population-in-europe.

17. As of 2015, 1,856,000 French citizens make their home in the overseas departments, while 66,318,000 reside in metropolitan France.

18. This program is generally referred to as BUMIDOM, for Bureau pour le Développement des Migrations dans les Départements d'Outre-Mer.

19. See Beauchemin, Hamel, and Simon 2009, which is based on the 2008 census. Using data from the "Baromètre des Discriminations" study conducted by TNS-Sofrès, the Representative Council of Black Associations estimates the number of blacks in overseas and mainland France at 1.88 million, or 3.86 percent of the general population; most are of sub-Saharan African origin (Conseil Représentatif des Associations Noires 2007). Figures for Martinique and Guadeloupe are based on the 2012 Insee census.

20. On French racism and discrimination against non-white "colonial troops" during World War I and World War II, including the famous *tirailleurs Senegalais*, soldiers originally enlisted in Senegal, see Fogarty 2008.

21. For excellent reviews of the field, see Crenshaw 1995; Valdes, Culp, and Harris 2002.

22. Yet unlike the United States, where the founders of the nation referred to themselves as white and used racist ideologies to justify slavery, white-supremacist racism emerged relatively late in European history. This distinction is important, as it highlights the fact that ethnic labels and boundaries—such as "Gaul" and "Celtic"—predate modern racial categories in France and are more salient than the term "white" in the nation's collective memory.

23. "The title of French citizen will only be borne, in the expanse of this colony and its territories, by Whites. . . . No other individual can assume this title or exercise the functions or employment to which it is attached" (Keaton 2010: 110).

24. Elsewhere, Flaherty (2003: 19) also defines time work as "one's effort to promote or suppress a particular temporal experience."

25. On the persistent marginalization of Fanon in French scholarship, see Dayan-Herzbrun 2015.

26. My translation from the original French.

CHAPTER 1

1. Nevertheless, as Erik Bleich (2003) points out, geography cannot explain why, for example, matters of race and slavery are treated so differently right next door in Great Britain. France and Britain developed contrasting race politics despite similarities in their economic systems, democratic political structures, colonial empires, and involvement with overseas slavery. While Britain has established a variety of race-conscious policies, France has taken the opposite approach to antiracism. Bleich suggests that this difference can be explained as a result of contrasting race "frames" that have shaped the divergent course of antiracist policy in Britain and France.

2. Transatlantic slavery is sometimes referred to as the "triangular trade" to illustrate the relationship among Africa (where people were captured and sold to Europeans), the Americas (where they were transported and forced to labor without compensation), and Europe (which sent slaving ships to Africa and received lucrative crops and goods produced by enslaved labor).

3. One of the best online resources for studying the trade is the Transatlantic Slave Trade Database, which compiles records from more than thirty-five thousand enslaving voyages (see http://www.slavevoyages.org/tast/index.faces).

4. For detailed analysis of the French suppression of slavery, see Daget 1981.

5. Although the United Nations estimates that 21 million people are enslaved today, antislavery organizations evoke higher numbers. For example, the nongovernmental organization Free the Slaves estimates that 21 million to 36 million people are enslaved worldwide, of which 26 percent are subjected to sexual slavery. India has the largest enslaved population (14 million people). By comparison, there are currently sixty thousand enslaved people in the United States (see "Trafficking and Slavery Fact Sheet," available at https://www.freetheslaves.net/wp-content/uploads/2015/01/FTS_factsheet-Nov17.21.pdf).

6. Regarding anti-black racism in the Arab world, Davis (2003: 63) writes, "Arab antiblack racism has been flagrantly revealed in recent years in the persecution and enslavement of black Africans in southern Sudan, along with their genocide in Darfur, which was long a major export center of the Arab trans-Saharan slave trade as well as a site for farms that bred black slaves for sale like cattle or sheep."

7. On the etymology of the word "slave," see Davis 1996: 52, 2006: 49.

8. These figures are necessarily lower than the actual number of people enslaved, as the records themselves are incomplete (see "Assessing the Trade: Estimates," Transatlantic Slave Trade Database, available at http://www.slavevoyages.org/tast/assessment/estimates.faces).

9. For comparison, during the trans-Saharan trade, Arabs enslaved nearly 5 million people between 650 and 1600 (see Lovejoy 2012: 27).

10. "TransAtlantic Slave Trade," United Nations Educational, Scientific, and Cultural Organization, available at http://www.unesco.org/new/en/culture/themes/dialogue/the-slave-route/transatlantic-slave-trade.

11. Figures obtained from the Transatlantic Slave Trade Database. Note that France and Spain enslaved nearly the same number of Africans, with Spain sending at least 1,061,524 to colonial territories.

12. Constructivists such as Audrey and Brian Smedley (2012) theorize race as a worldview that emerged between the sixteenth century and the nineteenth century, during the development of European colonial expansion and the transatlantic slave trade. From this perspective, the purpose of the race concept was to classify populations that were already viewed as inferior, and, crucially, to justify their domination.

13. Davis (2006: 50–51) also points out that "in medieval western Europe, serfs and peasants were commonly depicted as subhuman and even 'Black,' as a result of their constant exposure to the sun, soil and manure."

14. While the modern concept of race is of relatively recent origin, there were conceptual precursors that conveyed hierarchical ideas about human difference. During the Spanish Inquisition of 1480, Jews and Muslims and their descendants were persecuted and eventually forced to choose between converting to Catholicism or departing Spain (Golash-Boza 2015; Quijano 2000).

15. As Patterson (1982: 7) describes the process, "Gradually there emerged something new in the conception of the black servant: the view that he did not belong to the same community of Christian, civilized Europeans. The focus of this 'we-they' distinction was at first religious, later racial."

16. On this point, see also the discussion in Lamont 2004. Here, she refers to the "decoupling of racism and blackness" among the French population, citing surveys from the 1980s that suggest that "negative feelings toward Blacks (as well as other racial minorities and European immigrants) are weaker than those toward North African immigrants" (Lamont 2004: 150). While Lamont acknowledges the existence of phenotypical racism in France, she insists that it is "less salient" than in the United States and that anti-black racism in particular is not "delegitimized" by French Republicanism. However, it is difficult to understand how such a conclusion could be reached, given the precedence of Frantz Fanon's theorization of France as a racist society that normalizes anti-blackness.

17. Audit studies of racism (known in France as "testing") have unveiled widespread bias against non-whites in contexts such as employment, housing, and entertainment (Cediey and Foroni 2007).

18. "Discrimination en boîte: SOS Racisme va porter plainte," Agence France-Presse, March 16, 2014.

19. To put these numbers into broader context, only 10 percent of the majority-white population, 16 percent of first-generation Asian immigrants, and 26 percent of immigrants overall report experiencing discrimination "sometimes" or "often" (Beauchemin et al. 2010).

20. There are some exceptions to the general pattern of ignoring French white supremacy, but they are few and far between. They can be found, most prominently, in historical studies of French colonialism and scientific racism. For example, Laurent Dubois's work on France's relationship to Haiti (Dubois 2004, 2012) examines white supremacy during the colonial and enslaving era. However, this body of literature on the history of French white-supremacist thinking and practice is rarely connected in a coherent way to French race relations today. Historians of French white-supremacist racism rarely characterize French society as still shaped by white supremacy. As an exception to this rule, a recent essay by Amandine Gay (2015), a filmmaker and writer, argues that white supremacy continues to exist in France.

21. The term "white privilege" has received some recent attention in the French press. In 2014, Amandine Gay wrote an important article for the online publication *Slate* on the need to link antiracism to the "deconstruction of white privilege." A few months later, *Libération* ran a feature

on white privilege (without citing Gay's work). Although neither article mentions white supremacy, both acknowledge the link among whiteness, resources, and power (see Faure 2015; Gay 2014).

22. Mills specifies that this racial contract—these epistemological and social practices of white supremacy—are *global*. Further, he argues that whiteness as a social construct involves the distortion and misrepresentation of the social world. "Part of what it means to be constructed as 'White' . . . to achieve Whiteness, successfully . . . is a cognitive model that precludes self-transparency and genuine understanding of social realities" (Mills 1997: 18).

23. Bodnar (1992: 24) overstates groups' capacities to freely construct collective memory by characterizing them as "fully capable" of creating separate memory, thus downplaying the role of social, institutional, and material constraints. This dimension is more fully analyzed in Brundage 2005.

24. Although Eyerman does not cite Patterson's work of 1971, the progressive-tragic dichotomy he identifies is a variation on the contributionist and catastrophic frames.

CHAPTER 2

1. On the controversy surrounding Pétré-Grenouilleau's comments, and his references to Dieudonné, see Dufoix 2006.

2. Unless noted otherwise, all translations from French are mine.

3. On debates over the particularity (or universalism) of Jewish suffering during the Holocaust in light of global modern human rights discourses, see Alexander 2004; Levy and Snaider 2004, 2006.

4. Henri Haget and Gilles Médion, "Le comique qui dérape," *L'Express*, January 19, 2004.

5. Stéphanie Binet and Blandine Grosjean, "La nébuleuse Dieudonné," *Libération*, November 10, 2005.

6. The program *On ne peut pas plaire à tout le monde* (You Can't Please Everyone) aired on the France 3 channel from 2000 to 2006.

7. "J'encourage les jeunes gens qui nous regardent aujourd'hui dans les cités pour (leur) dire: convertissez-vous comme moi, essayez de vous ressaisir, rejoignez l'axe du Bien, l'axe américano-sioniste."

8. The message read, "Ça te ferait rire si on faisait des sketches sur les odeurs des Blacks?"

9. Dieudonné, "Le sionisme, c'est le sida du judaïsme," Agence France-Presse, February 19, 2005.

10. In an interview on the LCI radio station, Dieudonné attempted to defend his statement by saying that he had been "talking about the exploitation of the memory of the Shoah" and by claiming that the term "memorial pornography" had already been used by the Israeli historian Idith Zerthal. On this point, see Catherine Coroller, "Antisémitisme: Dieudonné de nouveau mis en cause," *Libération*, February 19, 2005.

11. These four dates have been celebrated since 1983 and have been designated official holidays. The national day for commemorating slavery, however, is not a holiday.

12. The laws are named for Jean-Claude Gayssot, a politician in the French Communist Party, and for Christiane Taubira, a representative from French Guiana.

13. Widespread celebrations and commemorations were held throughout France in 1989 in recognition of the bicentennial of the French Revolution. Ironically, the occasion provided an important national context for people of African descent to contest the dominant representation of French identity. Significantly, little public attention was paid to West Indian culture, history, or achievements. As a result, many Antillais observed the festivities with ambivalence and resentment (Beriss 2004: 27–29).

14. In 2009, the name of the Committee for the Memory of Slavery was officially changed to the Committee for the Memory and History of Slavery, reflecting an effort on the part of the government to include historians in a more central capacity.

15. *Loi no. 2005-158 du 23 février 2005 portant reconnaissance de la Nation et contribution nationale en faveur des Français rapatriés.*

16. *Circulaire du 29 avril 2008 relative aux commémorations de la traite négrière, de l'esclavage et de leurs abolitions.*

17. Absent from most accounts of the relationship between the memory work of Jews and Afro-descended people is an acknowledgment that references to parallels between slavery and the Holocaust include boundary-bridging feelings such as solidarity (due to a sense of shared suffering) and mutual understanding. In their study of U.S. public opinion toward comparisons to the Holocaust, Katherine Bischoping and Andrea Kalmin (1999) use survey data to find that African Americans are significantly more likely to draw comparisons between the Holocaust and slavery.

18. See the text of the petition "Liberté pour l'histoire," available at http://www.lph-asso.fr/index.php?option=com_content&view=article&id=2&Itemid=13&lang=fr.

19. See http://www.viepublique.fr. The Direction de l'Information Légale et Administrative (Office of Legal and Administrative Information [DILA]) is a central office under the oversight of the government's secretary-general (*secrétariat général du gouvernement*). It is run by La Documentation Française, the official publisher of all official reports, speeches, and legislation in France. DILA was established in 2002 by the *Arrêté du 5 juillet 2002 relatif à la création au secrétariat général du gouvernement (direction de La Documentation Française)*; see "vie-publique.fr" (JORF, no. 158 [July 9, 2002]). DILA compiles and publishes three types of documents: (1) legislation, (2) administrative information, and (3) official texts. The office maintains eleven websites related to public institutions in France, including the sites at journal-officiel.gouv.fr, ladocumentationFrançaisfrançaise.fr, service-public.fr, and legisfrance.gouv.fr. The vie-publique .fr site was originally launched in 2002 and revamped in 2008. Its stated purpose is to stimulate public debate through the dissemination of information about French laws and institutions. Among other resources, Vie-publique.fr maintains a database of "discourses", which includes *all* publicly available reports, speeches, and statements made by people DILA refers to as "principal actors of public life": see http://www.vie-publique.fr/discours. These include the president, members of the government (the prime minister, ministers, and secretaries of state), party officials, and leaders of labor unions. In addition to the database of *discours*, the website maintains a collection of dossiers concerning a variety of subjects with the objective of "offering a neutral and objective visibility on the evolution of public politics" by compiling "articles introducing select documents of reference (laws, reports, studies, official speeches), put into perspective through chronologies." These dossiers, which include texts produced by DILA designed to summarize and orient the readers' understanding of public issues, are not part of this chapter's analysis.

20. The first text in the database during this thirty-year period appeared in 1981. There were no speeches identified in 1980. I excluded references that were primarily about modern-day slavery or child labor and texts that used the term "slavery" metaphorically. The data set includes full text of public speeches, official statements (*déclarations*), and live interviews on television and radio stations. Only texts with direct references to colonial slavery and transatlantic slavery by public officials were included. Press releases (*communiqués* and *communiqués de presse*), tribunes, interviews with newspapers, campaign platforms, and any text missing a precise date (at least month and year) were excluded. If the interviewer asked a question that referred partly to slavery, but speaker did not talk about it, it was not included in the data set. Identical speeches were counted only once. Some speeches mentioning slavery were identified by the database on viepublic.fr but were not available and thus not included in this analysis. In such cases, the error message read, "Ce document n'est pas libre de droit pour sa diffusion ou sa version électronique n'est pas disponible. Il convient de vous rapprocher de l'émetteur pour sa consultation" (This document is not royalty-free for diffusion or its electronic version is not available). Most of the speakers were national-level representatives or elected officials, but the data set also includes speeches by presidential candidates, party officials, and labor union representatives such as the CGT's

Secretary-General Thibault. All but one of the texts in the data set indicates the city in which the speech was made (or, in the case of written statements, where the text was produced).

21. See the *Grand Robert de la langue française*.

22. Another term linked to black color, *bois d'ébène* (ebony), was used by slave traders to refer to the enslaved. The first known reference dates to 1833.

23. The *Grand Robert de la langue française* defines the adjective *négrier, ère* as "having to do with the trade of Blacks" (*relatif à la traite des noirs, qui s'occupe de la traite des noirs*), while the noun form refers to "those who deal with the trade of Blacks" or "those who were involved in the trade of Blacks, buying, transporting and selling Black slaves" (*celui qui se livrait à la traite des noirs* or *achetait, transportait et vendait des esclaves noirs*").

24. April 7, 1998.

25. June 20, 1996.

26. May 14, 2006.

27. Historical narratives about the complicity of Arabs and black Africans in practicing slavery were very rarely mentioned in political texts.

28. April 26, 1998.

29. April 7, 1998.

30. March 8, 2000.

31. May 10, 2006.

CHAPTER 3

1. According to the association's documentation, the panels are rented to organizations for 1,219.59 euros, plus transportation and fees, which are also the responsibility of the individual or group displaying the exposition.

2. The seventh panel, titled "The Black Code: A Legalization of Slavery?" explicitly links the promulgation of the code in 1685 to the regulation of blacks in the colonies. The panel begins with the observation that "the Black Code . . . legally made the slave a being stripped of all civil rights: it is the 'merchandise' [*bien meuble*] of its owner." Jean-Baptiste Colbert, a French politician, and King Louis XIV are identified as the figures behind the conception and promulgation of the laws. The panel explains the second article of the Black Code, which instructed enslavers to provide adequate food, clothing, and care during times of illness, saying: "By introducing a certain protection for the slave against the exactions of the masters, the Black Code could be seen as a 'humanitarian' act, even if this gives us pause!"

3. *Gro'ka* (gwoka) is a traditional form of Guadeloupean music and dance that developed during slavery and became a key element of plantation culture (and slaves' cultural resistance) in Guadeloupe.

4. "Denise" is a pseudonym.

5. Hair that is relaxed (*défrisé* in French) has been straightened using chemicals designed to eliminate the natural "kink" of hair typical of African-descended people.

6. *Boudin*, also referred to as *boudin noir*, is a type of blood pork sausage typical of Antillean cuisine. It is also found in mainland France and Belgium. *Accras* are codfish fritters that are usually served with a vinegar-based pepper sauce.

7. I attended at least one commemorative event for each organization represented in the sample except the Centre d'Étude et de Recherche des Français d'Outre-Mer (Study and Research Center for French from Overseas) and the Régie Autonome des Transports Parisiens (Autonomous Operator of Parisian Transports) DOM-TOM. To gain insight into CM98, I oversampled members of the group and increased my fieldwork at its events. Thus, seventeen of the fifty-two interviews I conducted with commemorative organizers were with leaders and members of CM98.

8. In general, CM98 uses the term *fabrication* to refer to the socialization of slaves and their descendants within plantation society and the intergenerational transfer of behavior and men-

talities tied to that social and historical origin. I alternatively translate their usage of *fabrication* as "socialization" or "construction," depending on the context.

9. On the distinctiveness of U.S. racial classification, see Schor 2009.

10. According to a COFFAD spokesperson, the group formed during the 1980s but was established between 1991 and 1992. Faes and Smith (2006) report that it gained official recognition as a 1901 Law association in 1994.

11. "Frédéric" is a pseudonym.

12. COFFAD was criticized for the association between some of its leaders and Dieudonné, the controversial French comedian of mixed European and African heritage who has been widely vilified for his anti-Zionist remarks.

13. The respondent asked to remain anonymous.

14. This interview was one of several that was conducted in English. (Vergès is bilingual.)

15. In our interview, Vergès went on to describe the difficulties that geography poses in French collective memory. In response to my question about whether there had been a reaction to the march, she said, "I'm not sure if the government cared. But there were things in the newspaper, TV. I think it was not measured. People didn't really measure what was happening. For French public opinion, this happened in antiquity . . . so you don't talk about that. So there was some kind of confusion about what happened. But French history is very geographically contained within the border of continental France. So it's . . . the Guerre de '14, the Seconde Guerre Mondiale, the Croisades, Saint Louis, Clovis, but not this people . . . [n]ot overseas. Except for Algeria."

16. According to Lubin, the May 10 Coordinating Committee also works with the Mouvement International pour les Réparations (International Movement for Reparations).

17. Tobie Nathan is a professor of psychology at the Université de Paris XVIII and one of the leading theoreticians and practitioners of ethnopsychiatry in France. A formal interview and correspondence with Viviane Romana, wife of Serge Romana, confirmed that she was a former student of Nathan's but that she subsequently took a different path after she established her own career as a clinical psychologist specializing in Antillean families. He has been actively involved in the CRIF and was appointed *conseiller de coopération et d'action culturelle* for the French Embassy in Israel in 2004.

18. Camus (2006: 653) describes the French Caribbean lobbying group Collectif-DOM as a "black association," even though the group's leaders opposed the creation of CRAN and have criticized black identification as "racist" (see Célestine 2009b: 20). On the consequences of "race-blindness" for activists representing French of sub-Saharan African and Caribbean origin, see Keaton 2010.

CHAPTER 4

1. "Tout en continuant à lutter pour la spécificité du groupe, les Antillais en France et les Portoricains aux Etats Unis ont été et continuent d'être soumis à une forme de pression face à l'émergence de labellisations ethniques ou raciales globalisantes, 'Noirs' en France ou 'Hispaniques/Latinos' aux Etats-Unis, mettant en jeu leur 'spécificité.'"

2. Lozès, Tin, and Ndiaye are all former leaders of the Cercle d'Action pour la Promotion de la Diversité en France (Action Circle for the Promotion of Diversity in France).

3. The prevalence of public speech in the commemorations I observed in my fieldwork is, in part, a reflection of the choices I made in deciding which events to attend. However, public speeches are a standard feature in the French commemorative repertoire, providing mnemonic entrepreneurs with an opportunity to describe their interpretation of the past.

4. The word *esclavagiste* can mean "enslaver," "slave driver," or "someone who is pro-slavery."

5. The reference to *la trempe de l'épée* is from Césaire 1947.

6. Présence Africaine developed out of a Pan-African literary magazine associated with the Negritude movement that was founded in 1949 by the Senegalese intellectual Alioune Diop. It is based in the Fifth District of Paris, near the venue of *The Slaves' March* event.

7. Shelby (2005: 209–211) describes five "modes" of thick blackness: (1) racialist (depictions of blackness as a biological category), (2) ethnic (emphasizing ancestry and cultural heritage), (3) nationality (identification with predominantly black nation-states or forms of ethnic nationalism in which people "think of themselves and their culture as derived from a particular geographic location"), (4) cultural (defines blackness in terms of practices, beliefs, and norms), and (5) kinship (signifies blackness using tropes of family and relatedness).

8. BUMIDOM refers to the state-sponsored program of mass-migration from the Antilles to mainland France that began in the 1960s.

9. *Domien* is a reference to the overseas departments (DOM).

10. In her analysis of Antillean associations' "strategy of differentiation"—efforts to distinguish themselves from other "blacks"—Célestine (2010) analyzed the boundary work of groups such as Collectif-DOM and CM98 as they attempted to distinguish themselves from CRAN. She points out that CRAN's efforts to intervene on the memory of slavery for May 10 events in 2006 provoked negative reactions from Antillean associations. Specifically, CRAN was denounced for conflating Antillean concerns with those of the Afro-French, racializing the history of slavery, and linking this history to black identity.

CHAPTER 5

1. Most people who are perceived as black and self-define as black in France are actually from sub-Saharan Africa and are not descendants of transatlantic slaves.

2. Past research suggests that higher socioeconomic status correlates with greater knowledge about one's ancestral belonging. For example, Lieberson 1985 has shown that low-income rural whites in the United States more often describe themselves as "unhyphenated whites," without identifying a particular ethnic heritage.

3. Indeed, the ancestral and cultural diversity of Guadeloupean and Martinican people has been the focal point of the *antillanité* and *créolité* movements in French Caribbean literature that have reacted against the African (and black) identity at the heart of *négritude*.

4. *Chapé coulie* was also a term mentioned by respondents that indicated Indian ancestry. *Chapé* was often used as a modifier for various categories. In this case, *chapé coulie* would mean "someone who could *almost* pass for a *coulie*" (literally, it means "someone who just missed qualifying as a *coulie*").

5. In this context, *négresse* could be translated as "Negro woman." When used by members of the group about themselves, it almost never has a pejorative connotation and is often used as a compliment, although sometimes it is formulated in a backhanded way (e.g., calling someone a *belle négresse* translates as a "beautiful Negro woman," whereas using just the term *chabine* [a term for light-complexioned women with brown or copper-colored hair and eyes] is viewed in many cases as a compliment (even without the modifier *belle*).

6. Cheikh Anta Diop (1923–1986), a Senegalese intellectual, was well known for his research on precolonial African cultures and civilizations.

7. For a discussion of interracial and interethnic relationships during slavery in the United States, see Waters 1991: 61. In particular, she writes, "There were also consensual unions between Whites and Blacks in both the North and the South, and also unions between Blacks and Indians as well as with other ethnic or racial groups. . . . There is also much evidence that the degree of intermixing, both voluntary and involuntary, was quite high over the course of generations." It is unclear to me, however, that consent (and thus "consensual" black-white relationships) can be said to exist under a situation of oppression, enslavement, and natal alienation.

8. *Crépus* could be translated into English neutrally as "frizzy," but in colloquial African American usage, one would say "nappy" hair to denote the thickly coiled hair texture typical of African-descended populations.

9. On this topic, Lirus (1979: 24) writes, "En créole, 'nèg kongo' signifie corporellement un Noir non métissé, l'esclave africain, image détestée de l'avilissement subi. Encore de nos jours ces mots sont une insulte et s'adressent, comme 'par hasard,' à ceux qu'on considère comme non 'civilisé,' qui ont le plus souvent la peau très noir et les traits négroïdes."

10. A small number of respondents (5 percent) defined blackness in terms of categorical opposition to whiteness. For example, Raphael, a second-generation migrant, said that being black simply meant "not being white."

11. See Noiriel 1988: 13, which describes immigration as a *non-lieu de mémoire* in French collective memory.

CHAPTER 6

1. Some mainstream media outlets referred to the LKP in standard French as the Collectif contre l'Exploitation Outrancière (Collective against Outrageous Exploitation).

2. Criticism of capitalism was a central feature of the LKP movement, which partly explains the support the group was able to garner from the CGT and other labor unions in the DOM and mainland France. To take just one example, Domota was quoted as saying that "capitalism inexorably leads to barbarism" in an interview with *L'Humanité*, September 18, 2009.

3. "Aujourd'hui, s'attaquer à un tabou, en disant que la Guadeloupe est et demeure construite sur des rapports de classes et de races, cela choque alors que c'est la vérité," as quoted in Nedelkovic and Dieudonné 2009.

4. These claims (*revendications*) were organized into fourteen categories (including "Life Conditions," "Health," "Environment," "Housing," "Education," "Union Rights," "Agricultural Production," and "Management of Territory and Infrastructures"). Most famously, the group lobbied unsuccessfully for the French state and particular companies to pay 200 euros per month to Guadeloupean families to help offset the rapidly rising cost of living, a long-standing problem that became even worse during the global economic downturn.

5. In Antillean Creole, *profitayson* refers to exploitation.

6. For a comparison of African American and Jewish reparations claims, see also Howard-Hassmann and Lombardo 2007. With regard to causal narratives, the authors note, "The shorter the causal chain, and the fewer the actors involved in causing the harm, the easier it is for the link to be established" (Howard-Hassmann and Lombardo 2007: 29).

7. The wording of the question was "Est-ce que tu penses qu'il existe encore des conséquences ou des traces de l'esclavage aujourd'hui?" In almost every case, I used the words *conséquences* and *traces* when probing respondents on this theme. This choice was deliberate, given the relatively neutral valence of the word "consequence," as opposed to other terms that would have a positive or negative association. In the earlier phase of my fieldwork, I experimented with using the word *sequelle* (roughly translated as "aftereffect") when posing the question to respondents but decided to generally avoid it unless respondents used it first. On a few occasions, particularly when respondents did not seem to understand the question, I used the term *dégâts* (aftermath), but this was not ideal, given the decidedly negative connotations. However, with those caveats aside, my analysis shows that in the vast majority of the cases where the neutral word "consequences" was used in asking the question, respondents almost always provided a list of contemporary problems rather than "positive" effects of the slave trade. From a methodological standpoint, this could suggest that regardless of the specific wording of the probe, the line of questioning earlier in the interviews (particularly on themes related to problems facing Antilleans in overseas and mainland France) could have primed respondents to interpret the question in terms of negative group dynamics or challenges experienced by group members. More "posi-

tive" responses might have been observed if respondents had been primed with questions about the "best" characteristics of Antilleans, for example.

8. Respondents usually indicated a geographic locus spontaneously. In some, but not all, cases, I probed to clarify where respondents felt the slavery past had left a lasting effect. Further research should determine how Antilleans would respond if probed systematically on this question.

9. The respondent used the word *nègre*, but in this context it is clear that it was pejorative; thus, the proper translation is "nigger." As mentioned earlier, French and Antillean Creole have no specific word that means "nigger." The positive, neutral, and negative meanings of *negre* and *neg* are context-specific.

10. For discussion of Fanon's and Sartre's conception of the legacies of colonialism, see Jules-Rosette 2007: 279. Jules-Rosette writes, "The devastating consequences of colonialism outlined in Sartre's preface include its negative effects on the psyches and politics of the oppressors and the oppressed. Although they approach this program from different perspectives, Sartre and Fanon agree. . . . [T]he economic profits and wealth reaped from colonialism are a bitter pill swallowed by the colonizing nations as they absorb the guilt for their actions and the potential internal violence that they may cause in the long run."

CHAPTER 7

1. They elaborate: "A reparation scheme might for example, effect a transfer from taxpayers to identified individual victims, as in the case of Japanese American reparations. It might effect a transfer from identified wrongdoers to a group or institution that serves as a stand-in for deceased or unidentifiable victims, as when compensatory payments are made to Jewish charities or the State of Israel as representatives of deceased victims of the Holocaust. It might even relax both constraints, as in proposals for living taxpayers to pay money to living African Americans based on harms inflicted by dead people (antebellum Whites) on dead people (antebellum Blacks)" (Posner and Vermeule 2003: 691–692).

2. "De nos conversations avec les planteurs il résulte pour nous qu'ils ne se montrent si rebelles au progrès que parce qu'ils ont peur de tout perdre. Le jour où l'indemnité leur sera accordée, sur quelques fous, ils se soumettront sans plus de résistance" (Schoelcher 1842: 259).

3. "L'esclavage est le malheur des maitres et non pas leur faute, la faute est à la métropole qui le commanda, qui l'excita. L'émancipation est une expropriation forcée pour cause d'utilité humanitaire, comme l'a dit un habitant. L'indemnité est donc un droit pour les créoles. . . . Sans doute, la servitude a toujours été un abus, un acte de violence, un crime, et le crime n'engendre pas de droit; mais le crime politique engendre des faits qui ont leur valeur légale et commandent la réserve. . . . Ceux qui prétendent qu'il est permis d'arracher aux maitres leur propriété noire, purement et simplement, parce que cette propriété est et à toujours été illégitime, méconnaissent qu'elle est à toujours été légale, ils oublient que le pacte social qui la protège ne peut rien défaire violemment de ce qu'il a institué législativement" (Schoelcher 1842: 260).

4. According to Frédéric Régent (2007), former slave owners in Guadeloupe received 470 francs per slave, and Martinican colonists received 430 francs per slave.

5. Haiti's colonial debt was reduced to 90 million francs—a sum that Haiti was only able to pay in 1883—seventy-nine years after its independence.

6. See Marquand 2010.

7. According to Verdun (1993: 600), the African American reparations movement can be divided into five periods: "1) the Civil War–Reconstruction era; 2) the turn of the century; 3) the Garvey movement; 4) the civil rights movement of the late 1960s and early 1970s; and 5) the post–Civil Liberties Act era beginning in 1989."

8. See "What Is N'COBRA?" National Coalition of Blacks for Reparations in America website, available at http://www.ncobra.org/aboutus/index.html (accessed April 25, 2011). Here, the group defines reparations as "a process of repairing, healing and restoring a people injured

because of their group identity and in violation of their fundamental human rights by governments or corporations." N'COBRA bases its reparations claims on the qualification of chattel slavery as a crime against humanity (subject to international law governing human rights abuses) and the century of racialized oppression that followed it after abolition in the United States: "The Trans-Atlantic Slave 'Trade' and chattel slavery, more appropriately called the Holocaust of Enslavement or Maafa, was a crime against humanity. Millions of Africans were brutalized, murdered, raped and tortured. . . . It was followed by 100 years of government led and supported denial of equal and humane treatment including Black Codes, convict lease, sharecropping, peonage, and Jim Crow practices of separate and unequal accommodations. African descendants continue to be denied rights of self-determination, inheritance, and full participation in the U.S. government and society."

9. Although it is often stated that African Americans were promised "forty acres and a mule" following abolition, Verdun (1993: 611) shows that this is only partially true: "The forty acres and a mule may be more symbolic than substantive in its origins. Although legislation providing land to freedmen existed, and land was divided up by the Freedmen's Bureau in twenty and forty acre plots, there was never any legislation that provided freedmen with mules."

10. Shelly Campo, Teresa Mastin, and M. Somjen Frazer (2004) demonstrated that while blacks favored reparations more frequently than whites, attitudes toward reparations in the United States were much less polarized around race than reported in the media. Moreover, support for reparations was generally mediated by whether respondents felt that forms of compensation and restitution would improve or damage race relations. Dawson and Popoff (2004) found the opposite—that is, opposition to both economic and symbolic repair was overwhelmingly polarized around race, with the vast majority of whites opposing both and most blacks supporting both. Significantly, the authors found that blacks' support for reparations was explained in large part by their racial identity, consistent with Dawson's prior work on blacks' political attitudes being contingent on the salience of their black identity (particularly the extent to which they view their fate as linked to the group).

11. This figure includes thirteen leaders and members of CM98 and thirty leaders and members of other organizations.

12. "Racism Monitor to Sue over French Bank's Haiti 'Plunder,'" *France 24*, May 10, 2013, available at http://www.france24.com/en/20130510-france-racism-watchdog-lawsuit-haiti-plun der-slavery-reparations.

13. The 2002 history curriculum limits discussion of Atlantic slavery to CE2-CM1-CM2 history classes.

14. On the French occupation of the Ruhr River valley in 1923, see Fischer 2003.

15. COFFAD (2000) estimated that Western nations owed black populations $960 trillion, or 1,000 trillion euros.

16. The question posed to respondents was *"Qu'est-ce que tu penses de l'idée de réparations?"*

CONCLUSION

1. William Cohen (1980) acknowledged Napoleon's negrophobia, and recent work has brought new attention to Napoleon's anti-black racism (see, e.g., Reiss 2012; Ribbe 2005).

2. See https://www.facebook.com/OuvrirLaVoix (accessed March 8, 2016).

3. Tweet from September 8, 2015, https://twitter.com/my_quiche/status/641278112114864128.

4. On the differences between French and British approaches to representing slavery as "racial history," see Hourcade 2014, esp. chaps. 1, 5.

5. See Flandrin 2015.

6. On "dissensual" commemorations, see Wagner-Pacifici and Schwartz 1991: 408: "Attended by all but interpreted in different ways, the Vietnam Veterans Memorial occasions solidarity in the absence of common beliefs. It induces people who think differently to display the

same ritual respect toward the soldiers. While some scholars, notably Émile Durkheim (and followers, including David Kertzer [1988]), construe common action rather than common beliefs as the essence of solidarity, there remains a distinction to be drawn between monuments that induce uniform ritual respect without consensus in belief (like the Vietnam Memorial) and monuments that sustain both common belief and uniform ritual respect (like the Revolutionary War and the world war memorials). At stake in this distinction are two different conceptions of the past, two different ways of affectively responding to it, and two different ways of representing it. To consensual monuments goes the task of celebrating the past; to dissensual monuments goes the task of coming to terms with it, of integrating into the collective memory political divisions and military defeat."

7. "What differentiates between fragmented and multivocal types of commemoration may not be a political culture, a link between the past and present debates, or power of agents of memory. Rather, it seems to depend on whether groups of agents of memories forge networks of interactions, create feedback loops among the groups, and consolidate their initially fragmented commemorative practices into a multivocal yet single frame of commemoration" (Saito 2006: 372).

8. In pointing to the path dependency of commemorative practices, I draw on Olick 1999b. Olick uses Mikhail Bakhtin's concept of the "genre" to argue that "historically accrued 'types' of utterances" constitute patterns of speaking structured as a set of conventions against which or within which those utterances are produced and read" (Olick 1999b: 384). In other words, present commemorations are structured by past "utterances" (what I would simply term "historical representations").

9. For example, Mwasi-Collectif is an Afro-feminist group established in 2014 that uses social media, intellectual exchange, and public protest to bring attention to the particular experiences and challenges of black women in France: see "Afro-feminism in France: The Struggle for Self-Emancipation," available at http://www.awid.org/news-and-analysis/afro-feminism-france-struggle-self-emancipation, and "Les afroféministes sortent du rang et envahissent Twitter," available at http://www.grazia.fr/societe/phenomenes/articles/les-afrofeministes-sortent-du-rang-et-envahissent-twitter-755610 (accessed March 8, 2016).

APPENDIX C

1. Public figures include officials, party representatives, and leaders of labor unions.

2. Commemorators were not paid for their participation. Interviews were conducted with one to four leaders of each organization included in the main analysis. Commemorative informants included individuals who have produced commemorative events but are not themselves members of organizations included in the main analysis. Informants also included (1) members and leaders of groups that were not directly involved in memory work related to slavery but sometimes partnered with mnemonic entrepreneurs (e.g., the Comité d'Action Sociale en faveur des Originaires des Départements, the Conseil Représentatif des Institutions Juives de France, the Conseil Regroupant les Organisations Arméniennes de la France, Tous Créole), (2) individuals who had been involved in commemorative groups that are no longer active, and (3) commemorative groups that were not based in Paris.

3. These same procedures were used to analyze interviews with non-activists.

4. Determining the generational status of Antillean migrants is complicated by the circular migration patterns that characterize Antilleans' movement between their islands and mainland France. By "first-generation migrants," I mean Antilleans who spent most of their childhood growing up in the islands and migrated to Paris, usually to find work or pursue higher education. However, it is important to note that many Antilleans grow up "between" the West Indies and mainland France. In some cases, respondents were born in Paris for medical reasons (their mothers preferred the hospitals in Paris) but grew up in the islands. Other Antilleans would accompany one or both of their parents on their own attempts to find work in Paris, only to return to

Martinique or Guadeloupe when these opportunities did not pan out. For the purposes of this study, second-generation migrants were respondents who were born and raised entirely in mainland France. Such people are frequently (and usually pejoratively) referred to in Antillean circles as *Négropolitains*, a play on the words "Negro" and "metropolitan."

APPENDIX D

1. In the months following this event, I interviewed Gningue, Lubin, and Batamack.

2. It is interesting to note that the French version racializes slavery by invoking the term "black slaves" (*esclaves noirs*), whereas the English version refers simply to "slaves." The website includes this summary of the film in English: "The musical road movie, *Return to Gorée*, tells of African singer Youssou N'Dour's epic journey following the trail left by slaves and by the jazz music they invented. Youssou N'Dour's challenge is to bring back to Africa a jazz repertoire and to sing those tunes in Gorée, the island that today symbolizes the slave trade and stands to commemorate its victims. Guided in his mission by the pianist Moncef Genoud, Youssou N'Dour travels across the U.S. of America and Europe. Accompanied by some of the world's most exceptional musicians, they meet peoples and well-known figures, and create, through concerts, encounters and debates, music which transcends cultural division. From Atlanta to New Orleans, from New York to Dakar through Luxemburg the songs are transformed, immersed in jazz and gospel. But the day of their return to Africa is fast approaching and much remains to be done to be ready for the final concert" ("Synopsis," available at http://www.retouragoree.com/synopsis.html).

3. See http://www.dapper.com.fr.

4. *Tropiques Amers* (Bitter Tropics) was a five-part television series that appeared on the France 3 channel in 2007. The plot chronicled the lives and loves of a plantation owner in Martinique, his white wife, and his black (slave) mistress in the 1800s.

References

Ako, Edward O. 1984. "'L'Etudiant Noir' and the Myth of the Genesis of the Negritude Movement." *Research in African Literatures* 15:341–353.

Alexander, Jeffrey C. 2004. "On the Social Construction of Moral Unversals: The 'Holocaust' from War Crime to Trauma Drama." In *Cultural Trauma and Collective Identity*, ed. Jeffrey C. Alexander et al., 196–263. Berkeley: University of California Press.

Alexander, Jeffrey C., Ron Eyerman, Bernard Giesen, Neil J. Smelser, and Piotr Sztompka. 2004. *Cultural Trauma and Collective Identity*. Berkeley: University of California Press.

Anderson, Benedict R. 2006. *Imagined Communities: Reflections on the Origin and Spread of Nationalism*. London: Verso.

Araujo, Ana Lucia. 2010. *Public Memory of Slavery: Victims and Perpetrators in the South Atlantic*. Amherst, NY: Cambria.

———. 2012. *Politics of Memory: Making Slavery Visible in the Public Space*. New York: Routledge.

Bailey, Anne C. 2005. *African Voices of the Atlantic Slave Trade: Beyond the Silence and the Shame*. Boston: Beacon.

Balibar, Étienne, and Immanuel Maurice Wallerstein. 1991. *Race, Nation, Class: Ambiguous Identities*. London: Verso.

Barth, Fredrik. 1969. *Ethnic Groups and Boundaries: The Social Organization of Cultural Differences*. Boston: Little, Brown.

Barthel-Bouchier, Diane L. 1996. *Historic Preservation: Collective Memory and Historical Identity*. New Brunswick, NJ: Rutgers University Press.

Bashi-Treitler, Vilna. 2013. *The Ethnic Project Transforming Racial Fiction into Ethnic Factions*. Stanford, CA: Stanford University Press.

Beauchemin, Cris, Christelle Hamel, Maud Lesné, Patrick Simon, and the TeO Group. 2010. "Les discrimination: Une question de minorités visibles." *Population and Sociétés*, no. 466, April. Available at https://www.ined.fr/fichier/s_rubrique/19134/466.fr.pdf.

Beauchemin, Cris, Christelle Hamel, and Patrick Simon. 2009. "Trajectoires et origines: Enquête sur la diversité des populations de France." Documents de Travail no. 168. Institut National d'Études Demographiques, Paris.

Becker, Howard Saul. 1991. *Outsiders: Studies in the Sociology of Deviance.* New York: Free Press.

Bell, Derrick. 1992. *Faces at the Bottom of the Well: The Permanence of Racism.* New York: Basic.

Berg, Manfred. 2009. "Historical Continuity and Counterfactual History in the Debate over Reparations for Slavery." In *Historical Justice in International Perspective: How Societies Are Trying to Right the Wrongs of the Past,* ed. Manfred Berg and Bernd Schaefer, 69–92. New York: Cambridge University Press.

Beriss, David. 2004. *Black Skins, French Voices: Caribbean Ethnicity and Activism in Urban France.* Boulder, CO: Westview.

Best, Stephen, and Saidiya Hartman. 2005. "Fugitive Justice." *Representations* 92:1–15.

Biddiss, Michael D. 1970. *Father of Racist Ideology: The Social and Political Thought of Count Gobineau.* New York: Weybright and Talley.

Bischoping, Katherine, and Andrea Kalmin. 1999. "Public Opinion about Comparisons to the Holocaust." *Public Opinion Quarterly* 63:485–507.

Bleich, Erik. 2000. "Antiracism without Races: Politics and Policy in a 'Color-Blind' State." *French Politics Culture and Society* 18:48–74.

———. 2003. *Race Politics in Britain and France: Ideas and Policymaking since the 1960s.* Cambridge: Cambridge University Press.

———. 2004. "Anti-racism without Races: Politics and Policy in a 'Color-Blind' State." In *Race in France: Interdisciplinary Perspectives on the Politics of Difference,* ed. Herrick Chapman and Laura L. Frader, 162–188. New York: Berghahn.

Bodnar, John E. 1992. *Remaking America: Public Memory, Commemoration, and Patriotism in the Twentieth Century.* Princeton, NJ: Princeton University Press.

Boittin, Jennifer Anne. 2010. *Colonial Metropolis: The Urban Grounds of Anti-imperialism and Feminism in Interwar Paris.* Lincoln: University of Nebraska Press.

Bonilla-Silva, Eduardo. 1997. "Rethinking Racism: Toward a Structural Interpretation." *American Sociological Review* 62:465–480.

———. 2000. "This Is a White Country: The Racial Ideology of the Western Nations of the World-System." *Sociological Inquiry* 70 (2): 188–214.

Bourdieu, Pierre. 2001. *Masculine Domination.* Stanford, CA: Stanford University Press.

Bouteldja, Houria. 2016. *Les blancs, les juifs et nous: Vers une politique de l'amour révolutionnaire.* Paris: La Fabrique.

Bovenkerk, Frank, Benjamin Kilborne, François Raveau, and David Smith. 1979. "Comparative Aspects of Research on Discrimination against Non-white Citizens in Great Britain, France and the Netherlands." In *Problems in International Comparative Research in the Social Sciences,* ed. Jan Berting, Felix Geyer, and Ray Jurkovich, 105–122. Oxford: Pergamon.

Braxton, Joanne M., and Maria Diedrich. 2005. *Monuments of the Black Atlantic: Slavery and Memory.* Münster, Germany: Lit Verlag.

Breeden, Aurelien. 2014. "After London, Protesters Interrupt Showing of 'Exhibit B' near Paris." *New York Times,* November 28. Available at http://artsbeat.blogs.nytimes.com /2014/11/28/after-london-protesters-interrupt-showing-of-exhibit-b-near-paris/?_r=0.

Breuil-Genier, Pascale, Catherine Borrel, and Bertrand Lhommeau. 2011. "Les immigrés, les descendants d'immigrés et leurs enfants." In *France: Portrait social.* Paris: Insee Références.

Brown, Vincent. 2008. *The Reaper's Garden: Death and Power in the World of Atlantic Slavery.* Cambridge, MA: Harvard University Press.

Brubaker, Rogers. 2004. *Ethnicity without Groups.* Cambridge, MA: Harvard University Press.

Brundage, W. Fitzhugh. 2005. *The Southern Past: A Clash of Race and Memory.* Cambridge, MA: Harvard University Press.

Bruner, Edward M. 1996. "Tourism in Ghana: The Representation of Slavery and the Return of the Black Diaspora." *American Anthropologist* 98:290–304.

Burnard, Trevor. 2011. "The Atlantic Slave Trade." In *The Routledge History of Slavery*, ed. Gad J. Heuman and Trevor G. Burnard, 80–97. London: Routledge.

Campo, Shelly, Teresa Mastin, and M. Somjen Frazer. 2004. "Predicting and Explaining Public Opinion Regarding U.S. Slavery Reparations." *Howard Journal of Communications* 15:115–130.

Camus, Jean-Yves. 2006. "The Commemoration of Slavery in France and the Emergence of a Black Political Consciousness." *European Legacy* 11:647–655.

Cassely, Jean-Laurent. 2014. "La carte des villes 'apartheid': Celles où les équipes municipales sont totalement blanches." *Slate*, March 20. Available at http://www.slate.fr/france/84767/diversite-equipes-municipales-apartheid.

Cediey, Eric, and Fabrice Foroni. 2007. *Discriminations à raison de "l'origine" dans les embauches en France Une enquête nationale par tests de discrimination selon la méthode du BIT.* Geneva: Bureau International du Travail.

Célestine, Audrey. 2009. "Mobilisations collectives et construction identitaire: Le cas des Antillais en France et des Portoricains aux Etats-Unis." Ph.D. diss., Sciences Po Paris.

———. 2010. "Mobilisations et identité chez les Antillais en France: Le choix de la différentiation." *REVUE Asylon(s)*, no. 8, July 2010–September 2013, Radicalisation des frontières et promotion de la diversité.

Césaire, Aimé. 1947. *Cahier d'un retour au pays natal.* Paris: Bordas.

Chapman, Herrick, and Laura Levine Frader. 2004. *Race in France: Interdisciplinary Perspectives on the Politics of Difference.* New York: Berghahn.

Churchland, Paul M. 1984. *Matter and Consciousness: A Contemporary Introduction to the Philosophy of Mind.* Cambridge, MA: MIT Press.

Clarke, Kamari Maxine. 2006. "Mapping Transnationality: Roots Tourism and the Institutionalization of Ethnic Heritage." In *Globalization and Race: Transformations in the Cultural Production of Blackness*, ed. Kamari Maxine Clarke and Deborah A. Thomas, 133–154. Durham: NC: Duke University Press.

Clarke, Max, and Gary Alan Fine. 2010. "'A' for Apology: Slavery and the Discourse of Remonstrance in Two American Universities." *History and Memory* 22:81–112.

COFFAD. 1998. "Resolutions." Available at http://remy.clarac.free.fr/francais.

———. 2000. "Reparation." Available at http://remy.clarac.free.fr/francais.

Cohen, William B. 1980. *The French Encounter with Africans: White Response to Blacks, 1530–1880.* Bloomington: Indiana University Press.

———. 2013. *On Intellectual Activism.* Philadelphia. PA: Temple University Press.

Comité Marche du 23 Mai 1998. 2011. *Non an nou: Le livre des noms de familles guadeloupéennes.* Paris: Comité Marche du 23 Mai 1998.

———. 2012. *Non nou le livre des noms de familles martiniquaises.* Paris: Comité Marche du 23 Mai 1998.

Condon, Stéphanie. 2000. "Migrations antillaises en métropole: Politique migratoire, emploi et place spécifique des femmes." *Cahiers du Centre d'Enseignements, de Documentation et de Recherches pour les Études Féministes* 8–9:167–200.

———. 2005. "Transatlantic French Caribbean Connections: Return Migration in the Context of Increasing Circulation between France and the Islands." In *The Experience of Return Migration: Caribbean Perspectives*, ed. Robert B. Potter, Dennis Conway, and Joan Phillips, 225–244. London: Ashgate.

Condon, Stéphanie A., and Philip E. Ogden. 1993. "The State, Housing Policy and Afro-Caribbean Migration to France." *Ethnic and Racial Studies* 16:256–297.

Conklin, Alice L. 1997. *A Mission to Civilize: The Republican Idea of Empire in France and West Africa, 1895–1930*. Stanford, CA: Stanford University Press.

Conley, Dalton. 2003. "Calculating Slavery Reparations: Theory, Numbers and Implications." In *Politics of the Past: On Repairing Historical Injustices*, ed. John C. Torpey, 117–125. New York: Rowman and Littlefield.

Conseil Représentatif des Associations Noires. 2007. *Le ler baromètre des populations noires de France*. Available at http:/lecran.org/?p=243.

Constant, Fred. 2009. "Talking Race in Color-Blind France: Equality Denied, 'Blackness' Reclaimed." In *Black Europe and the African Diaspora*, ed. Darlene Clark Hine, Trica Danielle Keaton, and Stephen Small, 145–159. Urbana: University of Illinois Press.

Conway, Brian. 2009. "Rethinking Difficult Pasts: Bloody Sunday (1972) as a Case Study." *Cultural Sociology* 3:397–413.

Cooper, Anna Julia. 1925. *L'attitude de la France à l'égard de l'esclavage pendant la Révolution*. Paris: Imprimerie de la Cour d'Appel.

Cottias, Myriam, Crystal Fleming, and Seloua Luste Boulbina. 2009. "Nos ancêtres les Gaulois . . . La France et l'esclavage aujourd'hui." *Cahiers sens Public* 10 (2): 45–56.

Crenshaw, Kimberlé. 1995. *Critical Race Theory: The Key Writings that Formed the Movement*. New York: New Press.

Curran, Andrew S. 2011. *The Anatomy of Blackness: Science and Slavery in an Age of Enlightenment*. Baltimore: Johns Hopkins University Press.

Daget, Serge. 1981. "France, Suppression of the Illegal Trade, and England, 1817–1850." In *The Abolition of the Atlantic Slave Trade: Origins and Effects in Europe, Africa and the Americas*, 125–240. Madison: University of Wisconsin Press.

Davis, David Brion. 1996. *The Problem of Slavery in Western Culture*. Ithaca, NY: Cornell University Press.

———. 2006. *Inhuman Bondage: The Rise and Fall of Slavery in the New World*. Oxford: Oxford University Press.

Dawson, Michael C., and Rovana Popoff. 2004. "Reparations: Justice and Greed in Black and White." *Du Bois Review* 1:47–91.

Dayan-Herzbrun, Sonia. 2015. "Foreword." In *What Fanon Said: A Philosophical Introduction to His Life and Thought*, ed. Gordon Lewis, xi–xvi. New York: Fordham University Press.

DeGloma, Thomas. 2010. "Awakenings: Autobiography, Memory, and the Social Logic of Personal Discovery." *Sociological Forum* 25:519–540.

Delgado, Richard, and Jean Stefancic. 2001. *Critical Race Theory: An Introduction*. New York: New York University Press.

Dodier, Nicolas, and Janine Barbot. 2009. "Itinéraires de réparation et formation d'un espace de victimes autour d'un drame médical." In *Destins politiques de la souffrance: Intervention sociale, justice, travail*, ed. Thomas Périlleux and John Cultiaux, 101–119. Toulouse, France: Erès.

Dubois, Laurent. 2004. *Avengers of the New World: The Story of the Haitian Revolution*. Cambridge, MA: Harvard University Press.

———. 2012. *Haiti: The Aftershocks of History*. New York: Metropolitan.

Dufoix, Stéphane. 2006. *La politique des mémoires en France*. Paris: Controverses.

Durkheim, Émile. (1912) 1965. *The Elementary Forms of the Religious Life*. New York: Free Press.

Durpaire, François. 2002. *Enseignement de l'histoire et diversité culturelle: "Nos ancetres ne sont pas les Gaulois."* Paris: Hachette Education.

Edwards, Brent Hayes. 2003. *The Practice of Diaspora: Literature, Translation, and the Rise of Black Internationalism*. Cambridge, MA: Harvard University Press.

Esedebe, P. Olisanwuche 1994. *Pan-Africanism: The Idea and Movement, 1776–1991*. Washington, DC: Howard University Press.

Essah, Patience. 2001. "Slavery, Heritage and Tourism in Ghana." *International Journal of Hospitality and Tourism Administration* 2 (3): 31–49.

Essed, Philomena. 1991. *Understanding Everyday Racism: An Interdisciplinary Theory*. Vol. 2. Newbury Park, CA: Sage.

Ewick, Patricia, and Susan S. Silbey. 1995. "Subversive Stories and Hegemonic Tales: Toward a Sociology of Narrative." *Law and Society Review* 29:197–226.

Eyerman, Ron. 2001. *Cultural Trauma: Slavery and the Formation of African American Identity*. Cambridge: Cambridge University Press.

Faes, Géraldine, and Stephen Smith. 2006. *Noir et français!* Paris: Hachette Littératures.

Fanelli, Doris Devine. 2005. "History, Commemoration, and an Interdisciplinary Approach to Interpreting the President's House Site." *Pennsylvania Magazine of History and Biography* 129:445–460.

Fanon, Frantz. 1967. *Black Skin, White Masks*. New York: Grove.

———. 1968. *The Wretched of the Earth*. New York: Grove.

Faure, Sonya. 2015. "Les blancs, une majorité invisible." *Libération*, August 28. Available at http://www.liberation.fr/cahier-ete-2015/2015/08/28/les-blancs-une-majorite-invisible_1371285 (accessed March 8, 2016).

Feagin, Joe R. 2006. *Systemic Racism: A Theory of Oppression*. New York: Routledge.

Finley, Cheryl. 2002. "Committed to Memory: The Slave-Ship Icon and the Black-Atlantic Imagination." Departments of African American Studies and History of Art, Yale University, New Haven, CT.

Fischer, Conan. 2003. *The Ruhr Crisis, 1923–1924*. Oxford: Oxford University Press.

Flaherty, Michael G. 1999. *A Watched Pot: How We Experience Time*. New York: New York University Press.

———. 2003. "Time Work: Customizing Temporal Experience." *Social Psychology Quarterly* 66:17–33.

———. 2011. *The Textures of Time: Agency and Temporal Experience*. Philadelphia: Temple University Press.

Flandrin, Antonin. 2015. "Cinq choses à savoir sur le Mémorial ACTe, en Guadeloupe." *Le Monde*, May 10. Available at http://www.lemonde.fr/afrique/article/2015/05/10/cinq-choses-a-savoir-sur-le-memorial-acte-en-guadeloupe_4630682_3212.html.

Fleming, Crystal M. 2011. "The Educational Experiences of Caribbeans in France." In *Education in the Black Diaspora*, ed. Kassie Freeman, Ethan Johnson and Kelvin Shawn Sealey, 79–98. London: Routledge.

———. 2012. "White Cruelty or Republican Sins? Competing Frames of Stigma Reversal in French Commemorations of Slavery." *Ethnic and Racial Studies* 35 (3): 488–505.

Fleming, Crystal M., and Aldon Morris. 2015. "Theorizing Ethnic and Racial Movements in the Global Age: Lessons from the Civil Rights Movement." *Sociology of Race and Ethnicity* 1 (1): 105–126.

Fogarty, Richard. 2008. *Race and War in France: Colonial Subjects in the French Army, 1914–1918*. Baltimore: Johns Hopkins University Press.

Foner, Nancy, and Richard Alba. 2010. "Immigration and the Legacies of the Past: The Impact of Slavery and the Holocaust on Contemporary Immigrants in the United States and Western Europe." *Comparative Studies in Society and History* 52:798–819.

Frankenberg, Ruth. 2001. "The Mirage of an Unmarked Whiteness." In *The Making and Unmaking of Whiteness*, ed. Birgit Brander Rasmussen, Irene J. Nexica, Matt Wray, and Eric Klinenberg, 72–96. Durham, NC: Duke University Press

Frazier, E. Franklin. 1966. *The Negro Family in the United States.* Chicago: University of Chicago Press.

Fredrickson, George M. 2005. "Mulattoes and Métis: Attitudes toward Miscegenation in the United States and France since the Seventeenth Century." *International Social Science Journal* 57 (183): 103–112.

Garraway, Doris L. 2008. "Memory as Reparation? The Politics of Remembering Slavery in France from Abolition to the Loi Taubira (2001)." *International Journal of Francophone Studies* 11:365–386.

Gay, Amandine. 2014. "L'antiracisme commence avec la déconstruction du privilège blanc." *Libération*, December 14. Available at http://www.slate.fr/story/95643/antiracisme-privilege-blanc.

———. 2015. "Deny and Punish: A French History of Concealed Violence." *Occasion* 9. ("The *Charlie Hebdo* Attacks and Their Aftermath" special issue).

Géraud, Alice. 2015. "Un procès en appel antidiscriminations." *Libération*, February 24. Available at http://www.liberation.fr/societe/2015/02/24/un-proces-en-appel-anti discriminations_1209226.

Gillis, John R. 1994. *Commemorations: The Politics of National Identity.* Princeton, NJ: Princeton University Press.

Giraud, Michel. 2005. "Revendication identitaire et 'cadre national.'" *Pouvoirs* 2:89–100.

Gobineau, Arthur de. 1967. *Essai sur l'inegalite des races humaines.* Paris: Editions Pierre Belfond.

Golash-Boza, Tanya Maria. 2011. *Yo soy negro: Blackness in Peru.* Gainesville: University Press of Florida.

———. 2015. *Race and Racisms: A Critical Approach.* New York: Oxford University Press.

Goldberg, David Theo. 2009. *The Threat of Race: Reflections on Racial Neoliberalism.* Malden, MA: Wiley-Blackwell.

Gongaware, Timothy B. 2011. "Keying the Past to the Present: Collective Memories and Continuity in Collective Identity Change." *Social Movement Studies* 10 (1): 39–54.

Gordien, Emmanuel. 2013. "Les patronymes attribués aux anciens esclaves des colonies françaises." *In Situ.* Available at http://insitu.revues.org/10129

Griffin, Larry J. 2004. "Generations and Collective Memory Revisited: Race, Region, and Memory of Civil Rights." *American Sociological Review* 69:544–557.

Griffin, Larry J., and Kenneth A. Bollen. 2009. "What Do These Memories Do? Civil Rights Remembrance and Racial Attitudes." *American Sociological Review* 74:594–614.

Gueye, Abdoulaye. 2001. *Les intellectuels africains en France.* Paris: L'Harmattan.

———. 2006. "The Colony Strikes Back: African Protest Movements in Postcolonial France." *Comparative Studies of South Asia, Africa and the Middle East* 26:225–242.

———. 2010. "Breaking the Silence: The Emergence of a Black Collective Voice in France." *Du Bois Review* 7:81–102.

Halbwachs, Maurice. (1925) 1952. *Les cadres sociaux de la memoire.* Paris: Presses Universitaires de France.

Hall, Gwendolyn Midlo. 2005. *Slavery and African Ethnicities in the Americas: Restoring the Links.* Chapel Hill: University of North Carolina Press.

Hargreaves, Alec G. 1995. *Immigration, "Race" and Ethnicity in Contemporary France.* London: Routledge.

———. 2007. *Multi-ethnic France: Immigration, Politics, Culture and Society.* New York: Routledge.

Harris, Cheryl I. 1993. "Whiteness as Property." *Harvard Law Review* 106 (8): 1707–1791.

Hass, Kristin Ann. 1998. *Carried to the Wall: American Memory and the Vietnam Veterans Memorial.* Berkeley: University of California Press.

Higman, B. W. 1998. "Remembering Salvery: The Rise, Decline and Revival of Emancipation Day in the English-Speaking Caribbean." *Slavery and Abolition* 19 (1): 90–105.

Hill Collins, Patricia. 1990. *Black Feminist Thought Knowledge, Consciousness, and the Politics of Empowerment.* New York: Routledge.

Holsey, Bayo. 2004. "Transatlantic Dreaming: Slavery, Tourism and Diasporic Encounters." In *Homecomings: Unsettling Paths of Return*, ed. Fran Markowitz and Anders H. Stefansson, 166–182. Lanham, MD: Lexington.

Holub, Robert C. 1984. *Reception Theory: A Critical Introduction.* London: Meuthen.

Hopquin, Benoît. 2005. "Ni Chirac ni Villepin ne commémorent Napoléon, accusé d'esclavagisme." *Le Monde*, November 29, 2005.

Hourcade, Renaud. 2012. "Commemorating a Guilty Past: The Politics of Memory in the French Former Slave Trade Cities." In *Politics of Memory: Making Slavery Visible in the Public Space*, ed. Ana Lucia Araujo, 123–140. New York: Routledge.

———. 2014. *Les ports négriers face à leur histoire politiques de la mémoire à Nantes, Bordeaux et Liverpool.* Paris: Dalloz.

Howard-Hassmann, Rhoda E. 2004. "Getting to Reparations: Japanese Americans and African Americans." *Social Forces* 83:823–840.

Howard-Hassmann, Rhoda E., and Anthony P. Lombardo. 2007. "Framing Reparations Claims: Differences between the African and Jewish Social Movements for Reparations." *African Studies Review* 50:27–48.

Irwin-Zarecka, Iwona. 1994. *Frames of Remembrance: The Dynamics of Collective Memory.* New Brunswick, NJ: Transaction.

Jenkins, Richard. 1997. *Rethinking Ethnicity: Arguments and Explorations.* London: Sage.

Jules-Rosette, Bennetta. 2007. "Jean-Paul Sartre and the Philosophy of Négritude: Race, Self, and Society." *Theory and Society* 36:265–285.

Jung, Moon-Kie. 2015. *Beneath the Surface of White Supremacy: Denaturalizing U.S. Racisms Past and Present.* Stanford, CA: Stanford University Press.

Kammen, Michael. 1995. "Review." *History and Theory* 34:245–261.

Keaton, Trica Danielle. 2010. "The Politics of Race-Blindness." *Du Bois Review* 7:103–131.

Keaton, Trica Danielle, T. Denean Sharpley-Whiting, and Tyler Edward Stovall. 2012. *Black France/France Noire: The History and Politics of Blackness.* Durham, NC: Duke University Press.

Kertzer, David I. 1988. *Ritual, Politics, and Power.* New Haven, CT: Yale University Press.

Kovacs, Stéphane 2012. "France: 12 millions d'immigrés et d'enfants d'immigrés." *Le Figaro*, October 10. Available at http://www.lefigaro.fr/actualite-france/2012/10/10/01016-20121010ARTFIG00262-immigration-les-chiffres-de-l-insee.php.

Lamont, Michèle. 1992. *Money, Morals, and Manners: The Culture of the French and American Upper-Middle Class.* Chicago: University of Chicago Press.

———. 2000. *The Dignity of Working Men: Morality and the Boundaries of Race, Class, and Immigration.* New York: Russell Sage Foundation.

————. 2004. "Immigration and the Salience of Racial Boundaries among French Workers." In *Race in France: Interdisciplinary Perspectives on the Politics of Difference*, ed. Herrick Chapman and Laura Levine Frader, 144–161. New York: Berghahn.

Lamont, Michèle, and Nicolas Duvoux. 2014. "How Neo-Liberalism Has Transformed France's Symbolic Boundaries." *French Politics, Culture and Society* 32 (2): 57–75.

Le Baron, Bentley. 1966. "Négritude: A Pan-African Ideal?" *Ethics* 76:267–276.

Lecouteur, Amanda, and Martha Augoustinos. 2001. "Apologising to the Stolen Generations: Argument, Rhetoric, and Identity in Public Reasoning." *Australian Psychologist* 36:51–61.

Lerner, Gerda. 1993. *The Creation of Feminist Consciousness: From the Middle Ages to Eighteen-Seventy*. New York: Oxford University Press.

Levy, Daniel, and Natan Sznaider. 2004. "The Institutionalization of Cosmopolitan Morality: The Holocaust and Human Rights." *Journal of Human Rights* 3 (2): 143–157.

————. 2006. *The Holocaust and Memory in the Global Age*. Philadelphia: Temple University Press.

Lewis, David L. 2000. *W.E.B. DuBois—the Fight for Equality and the American Century, 1919–1963*. New York: Henry Holt.

Lewis, Mary Dewhurst. 2007. *The Boundaries of the Republic: Migrant Rights and the Limits of Universalism in France, 1918–1940*. Stanford, CA: Stanford University Press.

Lieberson, Stanley. 1985. "Unhyphenated Whites in the United States." *Ethnic and Racial Studies* 8 (1): 159–180.

Lirus, Julie. 1979. *Identité antillaise: Contribution à la connaissance psychologique et anthropologique des Guadeloupéens et des Martiniquais*. Paris: Éditions Caribéennes.

Lovejoy, Paul E. 1983. *Transformations in Slavery: A History of Slavery in Africa*. Cambridge: Cambridge University Press.

————. 2012. *Transformations in Slavery: A History of Slavery in Africa*, 2d ed. Cambridge: Cambridge University Press.

Lutte Ouvrière. 1998. "Cent cinquantenaire de l'abolition de l'esclavage: Les manifestations nationales en métropole." December 6. Available at http://www.culture.gouv.fr/culture/actual/abolition/metro.html.

Mailloux, Steven. 1998. *Reception Histories: Rhetoric, Pragmatism, and American Cultural Politics*. Ithaca, NY: Cornell University Press.

Marquand, Robert. 2010. "France Dismisses Petition for It to Pay $17 Billion in Haiti Reparations." August 17. Available at http://www.csmonitor.com/World/Europe/2010/0817/France-dismisses-petition-for-it-to-pay-17-billion-in-Haiti-reparations.

Mataillet, Dominique. 2007. "Combien sont-ils?" *Jeune Afrique*, April 2. Available at http://www.jeuneafrique.com/132911/archives-thematique/combien-sont-ils.

May, Reuben A. Buford. 2000. "Race Talk and Local Collective Memory among African American Men in a Neighborhood Tavern." *Qualitative Sociology* 23 (2): 201–214.

McAdam, Doug. 1982. *Political Process and the Development of Black Insurgency, 1930–1970*. Chicago: University of Chicago Press.

Michel, Johann. 2010. *Gouverner les mémoires: Les politiques mémorielles en France*. Paris: Presses Universitaires de France.

————. 2015. *Devenir descendant d'esclave: Enquête sur les régimes mémoriels*. Rennes, France: Presses Universitaires de Rennes.

Michelson, Melissa R. 2002. "The Black Reparations Movement: Public Opinion and Congressional Policy Making." *Journal of Black Studies* 32:574–587.

Mills, Charles. 1997. The *Racial Contract*. Ithaca, NY: Cornell University Press.

————. 1998. *Blackness Visible: Essays on Philosophy and Race*. Ithaca, NY: Cornell University Press.

———. 2015. "Global White Ignorance." In *Routledge International Handbook of Ignorance Studies*, ed. Matthias Gross and Linsey McGoey, 217–227. New York: Routledge.

Morning, Ann Juanita. 2011. *The Nature of Race: How Scientists Think and Teach about Human Difference*. Berkeley: University of California Press.

Ndiaye, Pap. 2008. *La condition noire: Essai sur une minorité française*. Paris: Calmann-Lévy.

Nedelkovic, Eddy, and David Dieudonné. 2009. "'Il n'y a jamais eu volonté d'inciter à la haine raciale,' affirme Domota," Agence France-Presse, March 11.

Nimako, Kwame, and Stephen Small. 2010. "Collective Memory of Slavery in Great Britain and the Netherlands." Paper presented at the American Sociological Association Annual Conference, Atlanta.

Noiriel, Gérard. 1988. *Le creuset français: Histoire de l'immigration, XIXe–XXe siècles*. Paris: Seuil.

Olick, Jeffrey K. 1999a. "Collective Memory: The Two Cultures." *Sociological Theory* 17:333–348.

———. 1999b. "Genre Memories and Memory Genres: A Dialogical Analysis of May 8, 1945 Commemorations in the Federal Republic of Germany." *American Sociological Review* 64:381–402.

———. 2007. *The Politics of Regret: On Collective Memory and Historical Responsibility*. New York: Routledge.

Olick, Jeffrey K., and Daniel Levy. 1997. "Collective Memory and Cultural Constraint: Holocaust Myth and Rationality in German Politics." *American Sociological Review* 62:921–936.

Olick, Jeffrey K., and Joyce Robbins. 1998. "Social Memory Studies: From 'Collective Memory' to the Historical Sociology of Mnemonic Practices." *Annual Review of Sociology* 24:105–140.

Otele, Olivette. 2012. "Bristol, Slavery and the Politics of Representation: The Slave Trade Gallery in the Bristol Museum." *Social Semiotics* 22 (2): 155–172.

Painter, Nell I. 2010. *The History of White People*. New York: W. W. Norton.

Patterson, Orlando. 1971. "Rethinking Black History." *Harvard Educational Review* 41:297–315.

———. 1982. *Slavery and Social Death: A Comparative Study*. Cambridge, MA: Harvard University Press.

———. 2005. "Four Modes of Ethno-Somatic Stratification: The Experience of Blacks in Europe and the Americans." In *Ethnicity, Social Mobility and Public Policy: Comparing the USA and UK*, ed. Glenn C. Loury, Tariq Modood, and Steven M. Teles, 67–122. Cambridge: Cambridge University Press.

Paxton, Robert O. 1972. *Vichy France: Old Guard and New Order, 1940–1944*. New York: Knopf.

Peabody, Sue. 1996. *There Are No Slaves in France: The Political Culture of Race and Slavery in the Ancien Régime*. New York: Oxford University Press

Peabody, Sue, and Tyler Edward Stovall. 2003. *The Color of Liberty: Histories of Race in France*. Durham, NC: Duke University Press.

Phillips, Catherine. 2010. "White, like Who? Temporality, Contextuality and Anti-racist Social Work Education and Practice." *Critical Social Work* 11, no. 2. Available at http://www1.uwindsor.ca/criticalsocialwork/white-like-who-temporality-contextuality-and-anti-racist-social-work-education-and-practice.

Pierre, Jemima. 2013. *The Predicament of Blackness: Postcolonial Ghana and the Politics of Race*. Chicago: University of Chicago Press.

Posner, Eric A., and Adrian Vermeule. 2003. "Reparations for Slavery and Other Historical Injustices." *Columbia Law Review* 103:689–748.

Quijano, Anibal. 2000. "Coloniality of Power, Eurocentrism, and Latin America." *Nepentla* 1 (3): 533–580.

Régent, Frédéric. 2007. *La France et ses esclaves: De la colonisation aux abolitions, 1620–1848.* Paris: Grasset.

Reiss, Tom. 2012. *The Black Count: Glory, Revolution, Betrayal, and the Real Count of Monte Cristo.* New York: Crown Trade.

Ribbe, Claude. 2005. *Le crime de Napoléon.* Paris: Privé.

Rivera, Lauren A. 2008. "Managing 'Spoiled' National Identity: War, Tourism, and Memory in Croatia." *American Sociological Review* 73:613–634.

Roberts, Dorothy E. 2011. *Fatal Invention: How Science, Politics, and Big Business Re-create Race in the Twenty-First Century.* New York: New Press.

———. 2012. *Fatal Invention: How Science, Politics, and Big Business Re-create Race in the Twenty-First Century.* New York: New Press.

Rolle-Romana, Viviane. 2010. *Presentation.* Available at http://www.cm98.fr/index.php?option=com_content&view=article&id=47&Itemid=56.

Romana, Serge. 2005. "Démission de Serge Romana du 'Comite Maryse Conde.'" Available at http://www.potomitan.info/lafwans/demission.php.

Rousso, Henry. 1987. *Le syndrome de Vichy: 1944 à nos jours.* Paris: Seuil.

Saito, Hiro. 2006. "Reiterated Commemoration: Hiroshima as National Trauma." *Sociological Theory* 24:353–376.

Schmidt, Nelly. 2003. "The Drafting of the 1848 Decrees: Immediate Application and Long-Term Consequences." In *The Abolitions of Slavery: From Léger Félicité Sonthonax to Victor Schoelcher*, ed. Marcel Dorigny, 305–313. New York: Berghahn.

———. 2012. "Teaching and Commemorating Slavery and Abolition in France: From Organized Forgetfulness to Historical Debates." In *Politics of Memory: Making Slavery Visible in the Public Space*, ed. Ana Lucia Araujo, 106–123. New York: Routledge.

Schoelcher, Victor. 1842. *Des colonies françaises: Abolition immédiate de l'esclavage.* Paris: Éditions du CTHS.

Schor, Paul. 2009. *Compter et classer: Histoire des recensements américains.* Paris: Presses de l'École des Hautes Études en Sciences Sociales.

Schwartz, Barry. 1996. "Memory as a Cultural System. Abraham Lincoln in World War I." *International Journal of Sociology and Social Policy* 17.22–58.

———. 2001. "Commemorative Objects." In *International Encyclopedia of the Social and Behavioral Sciences*, ed. Neil J. Smelser and Paul B. Baltes, 2267–2272. Oxford: Pergamon.

Sharpley-Whiting, T. Denean. 2002. *Negritude Women.* Minneapolis: University of Minnesota Press.

———. 2015. *Bricktop's Paris: African American Women in Paris between the Two World Wars.* Albany: State University of New York Press.

Shelby, Tommie. 2005. *We Who Are Dark: The Philosophical Foundations of Black Solidarity.* Cambridge, MA: Harvard University Press.

Silverman, Maxim. 1992. *Deconstructing the Nation: Immigration, Racism, and Citizenship in Modern France.* London: Routledge.

Smedley, Audrey, and Brian D. Smedley. 2005. "Race as Biology Is Fiction, Racism as a Social Problem Is Real: Anthropological and Historical Perspectives on the Social Construction of Race." *American Psychologist* 60 (1): 16–26.

———. 2012. *Race in North America: Origin and Evolution of a Worldview.* Boulder, CO: Westview.

Smelser, Neil J. 2004. "Psychological Trauma and Cultural Trauma." In *Cultural Trauma and Collective Identity*, ed. Jeffrey C. Alexander, Ron Eyerman, Bernard Giesen, Neil J. Smelser, and Piotr Sztompka, 31–59. Berkeley: University of California Press.

Smith, Matthew J. 2006. "Two-Hundred-Year-Old Mountains: Issues and Themes in the Historiography of the Modern Francophone Caribbean." In *Beyond Fragmentation: Perspectives on Caribbean History*, ed. Juanita D. Barros, Audra Diptee, and David Vincent Trotman, 113–139. Princeton, NJ: Markus Wiener.

Snow, David A., and Robert D. Benford. 1988. "Ideology, Frame Resonance, and Participant Mobilization." *International Social Movement Research* 1:197–217.

Sopo, Dominique. 2014. "Exhibit B: Le révélateur d'un malaise." SOS Racisme. Available at http://sos-racisme.org/exhibit-b-le-revelateur-dun-malaise.

Stokes, Melvyn. 2010. "Race, Politics, and Censorship: D. W. Griffith's *The Birth of a Nation* in France, 1916–1923." *Cinema Journal* 50 (1): 19–38.

Stovall, Tyler E. 1997. "Harlem-sur-Seine: Building an African American Community in Paris." *Stanford Electronic Humanities Review* 5 (2): n.p.

Sullivan, Shannon. 2014. *Good White People: The Problem with Middle-Class White Anti-racism*. Albany: State University of New York Press.

Swidler, Ann, and Jorge Arditi. 1994. "The New Sociology of Knowledge." *Annual Review of Sociology* 20:305–329.

Teeger, Chana, and Vered Vinitzky-Seroussi. 2007. "Controlling for Consensus: Commemorating Apartheid in South Africa." *Symbolic Interaction* 30 (1): 57–78.

Thomas, Dominic. 2007. *Black France: Colonialism, Immigration, and Transnationalism*. Bloomington: Indiana University Press.

Tillet, Salamishah. 2009. "Black Girls in Paris: Sally Hemings, Sarah Baartman, and French Racial Dystopias." *Callaloo* 32 (3): 934–954.

Tin, Louis-Georges. 2008. "Who Is Afraid of Blacks in France? The Black Question: The Name Taboo, the Number Taboo." *French Politics, Culture and Society* 26:32–44.

———. 2013. *Esclavage et réparations: Comment faire face aux crimes de l'histoire*. Paris: Stock.

Tribalat, Michèle. 2008. "Statistiques: La question des minorités en France." *Le Figaro*, November 18. Available at http://www.lefigaro.fr/debats/2008/11/25/01005-20081125ARTFIG00001-statistiques-la-question-des-minorites-en-france-.php.

Trouillot, Michel-Rolph. 1995. *Silencing the Past: Power and the Production of History*. Boston: Beacon.

Twine, France Winddance. 1998. *Racism in a Racial Democracy: The Maintenance of White Supremacy in Brazil*. New Brunswick, NJ: Rutgers University Press.

Valdes, Francisco, Jerome McCrystal Culp, and Angela P. Harris. 2002. *Crossroads, Directions, and a New Critical Race Theory*. Philadelphia: Temple University Press.

Valo, Martine. 2013a. "Guadeloupe and Martinique Threatened as Pesticide Contaminates Food Chain." *The Guardian*, May 6. Available at http://www.theguardian.com/environment/2013/may/07/guadeloupe-economy-theatened-pesticides-pollution.

———. 2013b. "Guadeloupe: Monstre chimique." *Le Monde*, April 17. Available at http://www.lemonde.fr/planete/article/2013/04/16/guadeloupe-monstre-chimique_3160656_3244.html.

Verdun, Vincene. 1993. "If the Shoe Fits, Wear It: An Analysis of Reparations to African Americans." *Tulane Law Review* 67:597–668.

Vergès, Françoise. 2004. "Mémoires visuelles et virtuelles à l'île de la Réunion (Visual and Virtual Memories in Réunion)." *Cahiers d'Etudes Africaines* 44:387–399.

———. 2006. *La mémoire enchaînée: Questions sur l'esclavage*. Paris: Albin Michel.

Vergès, Françoise, Maryse Condé, and Comité pour la Mémoire de l'Esclavage. 2005. *Mémoires de la traite négrière, de l'esclavage et leurs abolitions: Rapport à monsieur le Premier ministre.* Paris: La Découverte.

Vinitzky-Seroussi, Vered. 2002. "Commemorating a Difficult Past: Yitzhak Rabin's Memorials." *American Sociological Review* 67:30–51.

———. 2009. *Yitzhak Rabin's Assassination and the Dilemmas of Commemoration.* Albany: State University of New York Press.

Wagner-Pacifici, Robin, and Barry Schwartz. 1991. "The Vietnam Veterans Memorial: Commemorating a Difficult Past." *American Journal of Sociology* 97:376–420.

Washburn, Leah H. 1997. "Accounts of Slavery: An Analysis of United States History Textbooks from 1900 to 1992." *Theory and Research in Social Education* 25 (4): 470–491.

Waters, Mary C. 1990. *Ethnic Options: Choosing Identities in America.* Berkeley: University of California Press.

———. 1991. "The Role of Lineage in Identity Formation among Black Americans." *Qualitative Sociology* 14:57–76.

Weber, Max. (1922) 1978. *Economy and Society: An Outline of Interpretative Sociology.* Vol. 2, trans. Guenther Roth and Claus Wittich. Berkeley: University of California Press.

Weiner, Melissa F. 2012. "Towards a Critical Global Race Theory." *Sociology Compass* 6 (4): 332–350.

———. 2014a. "(E)Racing Slavery: Racial Neoliberalism, Social Forgetting, and Scientific Colonialism in Dutch Primary School History Textbooks." *DuBois Review* 11 (2): 329–351.

———. 2014b. "The Ideologically Colonized Metropole: Dutch Racism and Racist Denial." *Sociology Compass* 8 (6): 731–744.

Wertsch, James V. 2002. *Voices of Collective Remembering.* Cambridge: Cambridge University Press.

Woodson, Carter G. 1933. *The Mis-education of the Negro.* Washington, DC: Associated.

Wright, Michelle M. 2015. *Physics of Blackness: Beyond the Middle Passage Epistemology.* Minneapolis: University of Minnesota Press

Wuhl-Ebguy, Leïla. 2006. "Migrants de l'intérieur. Les Antillais de métropole: Entre intégration institutionnelle et mobilisations collectives." Ph.D. diss., Université Paris–Dauphine.

Zerubavel, Eviatar. 1996. "Social Memories: Steps to a Sociology of the Past." *Qualitative Sociology* 19:283–299.

———. 2003. *Time Maps: Collective Memory and the Social Shape of the Past.* Chicago: University of Chicago Press.

———. 2012. *Ancestors and Relatives: Genealogy, Identity, and Community.* New York: Oxford University Press.